Mint Tea and Minarets
a banquet of Moroccan memories

Welcome to Dar Zitoun,
Kitty Morse

by Kitty Morse

Photography by Owen Morse

First published in the United States by La Caravane Publishing

Text copyright © Kitty Morse 2012
Photography copyright © Owen Morse 2012

Photograph of mint tea © Patricia McArdle 2012

Photograph of Rahoule painting © Robert Doddridge 2012

Photograph "Azemmour. - 9. - Débarquement des Mulets"
Jh Boussuge, Casablanca 1908

Driss Chraïbi quotations taken from *Mother Spring*, translated by Hugh Harter, copyright
©1989 by Hugh Harter. Used with permission of Lynne Rienner Publishers, Inc.

Passages from the Qur'an are taken from *The Qur'an*, translated by M.H. Shakir.
All quotations reprinted with permission of publisher, Tahrike Tarsile Qur'an Inc.,
Elmhurst, NY. Eighth U.S. edition 1999

Maps taken from *The Empire of Morocco*, by James Grey ESQ.,
published by Fry and Kammerer, Philadelphia, U.S. 1810

Quotations on falconry taken from *Doukkala, fief de la fauconnerie au Maroc*,
by Lekhiar El Mostafa and Chergui Bouchaïb, Acharika Al Jadida Dar Attakafa publisher,
Casablanca, 1984

Layout & Design by Beau Kimbrel

ISBN 13: 978-0-9852164-4-3

La Caravane Publishing
P.O. Box 433
Vista CA 92085
USA

www.mintteaandminarets.com

Printed in China

Dedication

To the Spirits of Dar Zitoun

Map of
WEST BARBARY,
Including
SUSE & TAFILELT,
forming the Dominions of the present
EMPEROR of MAROCCO.

N.B. The letter A after the name of the province signifies Arabs, the letter S signifies Shellahs.

O C E A

A T L A N T I C

Azamure

El Burreja or Mazagan

Tet

Soke or Great Mar

El Weladia

Duar of Woled Aisah

Sahell

DUQUE

C. Cantin

Asfee or Saffee

Salt Lake

Bld Hunin fine breed of Horses

A B D A

Jebbel El Hadeed or Iron Mountains

R. Tansit

Seeli Buzuructen

S H E D M A

Suerrah or Mogodor

Sanctu or Seedy Megodel

Idaugourd

Tegriwelt or C. Ossint

Sanctu Tidsi

Ait Ziltan

Benitameer R

Aternie or C. de Geer

Tamarac Idautenin

Bugum

Agadeer or Santa Cruz

Agueru Meekine

Salt petre

MEDITERRANEAN SEA

Straits of Gibraltar
C. Spartel
Wed El Eude or Jews R.
Arzille

Ceuta
Tetuan

Pegnon de Gomera

Tarokirat

Melilla

E R R I F
A.

Arabs

R. Mulluvia

TLEMS

El Araiche
El Kasser Kabeer
Wed El Koser
Arcor R.
Ait Emire

Wazzan

DESERT
of
ANGA

Meheduma
or Mamora
GARB
Kassen
Ruins of Pharaoh
Mulevelah Sanctuary
El Kirwan
B.

Sla or Sallee
Rabat
Shella
Roman Ruins
Sebou R.
Mekenes

Zemur Shelleh

Fas

Zha R.

Arabs

Fedalla
el beeda
El Mansoria
R. Najar
BENI
HASSAN
A.

Zien B.

Beni Bessen

Fighig
Station for the M
and Timbuctoo Carav

DISTRICT
of
TEDLA
Carpet
Manufactory

TEMSENA
A.

SHAWIYA
A.

Bulawan
pass of Boats

Mines of
Antimony
& Lead Ore

Curious Manufactory
of Hayks

Taftlelt

River absor
in
loose San

Rahammena

NORTH

Superior breed of Goats

MOROCCO
El Kuntera or Bridg
Dimenir
Ruins of a Roman
Triumphal Temple
MAROCCO
Solah
Upper
Mines
Ain Toga
Fine breed of
Horses

Arabs

BLED FILLELLY

ATLAS MA

Shellul

abounding in Dates

E

Dikena
Mjot

R. Fillelly

Country

Sejt
Mess

ATLAS MA

BLED EL JERREDE

Linguistic Note

No formal convention exists for transliterating *darija*, the Arabic dialect spoken in Morocco, into the Latin alphabet. Like most of my French contemporaries who grew up in North Africa, I developed the habit of transliterating Arabic words phonetically using French sounds and have chosen to do likewise in this book. To facilitate reader comprehension, I have elected to add "s" to pluralize Arabic nouns and add "'s" to indicate possession (e.g., for the plural of *riad*, a traditional Moroccan house, I use *riads* instead of *rawdah*; and for the possessive, *riad's* instead of *dial riad*). For the same reason, I have elected to use "'s" to indicate possession in French nouns (e.g., for the word *greffier*, clerk of court, I use *greffier's* instead of *du greffier*). I bear responsibility for any inconsistencies.

Contents

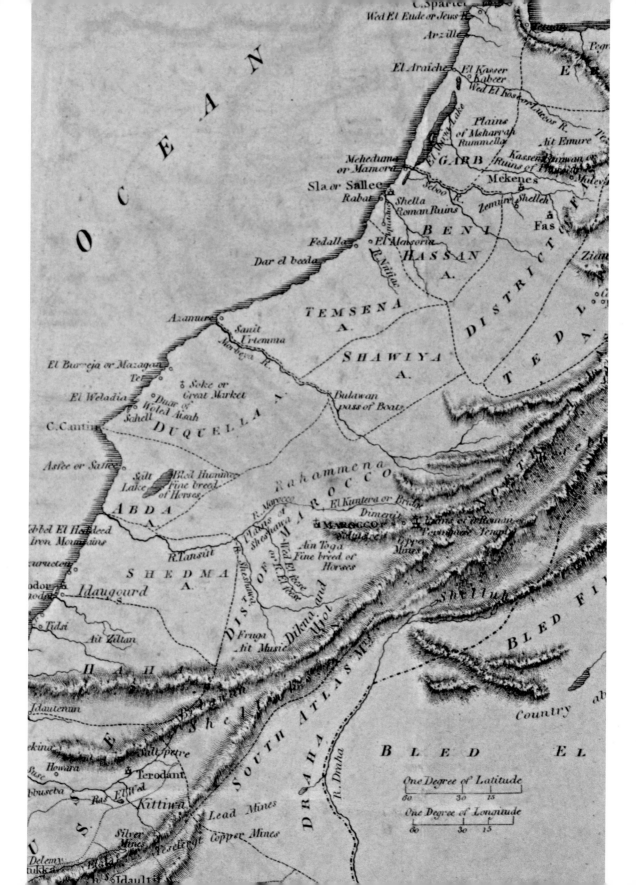

O C E A N

C. Spartel
Wed El Eude or Jews R.
Arzille
El Araiche
El Kasser Kabeer
Wed El Kosser Luccor R.
E
Plains of Msharrah Rummella
Ait Emure
Meheduma or Mamora
GARB
Kassen Zimwan or Ruins of
Mekenes
Sla or Sallee
Seboo R.
Zemure Shelleh
Rabat
Shella Roman Ruins
Fas
BENI
Fedalla
El Mansoria
R. Nafjur
HASSAN
Dar el beda
A.
DISTRICT
Ziau
TEMSENA
A.
Azamure
Sanit Urtemma
Morbeya R.
SHAWIYA
A.
TEDLA
El Burreja or Mazagan
Tet
Soke or Great Market
Bulawan pass of Boats
El Weladia
Duar of Woled Aisah
DUQUELLA
A.
Schell
C. Cantin
Rahammena
ROCCO
Asfee or Saffee
Salt Lake
Bled Hunune fine bred of Horses
R. Morocco
El Kuntera or Bridge
Dimeri
Ruins of Ritanan
Pennipont Temple
ABDA
A.
Plains of Sheshana
MAROCCO
Sidulare
Upper Mines
Jebbel El Hadeed Iron Mountains
R. Tansut
R. Sheshawd
Ain Toga Fine breed of Horses
Curucten
SHEDMA
A.
Wed El beere or El beer
Idaugourd
Shellui
BLED FIL
Tidsi
Ait Ziltan
Fruga Ait Musie
Dikna and Ajol
H   A   H   A
SOUTH ATLAS M.
Country ab
Idautenan
Shel
BLED
EL
Ekina
Howara
Saltpetre
Terodant
DRAHA
Busce
Ras Elwd
Kittiwa
Lead Mines
R. Draha
bbuseta
Silver Mines
Tesergont Copper Mines
One Degree of Latitude
60   30   15
Delemy
One Degree of Longitude
60   30   15
Idaults

1

Homecoming

There is for me a magic and an indescribable charm in the very consonance of the word Moghreb . . . meaning at the same time, 'the west, the setting sun, and the hour when the sun fades away.' It also signifies the Empire of Morocco, which is the most western of all the lands of Islam, that place on earth where the great religious impetus which Mohammed imparted to the Arabs faded out and died. Above all, it signifies the last prayer which, from one end of the Muslim world to the other, is recited at that hour of the evening — a prayer which originates in Mecca and, spreads . . . with universal prostration, across all of Africa . . . to cease only when it confronts the ocean, among the very last dunes of the Sahara, where Africa itself ends.

— from *Au Maroc (Into Morocco)* by Pierre Loti

A piercing ray of North African sun invaded the cabin as the aircraft banked steeply on final approach, giving me a dreamlike view of the Chaouia plain. Usually the sight of its fertile fields, dotted with modest dwellings as white as sugar cubes, would have me fantasizing about new adventures, both touristic and culinary. On that day however, it brought me to the verge of tears.

I knew Morocco, the land of my birth, as a potpourri of cultures and cuisines. Perched on the rims of the Mediterranean and Atlantic, it marked a crossroads of other worlds, other continents. Over the centuries, its traditions were sown and ripened with influences of travelers to Mecca, travelers to Europe, travelers into Africa's interior, around the horn, and to the Americas. Morocco's foreignness, tinged with seductive exoticism, fascinated visitors who returned again and again to learn from its diversity and revel in its bounty.

My stomach tipped in synchrony with the plane's wing, not from anticipation, but with dread. My father's last wish, my reason for coming to Morocco, filled me with apprehension. I glanced at the leather bag under the seat in front of me. Nestled among my personal belongings was the contraband — a canister containing Daddy's ashes. I stared out the window as I considered the next hour of my life as a daughter.

Fate and Britain's Royal Air Force plucked a young man from Hertfordshire at the beginning of World War II, made a Spitfire technician out of him, and sent him to another kingdom, this one ruled by a Sultan. *Mektoob*, it is written — fate. There he lived for more than fifty years.

Honoring my father's request placed me at odds with the Moroccan law that forbade cremation and the dissemination of ashes. I'd learned from an official at the country's consulate in London (the city where Daddy died) that, in the case of a non-Muslim decedent, it was possible to receive an exemption from the rule — provided a member of the family had the patience to wade through the required red tape. I decided to ignore the statute and smuggle Daddy's remains to his beloved Dar Zitoun, despite the demurrals of my two brothers, who were more law-abiding than I.

The thump of touchdown signaled my arrival at Mohammed V International Airport southeast of Casablanca. In minutes, I was inching toward passport control with other weary passengers. I'd been through the routine a hundred times. Yet that line ahead filled me with trepidation.

A stubbly-cheeked agent stared at me. Did I look as guilty as I felt?

"Here goes," I said, under my breath, to the one who had always been there, and was no longer.

The official took my passport and scrutinized the identity page. "Born in Casablanca? How long have you lived in the United States?" he asked.

"A long time — over twenty years."

"And the purpose of your visit?"

"My family owns a house here," I answered.

"Allez-y [Go ahead]." The sallow-faced man in uniform endorsed my plan, and my father's, with the loud whack of his entry stamp. In an instant, I sloughed the chrysalis of a traveler to reclaim my identity as a Casablancaise. I thanked the agent with as much insouciance as my fluttering heart could muster. Fellow travelers streamed past me in hopes of securing a good place in the queue at customs. I, on the other hand, was in no hurry to get there.

There wasn't a trace of leniency in the dark, piercing gaze of my next examiner. Why did he too linger so long on my passport? "You were born here?" he asked in an impersonal tone.

"Ana Beidaouia [I'm a Casablancan]," I answered in Arabic, with false bonhomie. The examiner patted my carry-on bag.

"Open it," he ordered. I did as he asked. The officer's scowl was enough to make even an innocent tourist feel guilty. Though ground bone was a far cry from kif or firearms, what I was doing was still technically illegal. The inspector's hairy hand probed the bag's depths. He shot an inquisitive look toward me as he produced a glass jar wrapped in tissue paper. "Confiture," I managed. "A gift for a friend." On a second descent, prospecting fingers latched onto the ash-filled canister and lifted it out. A shiver ran down my spine.

"And this?"

The container bore the orange logo of a popular laxative. My brothers had been shocked, but I was quite proud of my ingenuity with the packaging. Though it was certainly an indelicate conveyance, the container's ordinariness, I theorized, made it less suspect. Daddy would understand.

I held my belly and made a face. "Médicament pour l'estomac [stomach medicine]," I explained. Was my response too emphatic? I must have sounded convincing, however.

"Passez."

Inside the arrival hall, I half expected to hear my father's call: "Kitty! Over here!" Instinctively I scanned the crowd for the familiar grin beneath the graying painter's brush moustache. On that day, however, I witnessed only the emotional reunions of others. My eyes welled up with tears at the realization of a new and unwelcome loneliness. I clutched my leather bag more tightly.

In addition to the unhappy nature of the mission, my arrival sparked a feeling of momentary rootlessness, what the French dub *dépaysement*, a disorientation associated with unfamiliar surroundings. How could this be? This was my homeland, and I'd been coming and going annually for years.

Morocco still provoked a sensory overload of colors, odors, and sounds, like the cacophony of conversations in Arabic, Berber, Spanish, and French that swirled around me in the airport lobby. Jostling through a crowd as colorful as a spice merchant's display, my ears readjusted to the panoply of Mediterranean languages. Dar Beida (Casablanca) was one of the most cosmopolitan cities in Africa. Women in the latest Paris fashions clicked past me in high heels, leaving a scent of henna in their wake. The more conservative wore djellabah over blue jeans, with hair tucked carefully under modest hijab.

An ebony-skinned woman crowned in elaborate headdress and wrapped in yards of wildly printed cloth glided regally across the lobby. She stopped in front of me. "*Où est le bureau de change?*" she asked in the melodious French of a Mauritanian. I was happy to render assistance and happier still that she spoke to me in French. It proved I was still "Katy," still a *Casablancaise*.

The terminal echoed with women's ululations celebrating a pilgrim's return from Mecca. The trilled *youyous* moved me as much as a national anthem. All my years in the United States hadn't diminished the excitement of homecoming. The sounds of the revelers followed me all the way to the car rental desk, where an agent had just taken a call on his cell phone. I could have parroted the perfunctory string of salutations: "How are you? *Al hamdullilah* [Allah be praised]. And your health? Your children's health? Your parents' health? Allah be praised."

Tieless, sleeves rolled up, the agent paced behind the counter. I waited. My finger tapping on my passport finally got his attention. He put the caller on hold long enough to check my reservation and hand me a set of keys.

A tousled boy in oversized sneakers and torn shirt appeared from nowhere. "*Porteur?*" he asked. He was much too young to be an official porter. I recalled my father's admonition about vanishing luggage, so I'd keep a close watch. As for his fee, "*Comme tu veux* [As you wish]." The few dirhams he earned at the airport could well be his family's only source of income. Given the economic climate in the country, he was fortunate to have work at all. I knew of college graduates who swept floors in factories, or worse, sat idly at streetside cafés.

"*Française? Italiana?*" the lad asked.

"*Lah*, Beidaouia [No, Casablancan]."

"You're one of us!" he said, taking my suitcase. It must have weighed as much as he did. When we reached the car, I helped him muscle it into the trunk and then slipped him a generous gratuity. He counted his tip with the expertise of a teller. Contract fulfilled, I thought. Not quite.

"*Garro? Shwinggum?*" he asked, hoping to get a cigarette or stick of gum. My forceful "*Lah* [No]!" sent him off in search of other clients.

I threw my bag onto the passenger seat and set off on the road to my final destination, the town of Azemmour, a ninety-minute drive south. Weeks of sitting helplessly at my father's bedside at a clinic in Wimbledon made me long for the two-lane coastal road, where I could take charge once again.

Daddy and I left Casablanca's burgeoning suburbs behind. The air smelled of tilled earth and hay. To my right, between low-lying dunes, the Atlantic, twinkling and spraying salt-scented mist onto the beach, evoked memories of digging for clams as a child. There was one unforgettable evening when the bioluminescence of invading blue-green algae turned the waves radiant. We stayed up past midnight frolicking in the surf, our bodies silhouetted by the glow of microorganisms. I remember how this natural phenomenon struck fear in the fishermen, who blamed it on supernatural beings or genies, *jnoon*, that are an ancient and persistent fact of life in Muslim culture. My friends and I knew better, but we were young and cocky; we'd make fun of the fishermen for believing they could exorcise the *jnoon* by beating tambourines at a deafening pitch and yelling at the top of their lungs. Decades later I learned how many species of blue-green algae (Cyanobacteria) produce toxins that are hazardous to marine life as well as to animals and humans. If I'd known that when I was a girl, I would have joined the percussionists on the shore.

Much had changed since I'd last traveled that road, most notably, the expansion of posh villas in the beach communities of Dar Bouazza and Sidi Rahal, places where I'd spent many a summer weekend. I imagined the urban sprawl was the source of occasional traffic tie-ups, like the one that blocked my approach to the roundabout ahead. The owner of an overturned donkey cart struggled to right his vehicle. Unsympathetic drivers of Peugeots, Citroëns, and Mercedes honked, and for good measure, rolled down their windows to hurl insults: "Go back to your mother!" or "Out of the way, stupid animal!"

Shattered crates of cauliflower lay in the ditch. Excited cries from would-be rescuers and pilferers of errant produce cut through the pathetic braying of the donkey, then suffering a merciless whipping. I should have been immune to such cruelty, knowing that life's hardships left no room for compassion toward animals among Morocco's poor. Still, I pitied the beast. To skirt the distressing scene, I was forced to disobey a rule of the road and circle the roundabout in a clockwise direction. Luckily, I encountered only one other car in the course of the risky maneuver. As I drew abreast of the other vehicle, its bug-eyed driver twisted his index finger against his temple and screamed, "*N'ti mahbool* [You're crazy]!" Time to get away from the coast. I veered off onto a country road and headed inland.

Twenty minutes later, I reached the *route principale* just north of Bir Jdid, a town known for its meat market. In roadside butcher stalls, quartered sheep and cows dangled from stout iron hooks. Their severed heads, eyes fixed in unsettling gelatinous stares, lined an adjacent countertop. Everywhere, flies gorged themselves in sticky puddles of blood. A cause for revulsion in the United States, in Morocco, a common and expected part of the scenery. Aromatic smoke billowed around the shish kabob vendors. On earlier visits, Daddy heralded my return with a kilo of *kefta*, seasoned minced lamb and beef, or with a celebratory *gigot*, leg of lamb.

"Kate, fancy a *gee-go*?" he would ask, torturing the word with his anglicized French. I was tempted to drop in for old times' sake to purchase some of the cumin-scented patties nestled inside a pocket of flatbread. But I had precious cargo to deliver. The sandwich would have to wait. I drove on quickly, closing the distance between the Katy I once was and the fatherless daughter I had become. Ahead, the green flag that marked Friday prayers fluttered above the tiny white-domed shrine of a saint at Tnine des Chtouka, where a fork in the road marked the end of my journey.

Before crossing the bridge to another world — the palatial *riad* that Daddy had painstakingly restored over the course of twenty years — I followed a trail of memories to the edge of the Oum er-Rbia, Mother of Spring River. I took in the timeless view of the ramparts that had seduced my father, Clive Chandler, into buying the derelict residence of a former pasha. Transforming it into a majestic Moorish home called Dar Zitoun became his passion. High above the water, I located "The House of the Olive [Tree]" by its telltale arched window. Never again would Daddy and I sit together on its terrace sipping gin-and-Dubonnet cocktails while listening to the BBC on a shortwave radio and watching satellites drift across the clear night sky.

A whiff of fresh mint from a passing truck brought on a new surge of nostalgia. I placed my hand on the bag next to me. "Daddy, you're home," I whispered.

Kefta (Ground Meat Brochettes)

Makes about 10

½ pound beef sirloin
½ pound lamb
1 tablespoon preserved lemon pulp (see page 255)
½ onion, grated
15 sprigs cilantro, minced
10 sprigs fresh parsley, minced
1 tablespoon ground cumin
1½ teaspoons salt
½ teaspoon pepper
2 garlic cloves, minced
Extra cumin, for dipping
Harissa, North African hot sauce (see following recipe)

Have the butcher coarsely grind together beef and lamb. Combine meat with preserved lemon pulp, onion, cilantro, parsley, cumin, salt, pepper, and garlic. Pinch off a golf-ball size amount of this mixture and form into a spindle shape around a skewer. Proceed in this manner with remaining meat mixture.

Heat coals to the red hot stage, or preheat a broiler. Grill *kefta* 4 minutes per side, or to desired doneness. Serve with cumin and *harissa* on the side.

Harissa (North African Hot Sauce)

Makes about 1½ cups

The spiciness of this condiment depends upon the chiles you use — guajillo or poblano for a milder flavor, chiltepíns or red jalapeños for extreme heat.

8 large or 16 small dried chiles
1 red bell pepper, roasted, deribbed, and seeded
4 garlic cloves, peeled
1 tablespoon freshly squeezed lemon juice
½ cup extra virgin olive oil
1 teaspoon salt, or more, to taste
2 teaspoons ground cumin, or more, to taste

Using scissors, cut open and seed dried chiles. Chop them into small pieces and transfer to a bowl of warm water. Soak until soft, 25 to 30 minutes. Drain chiles and pat dry.

In a blender or food processor, combine chiles, roasted pepper, garlic, lemon juice, olive oil, salt, and cumin. Process until smooth. Transfer to a clean pint jar. Cover with a thin layer of olive oil. Refrigerate. Use within six months.

AZEMMOUR. - 9. - Débarquement des Mulets

Jh. Boussuge, à Casablanca

2

A House for Immortals

I'd somehow held myself together emotionally since Daddy died the week before, but in that moment at the bridge, all was lost. I sobbed uncontrollably as I drove across it en route to the oldest part of Azemmour — the walled medina, the kasbah.

Striving to compose myself before I ran into anyone, I took a deep breath to inhale the abiding peace that emanated from the Mother of Spring. Narrow dirt paths, packed to stone-like hardness through centuries of use, wound from the river's bank and snaked through fields of tomatoes, carrots, and mint.

The scenery was not altogether pristine. The incoming tide carried odd bits of flotsam and jetsam, and the outgoing laid bare scallops of unsightly algae. Although scrupulous when it came to the tidiness of their homes, Zemmouris, inhabitants of Azemmour, tended to be more cavalier in their attitude toward litter. They simply overlooked the blemish on the landscape. From experience, I knew that in a few days, I too would find the refuse less affecting.

As I entered the town, my father's exuberance seemed to spill over the ramparts. "Someday people will realize what a gem of a place this is," he predicted on my first visit to the backwater some thirty years before. I'd thought his eccentricity had gotten the better of him, but he was right. Each year saw more gentrification and civic improvements. Azemmour even played host to art and music festivals. Daddy's lovingly restored *riad* was one of the medina's outstanding curiosities. Everyone in town knew of Dar Zitoun.

Near *Azemmour centre*, a policeman gave me a friendly salute and held up traffic while I turned into a walled enclosure once reserved for donkeys and mules, where Daddy used to park his Peugeot. Messaoud, the attendant, offered his condolences. Word of my father's passing had traveled quickly.

Messaoud's woolen djellabah was large enough for a man twice his size. A clumsily wrapped turban left uncovered his seal-brown pate. In primitive sandals, his callused feet could almost pass for leather. Only during the rainy season had I seen him in shoes. He was as I had always known him, of indeterminate age, although his craggy features and hollow cheeks had become more pronounced since my last visit. His gaunt appearance made me fear that he might not be long for this world. Yet he was in good spirits, in keeping with his devotion to Islam and his strong belief in *mektoob*, fate.

His sparrow of a wife, Khadooj, emerged from a tin-roofed shanty, her face partially covered with a fringed scarf. She was more subdued than her husband, but equally sincere. Her voice cracked. "*Allah eeshoof* [God watches]," she consoled, to let me know that my father's death was God's will. Her two children, begrimed from playing in the unpaved lot, couldn't hide their delight — in anticipation of the treats they knew I carried. "*Bonbons?*" asked little Amal. I produced a package of hard candies from my purse. She and her brother scurried inside their ramshackle dwelling to devour their prize.

While I waited for Messaoud to designate a space for the car, the *muezzin* began his *adhan*, call to prayer: "*Allah-u'Akbar* [God is great]!" The spellbinding pronouncement resonated from a nearby minaret. Five times each day, between the pre-dawn hours and midnight, the *adhan* punctuates life in Morocco. I'd heard it thousands of times. On that day, however, its sound was hypnotic, and moved me as never before.

The call also prompted the disappearance of my *gardien de voiture*, parking attendant. I discovered him minutes later on a prayer rug, forehead to the ground, in a vacant bay of the garage. Neither barking dogs nor waiting patrons could interrupt his whispered recitations. I envied the ease with which he could retreat so completely into his inner space, harmonizing his mental state with the postures of prayer.

Moments later, Messaoud, oblivious to the delay, rejoined the physical world. He adjusted his turban before directing me into a slot between a produce truck and a moped. His son reappeared just when I needed him. Since the medina's streets didn't accommodate automobiles, I sent him off to hail a two-wheeled *carossa*, handcart. Soon he and an elderly man came rattling into the compound.

"Take the second archway and head downhill toward the river until you see DAR ZITOUN in wrought-iron letters," were the straightforward directions my father gave to visitors, seemingly oversimplified guidance in light of the medina's maze of streets and alleyways. But no one ever got lost. The *riad*'s name was all my porter required. "*Eeyeh, nref* [Yes, I know it]!" he said.

Except for a few *téléboutiques* and ubiquitous *barabool*, satellite dishes, the medina had changed little since the ramparts were constructed in the sixteenth century. An historic landmark of that era, the *ferran*, public oven, provided a fundamental service to Zemmouris of modest means who lacked the wherewithal for baking at home. Many well-heeled households made use of it too, out of a sense of tradition, or simply to catch up on the local gossip at the neighborhood's social hub.

Smoke emanating from the *ferran*'s runty, soot-stained chimney filled the lane ahead and irritated my eyes. Near the entrance to the grotto, a pile of firewood almost blocked my path. I paused in the doorway to watch the baker wield his long handle peel. Behind him on wooden planks, leavened pillows of unbaked dough, each imprinted with an identifying family symbol, awaited their rendezvous with the vaulted kiln for metamorphosis into crusty hubcaps of golden-brown *khobz*. The baker promised to set aside a couple from his private reserve for me. "Come back in two hours," he said, sliding a round of dough onto the radiant firebricks.

Two little girls brushed past me, headed home from a public fountain with buckets of water nearly as big as they. "*Nesraniya talfa* [Lost foreigner]," I heard one whisper. Her conjecture was on the mark, just not in the sense she imagined.

"*Andee dar h'na* [I have a house here]," I piped up. My Arabic surprised them.

I reached the small plaza just up the alley from Dar Zitoun. As usual, Zora, our neighborhood grocer, held court in her closet-sized *épicerie*. She kept her shop filled to capacity with bulging sacks of couscous, cans of sardines, and packets of candles. Sky-blue tanks of Butagaz fuel further diminished her already tight workspace. We shook hands over over containers of vanilla yogurt and boxes of French processed cheese arranged on the glass counter. Zora lowered her veil and kissed her crossed thumb and forefinger in a gesture of respect.

"*Meskeen papak* [Poor thing your father]," she said, dabbing her eyes. Another Zemmouri who held my father in high esteem. The string of condolences from Daddy's acquaintances reinforced the reality of his passing.

One of her daughters smiled at me. Poor Zora, I thought. She would need the services of an expert matchmaker to help her marry off her daughters, because finding mates for all six of them seemed an unlikely prospect in so poor a town.

"You want something, take it now and pay me later," she offered kindly.

I thanked her and then made for the blind alley not fifty meters away. Near its mouth was our familiar whitewashed façade. The massive door had acquired some additional pockmarks since my last visit. Like all doors in the medina, it bore the scars inflicted by mischievous stone throwers and amateur soccer players kicking who-knows-what against it. Some *joueurs de foot* interrupted their game with a polite "*Bonjour, madame*" just long enough for me to step down into our stairwell. The boys' French was rudimentary and my Arabic halting at best. Fortunately, we were always able to make ourselves understood.

As I approached the door, an indescribable sensation of loss, or emptiness, came over me. Here I was on the threshold of two worlds — the one that I grew up in and the one where I now lived. Had it been years or mere months since my last visit? My compression of time threw past and present into stark relief. I was, in effect, entering a new world, one without my father in it. Standing there before the huge door, I felt suddenly uncertain about how to proceed. I paused and then, following convention, rapped the knocker three times. Even through the dense wood, I could hear its metallic clang reverberate through the house.

"*Shkoon* [Who is it]?" came a familiar and sonorous query a minute later. The knock had brought our breathless housekeeper from the second floor.

"*Kreeb* [Someone familiar]," I replied. Security bolts rolled back and the door opened. Like the Oum er-Rbia and Dar Zitoun itself, Bouchaïb Melhaj, our dear *gardien* and *cuisinier*, watchman and cook, endured life's challenges with dignity. His slender build was similar to my father's, I realized with a start. His cropped hair and compact moustache were a little greyer than when I last saw him. A tear pearled behind his black-rimmed glasses.

"Katy! I always expected your father to recover from his illness and return to Dar Zitoun. Now, what are we to do?" he asked, wringing his hands. We embraced as I struggled to find words of reassurance.

"*Merci*, Bouchaïb. My father was very grateful for all you have done." My pathetic formality seemed to comfort him.

He set about unloading the waiting *carossa* and paying the porter. While he did so I kicked off my shoes to feel the coolness of the mosaic floor in the entryway. The double foyers, with their fusty smell and chiaroscuro, were like a birth canal about to deliver me into the brilliant atrium. "Dar Zitoun is a magical place," my father used to say. "Once I'm inside, I never want to leave."

At the riad's epicenter, the sound of the percolating fountain enfolded me. I sensed the reassuring presence of familiar spirits. "I've brought him back," I said under my breath. My brothers and I thought it best not to tell Bouchaïb about the ashes or the burial arrangements for fear of offending his cultural sensibilities.

He'd already set a couple of hard-boiled eggs, a saucer of ground cumin, a bowl of black olives, and some warm *khobz* on the atrium table. I asked him to cancel my order at the *ferran*. He opened a bottle of Oulmès sparkling mineral water and left me with my thoughts. With glass in hand, I took in the soothing ambiance of the inner courtyard. The atrium, the most charmed space in the *riad*, practically spoke of Daddy's unrelenting presence. I had never thought much about ghosts until that moment. As I moved toward the main staircase leading to the terrace, I pulled aside the curtain that concealed a consecrated space. "Sidi Makhfi, are you there?" I asked.

Long ago, when my father had first purchased Dar Zitoun, he informed me, "Kate, did you know we have a *marabout** buried in the house?" He recounted the legend: In the 1500s, Morocco's native Berbers lived in constant fear of Portuguese invasion. One day, an approaching armada of caravels brought the townspeople to arms. But the shopkeepers, tradesmen, and fishermen were no match for the Iberian onslaught. A few Berbers, however, led by one valiant Sidi Makhfi, continued to resist Portugese domination. When this Zemmouri counterpart to "Zorro" was killed in action, fellow insurgents interred his body on a plot of land that was later built upon by a wealthy merchant from the north. According to local oral historians, the grave lay directly beneath our *riad*'s stairs. Through the centuries, the tight space came to be associated with his tomb. He had no name other than Sidi Makhfi, The Invisible Man. After his death, he became a widely venerated *marabout* imbued with supernatural abilities. From time to time, pilgrims still visited the house to pay homage and seek his blessing. My father shielded the hallowed ground from view with an ornamental wrought iron gate and translucent silk curtain, partly in deference to the *marabout* and his devotees, though primarily to hide the rusty tools, tagine pots, and empty wine bottles he stored there.

Someone had left a half-burned candle and a box of matches on the step in front of the curtain. Bouchaïb's wife, perhaps? Leila regularly sought the counsel of *marabouts*. I knelt down to light the wick anew, finding consolation in sharing the ritual with the candle's owner. I did so in honor of Azemmour's early defender, but also for his twentieth century counterpart from Hertfordshire. Rest in peace, Sidi Makhfi. Watch over my father.

A craving for confections lured me back to the kitchen. Bouchaïb had come and gone without a sound, discreet as a Dar Zitoun spirit, leaving behind a saucer of dates stuffed with almond paste to round out my modest meal. I nibbled away at one of the plump and fragrant jewels as a gibbous moon hoisted itself above the river, like a promise yet to be fulfilled.

*marabout: A religious teacher or holy man. Also the tomb of a venerated saint

Dates Stuffed with Almond Paste

Makes about 2 dozen

1 cup whole blanched almonds
2 tablespoons water
6 tablespoons granulated sugar
4 tablespoons butter
1 tablespoon orange blossom water
¼ cup minced candied orange (see page 257)
24 large pitted dates, slit open lengthwise

Preheat oven to 350 degrees F.

Spread almonds on a lightly oiled baking sheet, shaking pan once or twice. Toast until lightly browned, 12 to 15 minutes. Cool. In increments, reduce almonds to a paste using a spice grinder or mortar and pestle. Alternatively, run almonds through a food grinder fitted with a coarse grinding plate and then, three or four times, with a fine grinding plate to achieve a smooth paste.

In a medium saucepan, combine water and sugar over medium-low heat. Cook, stirring, until mixture begins to foam. Remove from heat. Add butter and stir until melted. Add ground almonds, orange blossom water, and candied orange. Stir vigorously until paste separates from sides of pan. Set aside to cool.

Mold a heaping teaspoon of paste into a spindle shape and place inside a date. Compress sides of date so paste bulges out slightly. Using a knife, lightly score surface of filling. Continue in this manner until all dates are filled. Sprinkle lightly with granulated sugar and serve, or refrigerate for up to 3 months in an airtight container.

3

Mint Tea and Minarets

My dear Kitty, In the sunshine here at Dar Zitoun, life seems eternal — as indeed it is — but the making of a will is a doleful necessity, especially as you have been such a source of pride and comfort to me.
— from the testament of Clive Chandler

The hillside path leading down to the water's edge was slippery, and my emotional equilibrium more so. I longed for him — the kind, funny, real Clive Chandler — to steady my descent to the Oum er-Rbia. With the *riad* looming above me, my thoughts turned to the thousands of hours Daddy had put into its restoration. I should have been concentrating on my footing, if I hoped to keep my grand-gentleman-of-a-father-reduced-to-ash out of the mud. My stepbrother Nigel, just in from London, and brother Philippe from Edmonton, had gone ahead to engage a boatman for a "scenic excursion." They were waiting for me in the stern of a waterlogged skiff.

I took a seat in its prow. My glum siblings, aware of the plan from the beginning, acted like hostages of my intransigence and bore the look of conspiring mutineers. Their body language pointed to their uneasiness with the mission.

"We were crazy to listen to you," grumbled Philippe. "I don't know why we agreed to this. We'll all end up in the slammer." I kept silent while my mind replayed the deathbed scene at Wimbledon:

"Daddy, suppose you don't make it out of here?"

"Then take me back to Morocco," he whispered. "And sprinkle my ashes on the river." He caught a shallow breath, before adding with his usual dry humor, "And I want you to throw a party — just as long as I'm invited."

"You'll be the guest of honor," I assured him with heartsick cheerfulness.

My father's dying request had been unequivocal, and I was committed to carrying it out. "Give me your basket," demanded our navigator as I came aboard.

"I'd rather hang onto it," I replied, clutching the *couffin.* It suddenly felt leaden. What if someone on the bank was watching? Would our own boatman turn us in? To avoid such thoughts, I focused on the droplets that rained in rhythmic arcs from the blades of the oars, until the skiff drew even with the *riad*, midway between the Portuguese bastions that bookended the whitewashed medina. A garland of grey-green leaves dangled low enough from one of the gnarled branches of our wild olive tree to caress the river.

Our sea-level perspective diminished the prominence of the slender minarets in the kasbah's skyline. The distinctive towers were an architectural legacy of Islamic conquerors that introduced their religion to *Maghreb al Aqsa*, the Land where the Sun Sets, in the seventh century. Were it not for antennae and satellite dishes, the town would look much the way it did when Magellan made history by dropping anchor there during his circumnavigation of the globe. With the increase in local tourism, perhaps the medina would again make headlines.

"I guess Dad knew what he was doing when he bought that old ruin," Philippe suddenly opened up. My brother's abrupt change in mood made me wonder if he was trying to soothe his sister's ruffled feathers or mitigate his grief. "Kitty, do you remember the first time we saw the place?" He was referring to 1965, when the two of us returned to Morocco for the summer, in the year following our parents' separation and our relocation with our mother to the American Midwest.

"Everyone thought Dad was out of his mind," mused Philippe. Like most early visitors to Dar Zitoun, some of whom called my father "crazy," even his own children lacked enthusiasm for his plan.

"Remember the piles of rubble and the smell of guano?" added Philippe. "What a disaster!"

Zemmouri authorities apparently felt the same way, for soon after my father took title to the property, the *caïd*, mayor, issued an order demanding the structure's *démolition immédiate* to preserve public safety. "Daddy had a vision," I said in his defense. He had the last laugh too, by prominently displaying the infamous directive in the atrium of the restored *riad*.

No one at *La Perception d'Azemmour*, the office of the city tax assessor, believed a house with six bedrooms was merely a private residence, but a *fundook*, hotel. They taxed my father accordingly, in spite of his yearly protestations. The false impression was reinforced by Daddy's steady stream of international visitors, not all of them invited. On one occasion, a well-meaning policeman directed a German tourist to our front door. Finding it ajar, the gentleman climbed the stairs to the *salon*, where my father and friends were having aperitifs. "Excuse me, but could I get a room?" Everyone had a good laugh, including the embarrassed Berliner, who ended up spending the night as Daddy's guest. I imagined the anecdote would lose some of its humor once I had my first run-in with the taxman.

Taxes wouldn't be my only problem. A more fundamental question preyed upon my mind as a couple of moored fishing boats clacked against each other near the opposite shore. The ties that linked me to Morocco had weakened. Though I grew up in the country, as an adult, my annual visits from the United States were as a pampered guest. If I came back to live for extended periods, could I re-adapt? More important, would Dar Zitoun feel like home?

My attention was drawn to the geraniums that cascaded in pink clouds over our stone retaining wall. I made a mental note to transplant cuttings into clay pots on the terrace. I'd also have to do something about the beard of spent palm fronds that blocked the view from the atrium window. I was already thinking like a proprietor.

A skein of foraging swallows flapped and glided in erratic spurts above the *riad*. I took their arrival as a sign to discharge Daddy's ashes. With a nod from me, Philippe distracted our navigator. "*Cigarette?*"

The man eagerly shipped his oars and let the boat drift. He lit up and inflated his lungs with the delight of an addict, exhaling in a single dragon-like puff. He gave my brother a thumbs-up. "*Malbrook, mezzian* [Marlboro, good]," he declared, in praise of the brand.

While the two of them bantered, I leaned over the gunwale, hurriedly unscrewed the container's lid, and emptied its contents as close to the surface of the water as possible. Was this mixture of powder and fragmented bone all that was left of my poor father? The thought was jolting.

The river hungrily swallowed the evanescent ash. It comforted me to know that, although the ebbing tide would take my father out to sea, the rising tide would bring him back again.

Our captain was never the wiser. Lost in smoker's bliss, he followed the action of a soccer game playing out on a sandbar.

"It's turned windy," I said, inventing an excuse for our boatman to suspend the rest of our cruise and return to the point of embarkation. "Please take us back."

"*Walakeen* [But] . . ." he said, on his way to becoming ill tempered. I knew where he was going and cut him off.

"Don't worry, you'll be paid full price," I assured him.

He had to fight against the outgoing current to turn the skiff around. After several unsuccessful attempts to beach the craft, we were forced to jump into the shallows and wade through a blanket of algae. Mud sucked at my feet as if the river didn't want to let me go. Sodden and weepy, I longed for a glass of mint tea, always a balm for my spirits. Once back at Dar Zitoun, we settled into my father's favorite spot on the terrace. I could just make out whitecaps on the Atlantic, almost a kilometer away. Were they washing over Daddy's ashes in the estuary?

If Bouchaïb suspected the purpose of our nautical excursion, he never let on. He joined us soon after we sat down, bringing with him all the makings for mint tea. He poured boiling water over the Gunpowder green leaves inside an engraved silver pot and then, after allowing the brew to steep for a several minutes, added a generous bouquet of fresh mint.

Daddy wasn't as keen as I when it came to the Moroccan national beverage. For this expatriate Englishman, sipping mint tea was more a social obligation. According to him, *real* tea was of the black variety. "How about a cuppa?" he would ask every evening around five. A cup of Earl Grey with sugar and warm milk (in that order), there was nothing else like it as far as he was concerned. The tin with his favorite brand was still in the kitchen cupboard.

Bouchaïb dropped several chunks of sugar loaf into the pot and poured himself a glass to evaluate for taste. "*Parfait* [Perfect]," he proclaimed. He filled the remaining glasses with his usual finesse — raising and lowering the spout to lengthen and shorten the steaming, glittering ribbon of tea.

"*À Monsieur Changler*," he proposed, as he held his glass aloft. Many Moroccans had trouble getting their tongues to cooperate when it came to the "dl" in "Chandler."

Before Nigel, Philippe, and I could respond, the midday call to prayer erupted from loudspeakers on our neighborhood minaret. Soon, *muezzins* from more distant mosques lent their voices to the asynchronous *adhan* that rolled out in rounds over rooftop terraces. I waited for the chanting to draw to a close before following our toastmaster's lead. "*À Monsieur Changler*," I said in the same consonant-swapping way, in an attempt to lighten the solemnity of the moment. Nigel and Philippe followed suit. "*À Monsieur Changler*," they repeated in unison. This may not have been the "party" my father had in mind, but it was the best we could do.

"What are the plans for Dar Zitoun?" asked Nigel after a few moments of silence.

"Sell it, of course," interjected Philippe. "What else can we do? I can't fly in from Edmonton to patch a leaky roof."

I shifted uneasily in my seat.

"I'm not keen on being an absentee landlord, especially when it comes to property in Morocco. Are you, Kitty?" Philippe went on. My brother's indelicacy touched a nerve.

"Enough! This isn't the time!"

Parting with the family home so soon after Daddy's death seemed akin to turning our backs on him. More than that, it meant abandoning a precious chapter of my life, and I, for one, wasn't ready to close the book on Dar Zitoun. Our testy exchange must have been distressing for Bouchaïb. He headed for the stairs.

"I'm calling Owen," I said.

"Go ahead! Call Owen! You don't think he wants to keep this drafty old place?" Philippe shot back. He may have been right, but I didn't think so. My husband, the quintessential do-it-yourselfer, wouldn't need much arm-twisting to back me up.

I walked to the parapet overlooking the river. From that idyllic vantage point, logic and practicality vanished from my radar. "I need time to think. Give me until next summer." I suspected it would take at least that long to transfer title. "I'll handle everything concerning the house."

Nigel and Philippe seemed more wary of their sister as middle-aged-woman-in-crisis. They looked at each other before turning back to me. "Are you sure you're up to it?" asked Nigel.

Bouchaïb cast a worried look in my direction. He hadn't fled the scene after all. I nodded defiantly. "I am."

"I could use a beer," said Nigel.

"That's the best idea I've heard all day," seconded Philippe. "Bouchaïb tells me there's an *épicier* in town who sells alcohol on the QT. Let's track him down."

Dar Zitoun and I — and Bouchaïb — had won a reprieve. Though he didn't understand English, I was certain the man who'd watched over the house for more than thirty years understood the situation. Of all his titles: *cuisinier*, *gardien*, man Friday, butler, overseer, and *la mémoire de* Dar Zitoun (Dar Zitoun's historian), the *riad's* most faithful link to the past, none did justice to his overall job description.

"*Qu'est-ce que tu en penses* [What do you think]?" I later asked him. I didn't have to be more specific.

He answered, just as he had when applying for his position with my father three decades earlier: "*Je peux faire le nécessaire* [I can do whatever is necessary]," before adding, in what would become his new catchphrase, " . . . *comme quand votre père il était vivant* [just like when your father he was alive]."

Atay b'Nana (Mint Tea)

Makes 4 cups

4½ cups boiling water
2 teaspoons Gunpowder green or Chinese green tea
1 bunch fresh mint, *Mentha spicata,* washed under running water
½ cup granulated sugar (or to taste)

Rinse teapot with ½ cup boiling water. Discard water. Add tea and remaining boiling water. Steep for 2 to 3 minutes. Stuff pot with mint and steep another 2 to 3 minutes. Sweeten to taste and serve.

4

A Legacy of Restoration

My brothers drew up a daunting list of repairs before jetting off to rejoin their families. With the house to myself, I began to take stock of our common patrimony and to go through what personal effects Daddy kept in Azemmour. Nigel and Philippe's home improvement suggestions would have to wait.

The *riad* still hummed with a subtle energy that I attributed to my father. In the atrium, the tortured philodendron that he planted years before maintained its stranglehold on a pillar. The tenacious vine should have withered long ago, but like the once-condemned structure, it endured.

Around noon, an intense forest green radiated from the garden of ferns that Daddy had suspended in a wrought-iron basket below the skylight. The plants brought a sense of the wild to the atrium. A confusion of their roots and rhizomes hung down like untrimmed locks to tickle the water in "Bouchaïb's fountain," the one he'd unearthed years before from the rubble. "It took three days to dig it out," he boasted.

A ceramic frog, mouth open in silent croak, lay half-submerged in the central font. It didn't discourage a trespassing bunting from splashing about. Fellow interlopers cavorting among the luxuriant plants sent a flurry of dead leaves onto the floor of zillij, terra cotta tiles. They seemed to be more vigilant whenever Bouchaïb was around. Maybe they knew of the disoriented pigeons that had blundered into the atrium and ended up with top billing on the Melhaj family table — in *bestila au pigeon*, pigeon pie.

"Little bastards!" Bouchaïb griped, snapping a towel at the buntings whenever he passed the fountain. There wasn't enough meat on their little bones worth the effort of catching and cleaning them. But the birds didn't bother me. On the contrary, their spirited chirping lifted my spirits. The telephone interrupted their recital. "*Allô?*"

"Mademoiselle Chandler?" asked the voice.

"*Oui, c'est* Madame Morse," I corrected.

"*Je suis* Maître* Tanja, *le notaire* [I am Maître Tanja, the notary]."

"*Oui, bonjour,*" I replied guardedly.

"*Mes condoléances, mademoiselle,*" he continued. "I am sorry to bother you in your time of grief, but we need to discuss your father's testament. When will you be in Casablanca?" Frankly, I hadn't the strength to face probate just then. "I'll call you next week for an appointment, monsieur," I said to put off the dreaded rendezvous.

I moved to the rough granite fountain to dip my fingers into the water. For some reason, as I ran my hands over the velvety algae on its rim, my thoughts turned to Si Mohammed Ben Driss, a nineteenth century gentleman who became so besotted with Azemmour that he commissioned his architect to construct a grand *riad* on the banks of Oum er-Rbia. The edifice came to be known as Dar Basha, The House of the Pasha. Some in the medina used that name still.

---

*maître: "master," an honorific title for lawyers and notaries, as well as experts outside the legal field

Si Mohammed came from Tétouan, a region steeped in the culture of Al Andalus, that part of the Iberian Peninsula once governed by the Moors. I learned about him from one of his descendants during a New Year's gathering at the *riad* shortly after my father had acquired title.

The self-appointed Ben Driss family genealogist related the story: Lalla Meryem, Si Mohammed's wife, fell into a state of melancholy soon after relocating to Azemmour. She yearned for the sophisticated flavors and refined cuisine of her native Tétouan. In an effort to lift her spirits, her husband imported dark-skinned kitchen slaves, called *dadas*, to instruct local girls in the secrets of Andalusian cooking.

A Culinary Institute of Azemmour! In other words, the *riad*'s reputation for *haute cuisine* predated Bouchaïb's tenure. It was a legacy of Lalla Meryem. And through a combination of my Hungarian stepmother Hedda's membership in La Chaîne des Rôtisseurs, an honorary gastronomic society, my father's eclectic circle of international friends, and my own career as a cookbook author and leader of culinary tours, that reputation spread far beyond Morocco's borders. As for Bouchaïb, a guest of my father's, a visiting princess from the United Arab Emirates was so impressed by his talent in the kitchen that she tried to lure him to the Gulf. Luckily for us, he declined.

A neighbor who'd catered parties at Dar Zitoun whenever Bouchaïb was on vacation, appeared at our door cradling a tagine of *mrouziya*. Aromatic steam escaped from the gap between the conical lid and the base of Mina's cooking vessel. The meltingly tender pieces of lamb, bathed in an ambrosial honey/raisin sauce, sang of cinnamon and ginger. It was one of my father's favorites. Mina brought it over in memory of him.

"I don't think you know the story of this recipe," she said. "My grandmother picked it up right here at Dar Zitoun, from Lalla Z'hoor, the *dada* who worked for Hadj Ben Amar." The name Ben Amar rang a bell. Where had I seen or heard it before? Of course, on a copy of Dar Zitoun's title! Ben Amar was the man from whom my father bought the *riad*.

I was delighted to learn that Mina trained in the *dada* tradition under her grandmother's tutelage. Her aptitude for all things culinary as well as her Black African features were clues to her profession. Like many *dadas*, she probably descended from Haratin Berbers, tribesmen from the south, whose ancestors were slaves from Mauritania and Mali. Contemporary *dadas* like Mina worked as freelance caterers, commanding both respect and high fees for their services.

"Lalla Z'hoor, she taught many Zemmouri girls how to cook," she explained.

I tried to imagine Dar Zitoun's kitchens (or rather, Dar Basha's kitchens) generations before Bouchaïb and I took over, in the era when *dadas* reigned supreme. I envisioned one of them directing her apprentices:

"*Bnat* [Girls], when you dab *warka* dough on your griddle, it should look like the hoof print of a camel — like this."

"Yes, *dada*."

"*Bnat*, watch me carefully. Add just a pinch of saffron to the tagine sauce. This much. More than that will make it bitter. You understand?"

"Yes, *dada*."

"Dar Basha had the largest ovens in the medina," Mina informed me. "My grandmother and Lalla Z'hoor, when they cooked for a wedding *diffa* [banquet], they could roast six lambs at a time, right there, next to the *hammam* [steam bath]."

Hammam! I'd never paid much attention to the cluttered chambers that lay beneath the atrium. Ever since I could remember, my father used the space to store building materials.

"My grandmother told of being invited to Hadj Ben Amar's *hammam* every week on the night before *Masjid Al-Jum'a* [Friday communal prayer at the mosque]."

"Shall we go down for a look?" I asked, with a gesture toward the squat door that led to the river. Her face broke into a broad smile.

"Oh, yes!" she exclaimed, as if she'd waited her whole life for the opportunity. Her enthusiasm was engaging. She and I descended the uneven stairs past the access door to the cistern. Intrepid Mina brushed aside cobwebs to advance through an archway. She sidestepped piles of zillij, rusted scaffolding, and a drum of the slaked lime for whitewashing the *riad*'s exterior. Judging from the state of the plaster walls, we would soon be in need of it. I followed Mina with the curiosity of an archaeologist's assistant.

"This is just how my grandmother described it," she said. "Here are the ovens. And on this side, look, Katy, this is the *hammam*." She pointed to a dark, uninviting grotto.

I'd been down there before, but never in the company of such a knowledgeable guide. I marveled at the simplicity of the Turkish bath, so different from elegantly appointed American spas with their network of copper lines, chrome plated faucets, and washerless valves. Our *hammam*'s plumbing consisted of a single clay pipe to channel rainwater from the terrace to the cistern, from which Hadj Ben Amar's servants could draw water for domestic use. My father sealed off the opening to the underground reservoir for fear some wild or domesticated creature would tumble in.

Mina's narrative brought to mind an Orientalist tableau: women splashing warm water, scrubbing each other's backs, and working thick henna paste into their hair.

"Not many *hammam*s overlook the river," observed Mina. "No wonder my grandmother loved it here." The possibility of making the Turkish bath operational again crossed my mind. My brothers would have been furious with me for entertaining the idea.

Half a century of neglect hadn't discouraged the "eccentric Englishman" from restoring the *riad*. Why wouldn't *l'américaine* be up to the task of reweaving the warp and weft of her father's dream?

Mina's Mrouziya (Honey Spiced Lamb)

Serves 6

Mrouziya is traditionally served on *Aïd el Kebir*, the religious feast that commemorates the sacrifice of Ibrahim (Abraham). The word itself is derived from *Maurusia*, the ancient Greek appellation for northwest Africa.

4 pounds lamb shoulder or leg of lamb, cut into chunks
3 tablespoons *ras el hanoot* spice blend (see page 156)
2 to 3 cups water
½ cup vegetable oil
2 tablespoons *smen* (see page 268)
½ cup honey
¾ cup raisins, plumped in warm water and drained
2 tablespoons sesame seeds, toasted

Preheat oven to 325 degrees F. Coat meat with *ras el hanoot* and place in a tagine pot or cast iron pan with a heavy lid. Add 2 cups water, oil, *smen*, and honey. Cover tightly. Bake until meat falls off the bones, 3 to 4 hours. Check for dryness halfway through. Add more water if necessary.

Transfer meat to an ovenproof dish and keep warm. Skim fat from sauce. Place tagine over medium high heat and add raisins. Cook until sauce reduces by one-third, 10 to 12 minutes. Return meat to pan and heat through. Garnish with toasted sesame seeds. Serve with crusty bread.

5

The Souk

"Jav-eeeeel!" cried the itinerant bleach vendor on his early morning rounds, pushing his battered cart over the uneven pavement. I awakened with a start to the reveille.

"Ja-veeeel!" His second call got me out of bed. I pulled back the curtain. The peddler below was topping off a plastic bottle a neighbor submitted to him for refilling. On an adjacent rooftop, a malnourished watchdog, prisoner of his elevated domain, gnawed on a crust of stale bread.

Tuesday was souk day, the day of the open-air market. I slipped a djellabah over my t-shirt and jeans and ran downstairs for a cup of *café au lait* with Bouchaïb. He handed me a shopping list; looked like I'd be heading out alone with my two ratty *couffins*, straw baskets.

"The souk, it's too dusty," he declared. "I prefer the new *supermarché* in El Jadida."

That was heresy! For me, souks, from the relatively sophisticated el-Attarin spice souk in Fez to our own provincial market in Azemmour, held no end of culinary intrigue. And shopping in them helped me readjust to the rhythm of Moroccan life.

Zemmouris were out in force on the idyllic spring morning. A *grand taxi* disgorged six rumpled passengers from the surrounding countryside. They joined the flow of human traffic, interspersed with produce-laden carts, bicycles rigged with bulging straw panniers, and an intrepid moped operator ferrying a ladder on his shoulder. All clogged the main thoroughfare leading to the souk. A policeman blew his whistle amid the chaos, to no apparent effect.

I jumped back to avoid a cyclist who rode against the current, a live chicken hanging upside down from his handlebar. He swerved around me and vanished into the crowd. I couldn't help wondering how the stress of the harrowing commute would affect the flavor of the fowl. Whether donkey, dog, or chicken, Morocco is no paradise for animals.

The decibel level increased as I approached the souk. A discordant "Cheb Khaled! Cheb Khaled!" blared from a battery-powered bullhorn belonging to an unshaven man in a sweatshirt emblazoned with an image of Leonardo Dicaprio embracing Kate Winslet. The barker's call attracted three boys who cut in front of me in order to get to the Khaled CDs. He was a popular Algerian singer and a pioneer of *rai*, a style of music that melded Spanish, French, African-American, and Arabic traditions. *"Aïsha, Aïsha, Ecoute-moi* [*Aïsha, Aïsha, listen to me*]," went the song's unforgettable refrain. I bobbed my head to the beat.

A cut-rate CD I purchased the year before was defective and wouldn't play. That prospect didn't bother the tech-savvy youngsters who snapped up pirated CDs and DVDs — from computer programs to just-released American films — all smuggled in from Ceuta, Spain's autonomous peninsula on Morocco's Mediterranean coast. Though officially condemned, contraband was unofficially tolerated.

Copyright infringement didn't concern the middle-aged police officer browsing through the selections. He seemed more intent on finding a recording of legendary Umm Kalthum, the "Nightingale of the Nile," than exposing unauthorized copies.

The treasures I sought that day were edible in nature. Within a stone walled perimeter, the cornucopia of the Doukkala plain overflowed from wooden crates, wicker baskets, and burlap sacks. I dug for Bouchaïb's list to begin my haphazard pursuit of produce.

A mountain of artichokes waylaid me. Our *cuisinier* hadn't ordered any, but I couldn't resist them. I chose four grey-green globes and asked the farmer to remove the stems. He wagged his finger at me. The callused *zabibah*, prayer mark, on his brow identified him as a pious man, who faithfully touched his forehead to the ground many times each day.

"*Shoof* [Watch this]." With his pocketknife, he peeled away a stem's fibrous outer layer. "*Kool koolshee* [Eat everything]," he instructed, of the stalk's meaty xylem and phloem. "It's as good as the heart." I bowed to his far greater expertise. Before we could complete the transaction, he pushed forward a basket of fava beans. "How about half a kilo?" They weren't on Bouchaïb's list either, but I couldn't pass them up. I helped the vendor select the smallest of the bright green pods, ones I could cook whole — along with olive oil, garlic, and cilantro.

An adjacent merchant hawked vine-ripened tomatoes. Lacking the intensity of that Doukkala-grown commodity, cooks in other countries sometimes have trouble capturing the true flavor of Moroccan dishes. In my view, local tomatoes are distinctive enough to be worthy of AOC status, *Appellation d'Origine Contrôlée*. Unfortunately, this honor is reserved for the finest agricultural products grown only in France or one of its territories.

Bouchaïb made fun of me because of my breakfast of choice — sautéed tomatoes on toast. I had long tried to interest him in something more healthful than his beloved honey pastries washed down with a glass or two of cloyingly sweet mint tea. It was no wonder he had lost his teeth by his mid-forties. One morning, however, I caught him in the act, polishing off a *tomate grillée* on a slice of toasted *khobz*. "*Pas mal* [Not bad]," he conceded.

As for the red beauties in front of me, I'd stuff them with a mixture of couscous and diced vegetables. I let the vendor make a selection for me. As he set tomatoes on the scale, I noticed how soil had impregnated the fissures of his sausage-like fingers. Assorted iron weights he plunked onto an opposing pan brought the two sides into balance.

"*Arb'een d'rial* [Forty *rials*]," the man informed me, using the archaic numismatic term for a currency that had fallen out of circulation three-quarters of a century earlier, but was still the exchange favored by rural folk to compute prices. Asking for a tally in dirhams would have drawn a blank stare. Fortunately, calculating in *rials* is a skill I'd acquired in childhood. It is an aptitude uncommon among westerners that never fails to impress.

In my head I multiplied forty *rials* by five to determine the price in old francs and then divided that amount by one hundred to arrive at dirhams. Therefore *arbeen d'rial*, forty *rials*, was equal to two dirhams, about twenty cents. The fellow was almost giving his produce away. I couldn't help but compare souk prices with those at my local farmers' market in California. I pressed two coins into the man's leathery palm.

"*Fabor* [gift]," he said, handing me a bunch of parsley.

I took a buffeting from other preoccupied shoppers and plodding pack animals for trying to do two things at once — negotiate the twisting aisles and decipher Bouchaïb's writing. I paused to scrutinize his phonetic French:

"*Bom di tir*," *pomme de terre* — potatoes,
"*Poav*," *poivre* — pepper,
"*Lezeuf*," *les oeufs* — eggs, and
"*Lezonions*," *les oignons* — onions, I understood.

"*Budanjal*," *aubergine* — eggplant, proved more of a challenge because Bouchaïb had switched mid-list from French to Arabic. I guessed at what lay in the offing for the purple-skinned fruit — tagine *baraniya*, a distant cousin of a dish first prepared for the extravagant wedding of a ninth-century caliph to the daughter of his grand vizier. The bride's nickname was Buran.

The meaning of the next word on Bouchaïb's list, "*borro*," eluded me until I repeated it out loud several times, "*Borro, borro, borro*. Ah, *poireaux* [leeks]!" Bouchaïb's impressionistic list was again *en français*.

A young woman sat cross-legged under a makeshift awning behind a mountain of onions. Samira had the sunniest disposition of anyone I knew. That morning, she seemed radiant. An infant slept amid the folds of her djellabah. I congratulated her on the latest addition to her family.

"Three children, that's it," she said with a laugh. "I told Mustapha, '*Safee* [Enough].'" She and her husband rented a house near ours, but grew leeks and a few herbs on a small plot of land her family owned outside town.

"Last year, you were here with your father," she said, "he was carrying an old clock. You remember? I am sorry he is gone." I had forgotten about the clock. Whenever we came to the souk, my father gravitated toward the junk dealers. He would rummage there by the hour, looking for antique knickknacks, many of which lined the shelves in our salon. Sudden wails from Samira's baby threatened to cut short our conversation, but she silenced his cries with her breast.

The few leeks left in her basket were as thin as ballpoint pens. All they needed was cleaning, boiling, and a good dousing with Bouchaïb's incomparable garlic vinaigrette. The young mother refused payment.

"*Blesh* [It's not necessary]," she told me. "Would you mind dropping by one evening? It's about my sister. She wants to join her husband in Spain, but can't understand the forms from the consulate." I welcomed the opportunity to visit Samira and Mustapha in their cozy living quarters, setback as they were from a medina alleyway, behind a shabby Hobbit-like door.

"I'll be glad to help," I replied. Those were hard economic times. Thousands of husbands, brothers, and fathers left their families to work in Europe. Her brother-in-law had done well enough to send for his family. I would have agreed to translate even without Samira's edible retainer because of the psychological boost it offered — by providing continuity between my father's life and mine.

"*Ga'raa!*" cried a man standing over his crop of hassock-shaped squash the size of beach balls. With the flourish of a carnival performer, he whacked off a wedge of one of them, stabbed it with his blade, and held it out for my inspection. Beads of moisture formed on the surface of its apricot-colored flesh.

"*Besh hal* [How much]?" I asked. His scale settled at exactly one kilo. How did he manage that? I was digging through my purse for payment when I felt a tap on the shoulder.

"Mademoiselle Changler, I am Hadj Mustapha, the *samsar* [real estate agent]," said the man in blue jeans and open-toe sandals. My quizzical expression made him add, "I have a client who is interested in your house. I can bring him by this afternoon." With that, I recognized the face behind the knock-off designer sunglasses. He was one of the agents who monitored the medina's real estate. Bouchaïb had once pointed him out.

"But monsieur," I replied, somewhat startled by his proposition. "Dar Zitoun is not for sale." My statement fell on deaf ears.

"Good, I'll come by sometime and we can talk," he went on.

The souk was neither the time nor place for such a discussion. The question wasn't whether or not he had an interested party, but what my brothers and I intended to do with the house. An inner voice implored, "Keep it in the family."

"Do as you wish, monsieur," I replied. "And now, if you will excuse me, I have errands to run."

The chance encounter made me realize just how uncomfortable I was with the prospect of selling Dar Zitoun. Talking about the possibility with my brothers was one thing, but discussing it with a real estate agent was quite unsettling.

I held my breath from one end of the live poultry market to the other. Bouchaïb allowed only *djej beldi*, free-range chickens, into our kitchen, ones he obtained from a friend's farm. Of the egg purveyor at the souk, on the other hand, Dar Zitoun's persnickety *cuisinier* approved. The veiled woman reached under a blanket of straw to retrieve the eggs I requested, carefully transferring them to a cone fashioned from the pages of a newspaper. I always thought of a freshly laid egg as nature's most perfect gift, an opinion I formed during childhood in the garden of an elegant villa in Casablanca.

* * *

For apartment dwellers like my brother Philippe and me, there was nothing more exciting on a Sunday afternoon than being set free in the park-like grounds that surrounded the home of my grandmother's dearest friend Manou.

The main attraction for us was a hen house that dated back to World War II. Egg rationing ended shortly after the war, but Manou continued raising chickens in spite of a municipal ordinance outlawing the practice. "I need fresh eggs," she declared. "How can I make a decent quiche without fresh eggs?"

No one, not even city officials, dared argue with her. On those magical Sundays, our hearts beat faster as we stepped under the arch of purple bougainvillea that shaded her gate and waited for Laoucine, the gardener, the only member of the household staff out of uniform. The wizened old man was as bent as one of the fig trees in Manou's orchard. "Laoucine, did the chickens lay any eggs today?" we would ask, bright-eyed in anticipation.

"*Yallah* [Come on]," he replied, limping though the garden with us in tow. Philippe and I waited outside the wire enclosure until Laoucine shooed the indignant hens from their nests. We were soon racing back to Manou's living room cradling our nacreous finds.

"The chickens must have known you were coming," she would say, winking at my mother. "Now, are you ready for your *goûter* [afternoon snack]?"

"*Oui,* Manou!"

Flanked by slobbering boxers, Mic and Mac, she led us into her formal dining room and seated us around the massive, carved teak table she'd acquired in Indochina. As a rebellious eighteen-year-old, she'd run away from home to marry an officer in the French army who was then stationed in the Far East. The dragons and other mythical Asian creatures embroidered on her ornate silk screens filled us with wonder. We fell quiet as angels admiring them, doing our mother proud. No sooner did we unfold the monogrammed napkins than Manou summoned her cook with a touch of a buzzer within easy reach of her foot. Jamila appeared with Manou's signature *pudding de petits pains au chocolat*, to which she'd added bits of *orange confite* especially for our *goûter*. She acquired the recipe for the candied fruit from my grandmother.

"Now you understand why I raise hens," said Manou. "Desserts are always better when we use fresh eggs."

* * *

The egg vendor tapped me on the hand to bring me back to the transaction. She tucked in the top of the paper cone to add an extra modicum of crush resistance to the package.

What would I make? A quiche studded with caramelized leeks? Or, if I felt particularly ambitious, perhaps Manou's pudding. Thinking about recipes was a welcome interlude from contemplating probate or steering clear of the *samsar*. I was in my element. I overheard a woman asking for the price of eggplant. I pushed forward after she concluded her transaction to verify the price for myself.

"*Besh hal l'kilo dial budanjal* [How much for a kilo of eggplant]?" I enquired.

"*Mia ou steen d'rial* [160 *rial*s]."

The merchant had inflated the price.

"Surely you mean 100 *rial*s, the same price you quoted the last customer?"

"*Wakha* [Okay]," he said unashamedly. Pressing one's advantage, especially when it came to *nesraniyas*, foreigners, was a national pastime. I handed him a few dirhams and crossed *budanjal* from the list, leaving only "*poivre*" unaccounted for. I headed for the spice alley. Fifty grams of peppercorns were soon pinging on the brass pan of a balance.

I was getting hungry. The enticing aroma of fried fish didn't help matters. Nor did the enthusiasm with which local connoisseurs devoured crisp *petite friture*, small fried fish, composed of sardines and *solettes*, baby sole. "Be careful about eating at the souk," Bouchaïb repeatedly warned. "Your stomach isn't used to it." The fare must have been particularly good to pack the al fresco eatery to overflowing. But something about the smell of the oil in the blackened cauldron raised a red flag. I decided to press on.

At the fish market, one never knew what the day's catch would be — mackerel, sea bass, monkfish, tuna, or shark. Near a civic fountain, a worker scaled and gutted mackerel. The innards went to waiting felines. One of them, a crusty-eyed kitten produced a barely audible meow.

On a bed of crushed ice, a fishmonger displayed squid, eel, and half a dozen still quivering sole linked through the gills with a palm frond.

"*Ashabel?*" I asked, on the remote chance that he had set aside a specimen for a discriminating customer.

"Ahmed, *andek ashabel* [do you have *ashabel*]?" he hollered to a colleague lugging a twenty-liter bucket.

"*Ehyeh* [Yes]!" the man called back. I was in luck. Inside the sloshing container was a clear-eyed, red-gilled dream of a catch, a species of shad once prevalent in the estuary before upstream dams inhibited spawning.

"How much?" I asked with trepidation. The merchant had the upper hand and he knew it.

"*Alef d'rial l'kilo.*" One hundred dirhams per kilo, close to five dollars a pound, a hefty price by any standard. But I wouldn't get many more opportunities like that. The *ashabel* tipped the scales at three kilos. The fishmonger would be collecting a king's ransom. Nevertheless, the transaction was a coup for me as well. Azemmour suddenly seemed a lot more welcoming as I headed for home.

Just up the lane from our door, I came across Radia on her stool. The old woman earned a living selling *babboosh*, diminutive snails, much smaller than commercial escargots. She culled them each morning from hedgerows across the river. The children that ringed her cauldron sipped oregano-scented broth from chipped bowls and used straightened safety pins to tease mollusks from their delicate striated shells. Radia held up her ladle.

"*Non merci.*" I was in a hurry to get home. I rehearsed the poker face I would wear when Bouchaïb met me at the door. The chain of events played out in my mind: Bouchaïb relieves me of the *couffins* while I repair to the terrace for a glass of Oulmès to await the inevitable discovery of the *ashabel*, signaled first by Bouchaïb's high-pitched "Ka-ty" (emphasis on the second syllable), and second, by his inimitable hoarse, cackling laugh.

Tagine Baraniya

Serves 4

2 lbs lamb chops or beef short ribs
2 teaspoons ground ginger
¼ teaspoon freshly ground pepper
6 tablespoons olive oil
2 onions, finely chopped
½ bunch cilantro, tied with cotton string
10 sprigs fresh, flat-leaf parsley, tied with cotton string
8 threads Spanish saffron, toasted and crushed
1 cup beef broth, warmed
2 globe eggplants, peeled and cut into ½-inch-thick slices
1 (14¼ ounce) can Italian plum tomatoes
2 tablespoons tomato paste
Salt and freshly ground pepper to taste
2 cloves garlic, minced, for garnish
Minced parsley, for garnish

Preheat oven to 375 degrees F. Coat meat with ginger and pepper. In a tagine pot or Dutch oven over medium high heat, heat 3 tablespoons of olive oil. Brown the meat for 3 to 4 minutes. Add onions and cook until translucent, 2 to 3 minutes. Add cilantro and parsley. Steep saffron in broth and pour into Dutch oven. Cover and bake until meat is tender, 1½ to 2 hours. Transfer meat to a covered dish and keep warm. Discard parsley and cilantro, but reserve the pan juices.

Meanwhile, place eggplant slices on a clean towel. Sweat for 10 to 15 minutes. Pat dry. In a skillet, heat remaining olive oil over medium high heat. Fry eggplant until golden brown. Drain on paper towels and keep warm.

To the reserved pan juices in the Dutch oven, add tomatoes, tomato paste, and half the fried eggplant. Mash lightly. Season to taste with salt and pepper. Return meat to the Dutch oven and bake 30 minutes longer. Garnish with reserved eggplant slices, garlic, and parsley. Serve with crusty bread.

Pudding de Petits Pains au Chocolat à l'Orange Confite

(Chocolate Croissant Pudding with Candied Orange)

Serves 8

Petits pains au chocolat are often called "chocolate croissants" in the United States

2½ cups whole milk
¼ cup sugar
1 pound chocolate croissants, cut in ½-inch cubes
3 eggs
2 tablespoons butter, melted
¼ teaspoon salt
½ teaspoon vanilla
¼ teaspoon cinnamon
¾ cup diced candied orange rind (see page 257)
1 cup whipping cream, whipped with 1½ tablespoons granulated sugar
Dark chocolate, grated, for garnish
Candied orange rind, julienned, for garnish

Preheat oven to 350 degrees F. In a pan, heat milk until lukewarm. Add sugar. Transfer to a mixing bowl and fold in cubes of *petits pains*. Let stand 15 minutes.

In a separate bowl, beat eggs, melted butter, salt, vanilla, and cinnamon. Gently combine with *petits pains* mixture.

Grease a 9-inch flan pan (or 8 individual ramekins) with butter. Distribute half of the diced candied orange over the bottom. Using a ladle, add the pudding mixture and sprinkle with remaining diced rind. Set the pan or ramekins inside a large roasting pan. Using a measuring cup or kettle, add enough boiling water to reach halfway up their sides. Bake 50 to 55 minutes, or until a knife inserted into the pudding's center comes out clean. Let stand 10 minutes. Serve warm with whipped cream, grated chocolate, and extra candied orange rind on the side.

6

The Poison That Spreads

Things didn't go according to plan.

"The *samsar* is waiting for you," whispered Bouchaïb as he relieved me of my purchases.

"But I just saw him at the souk," I mouthed in disbelief.

My *ashabel* surprise ruined! Bouchaïb abandoned me to the tête à tête with the new man in my life. As I passed the kitchen I stuck my head through the doorway.

"*Merci*, Bouchaïb," I muttered, rolling my eyes.

The man who seemed to be shadowing me that morning was seated on the far side of the atrium enjoying a foul smelling cigarette. I was hopeless when it came to conducting business in Morocco. Luckily, I never had to. That was my father's province. Yet there I was, standing between his legacy and the dreaded *samsar*. Bouchaïb didn't dare involve himself on my behalf for fear of alienating a well-connected Zemmouri. So I was on my own. Translated literally, the word *samsar* means "the poison that spreads." I was beginning to understand why. I bottled up my apprehensions, willed some imaginary confidence into my step, and marched over to match wits with Hadj Mustapha.

"Hadj, we meet again," I said, forcing a smile. His honorary title denoted his pilgrimage to Mecca. Since our meeting at the souk, he'd made a quick change into an elegant white djellabah, an oufit more in keeping with his elevated social status.

Not much in the medina escaped his notice, especially news of a homeowner's passing. When a death in a family left a *riad* in abeyance and a notary was needed to search for its rightful heirs, the *samsar* would swoop in like a vulture. Here was a man who could sense weakness. The thought of being vulnerable to his wiles knotted my stomach. I stated my position as assertively as I could: "You need to understand, Hadj, I must talk to my brothers before I can put Dar Zitoun on the market."

"Yes, of course, mademoiselle," he said, dragging on his cigarette. "I've only come for a preliminary inspection."

"Madame," I corrected him for a second time.

I quite understood why he wanted a jump on the competition. It wasn't often that a place like ours became available. And with the increase in tourism and a sprawling five-star beach resort just south of Azemmour in the planning stages, European buyers would soon be arriving in droves. There were fat commissions to be made.

The restless agent took a turn around the atrium. "Beautiful," he cooed. "Many people from Marrakech are looking for a home like this — a place to escape the summer heat."

A frenzy of real estate speculation was sweeping through "The Pink City." Foreign investors spent millions of dirhams on derelict properties and poured millions more into elaborate renovations. Stylish B&Bs in the historic medina had grown to more than five hundred. This explained the dramatic overall increase in prices to levels inconceivable just three or four years earlier. Overnight, *riad*s, few of them the equal of Dar Zitoun in provenance, were being transformed into lavish vacation homes or trendy boutique hotels.

"When Azemmour's medina is discovered, every *samsar* will become wealthy!" he gushed. He moved toward the fountain. "Mademoiselle, you must have this scrubbed with *eau de Javel*." Much of the charm in the atrium's focal point lay in the mottled coat of algae nurtured by riverfront dampness. It would remain as it was.

"We like it that way, Hadj," I replied politely. He shrugged his shoulders. Next on his radar were the panels in the twelve-foot double doors to a downstairs guestroom. He moved to within inches of the woodwork and lifted his glasses.

"Very nice," he said, tracing the stylized floral motif with his finger. "Your father hired artisans for this?"

"From Fez. They painted the same pattern on this lintel." I drifted to the opposite side of the atrium in the hope of drawing him closer to the foyer, but he didn't cooperate. Instead, he meandered to the foot of the main staircase. "May I go up?"

"*Après vous*, Hadj," I said resignedly.

As the out-of-shape *samsar* wheezed his way to the second floor, I recounted the story of our resident saint, Sidi Makhfi. Hadj Mustapha stopped so abruptly I couldn't avoid bumping into him.

"Monsieur, are you all right?"

He didn't answer. Was he meditating? It was hard to see his face in the dimly lit stairwell. He continued his ascent to the terrace. After taking a few seconds to catch his breath, he confided, "You know, we Muslims must beg forgiveness whenever we step over someone's tomb, so I said a prayer to Sidi Makhfi." His reverence almost atoned for his pushiness.

I knew little about the *samsar* other than what Bouchaïb told me — he had two wives, one in the medina and the other ensconced in an apartment in El Jadida. "When one wife is fed up with him, he goes to live with the other," Bouchaïb enlightened me. "The law requires that he spend the same amount of money on each woman. The *samsar*, he is a wealthy man."

My visitor turned into the salon, where his attention was immediately diverted by a faded portrait of King Hassan and Queen Elizabeth, a reproduction of an official photograph taken on one of her majesty's state visits to Morocco. "The English and the Moroccans, they are like this," said the *samsar*, crossing his index and middle fingers.

I had no way of knowing whether or not this was true. However, by emphasizing the bond between the two peoples, Hadj Mustapha clearly hoped to make the case for a corresponding relationship between the two of us. In general, Moroccans held the British in relatively high esteem because they were unconnected to the country's colonial past. This explained why my father was able to transition so easily between the French Protectorate and the independent state of Morocco, a difficult period of modern history that saw many of his French and Spanish counterparts return to their native soil.

The *samsar* craned his neck at the intricately decorated cedar panels on the ceiling. Their exquisite Persian designs dated back to the time of Si Mohamed Ben Driss, the *riad*'s original owner.

"The beam, there, it is cracked. It must be repaired."

"But Hadj, it's been like that for as long as I can remember. Why not leave it alone?"

"Because the roof could cave in," he replied matter-of-factly. "I know someone who can take care of it, all in one day. And the *mashrabiya* too."

"And what's wrong with the *mashrabiya*?"

Sunlight filtered through the interstices of the turned-wood partition that divided the split-level salon. The screen was a traditional element used to enclose the harem in a Moorish palace. It kept the inviolable space free from men's prying eyes while, at the same time, affording the distaff members behind it a fractured image of events whenever the head of household entertained guests.

"Why, a spindle is missing from the corner," observed the *samsar*. I couldn't believe that any buyer would concern himself with such a tiny imperfection. The *samsar's* petty criticisms were beginning to feel like little punches.

"I'll keep your handyman in mind," I replied wearily. He didn't hear a word I said. His attention was on a framed photograph that had been taken on the day Daddy was made a Member of the British Empire. The *samsar* squinted at the glossy picture of my father wearing formal attire he'd rented from London's exclusive Moss Brothers men's store. I remembered how Daddy in top hat and morning suit had given me a fit of the giggles.

* * *

On the red-letter day of his investiture, a limousine transported us down The Mall, right up to the gates of Buckingham Palace. I had to pinch myself. A squad of police officers armed with under vehicle mirrors gave our limo a good going over before allowing it to proceed onto the palace grounds, where a member of the Royal Household in crimson jacket and white stockings awaited. We followed him up a curved, marble staircase, along resplendent galleries of priceless objets d'art, and into a magnificent ballroom — The Ballroom.

Like a child attending her first live performance at the theater, I tried to take it all in, from the ramrod straight Life Guardsmen in their plumed helmets to the massive crystal chandeliers. An orchestra was playing the improbable selection *Teddy Bears' Picnic* when we arrived, but soon struck up the more familiar *God Save the Queen*, which made our anticipation almost unbearable. And then, just like that, a smiling Elizabeth II stood before us in a sleeveless blue dress. How vulnerable she appeared, even with two fearsome Gurkah Orderly Officers by her side.

A hush settled over the audience as she placed her purse on a nearby gilt chair before offering words of welcome to her subjects. Honorees approached the Queen, one by one, as the Lord Steward called their names. Olympic decathlon champion Daley Thompson was among the first to be recognized, as was acclaimed actor Leo McKern, sporting vivid green socks, no less. I nudged my brother. A number of other names were read before it came to Daddy's turn. He must have practiced the requisite five-step-and-bow approach fifty times the night before. I hoped he wouldn't flub it, like one unfortunate honoree that preceded him. I could see the Queen's lips move as she pinned a medal on Daddy's chest, but I couldn't hear a word. Though his back was to us, I was sure he'd said something in reply, judging from her nod and smile.

"What did the Queen say?" we asked him after the ceremony.

"She wanted to know what the weather was like in Casablanca."

He'd been given strict orders from someone in the Royal Household to steer clear of long-winded answers when responding to a question from his Sovereign. Understandable jitters brought on by the pomp and circumstance of the occasion made sure of that.

"Hot, Your Majesty," quoth Daddy.

* * *

"Funny hat. Just like our fez," opined Hadj Mustapha, commenting on Daddy's top hat. On this point, I was in agreement. I was about to launch into a docent's narrative for the *samsar*'s benefit, but thought better of it. He wasn't a good listener. What were my reminiscences to him, whose eyes were so fully on the prize?

"You'll have to redecorate this room in the Moroccan style," he continued, turning toward me with smoke-infused proximity.

Friends often joked that Dar Zitoun was frozen in a 1960s time capsule, full of flea market finds. Granted, the Swedish modern armchair my father used to sit in while catching the BBC News on shortwave radio looked a little incongruous in a Moorish *riad*. But it was part of the eclectic mélange that perfectly reflected Daddy's personality. Bright patchwork cushions on wrought iron chairs invited comfort and intimacy, unlike the hard, overstuffed divans that lined the walls of traditional Moroccan living rooms that I found a hindrance to intimate conversation.

"It would be best to emulate the Moroccan model," suggested the *samsar*. "I would start with several divans upholstered in damask."

"Let me think about it, Hadj," I humored him.

His strategy was clear — critique-resolve-profit. The slimy fountain, the cracked beam, the defective *mashrabiya*, the unsuitable furnishings. Enough!

I felt bereft of support without my father, who had an uncanny ability to remain sanguine in the presence of such pompous characters. To get away from the *samsar* I stepped out onto the terrace to pluck a few snails from the rosebush Daddy smuggled in from Hertfordshire. I hurled the pests into the river. Would that I might be rid of my visitor so easily.

My self-appointed home staging expert momentarily lost his tongue as he approached the parapet that overlooked the Oum er-Rbia.

"*Allah*," he uttered. His professorial tone softened. "Mademoi — madame, you tell me you have two brothers. Well, consider now that you have three."

I had to give him credit for coming up with a compliment so imaginatively contrived. I stifled a laugh.

"*Shokran*, Hadj, you are most kind."

The "Glaoui's room" was next on the tour. It contained a curiosity I thought sure to interest — an antique brass bed with an inlaid mother-of-pearl headboard that my father purchased from an acquaintance of Winston Churchill's, who claimed it had once belonged to T'hami El Glaoui, *Lord of the Atlas*, pasha of Marrakech. That the bed may have served as the intimate playground for the legendary chieftain, with his harem of ninety-six women, made it a conversation piece to say the least, and certainly a point in its favor. I was wrong. The *samsar*'s face flushed.

"That traitor! That *collaborateur!*" he sputtered. After the French established the Protectorate in the years leading up to World War I, they allied themselves with El Glaoui, one of the most powerful men in the country. His fellow Berbers approved of the alliance, but nationalists of the *samsar*'s persuasion deemed El Glaoui's actions treacherous. I didn't dare reveal how members of my mother's family, like most French citizens, held the pasha in high regard.

* * *

For my maternal grandfather Pépé, El Glaoui was a man of mythical allure. Pépé regaled us with first-hand accounts of the pasha's opulent lifestyle, especially the fabled *diffas*, the tribal banquets that took place at the Kasbah of Telouet, his private fiefdom in the Atlas Mountains. On graduation from the prestigious Ecole des Langues Orientales in Paris, Pépé was posted to Marrakech. His fluency in French and Spanish, as well as Arabic and Berber, made him an indispensable liaison between French colonial authorities and the pasha.

My grandparents lived a charmed life under El Glaoui's protection until the day my grandmother found a venomous snake curled up in her youngest daughter's crib. Soon thereafter the family moved to Casablanca, where Pépé relinquished the privileges and intrigue of a French civil servant for the life of a struggling entrepreneur. I thought it fitting that Daddy should purchase the pasha's brass bed, an indirect memento of my grandfather's colorful career.

* * *

I changed the subject to prevent the *samsar* from a complete meltdown. "How do you like the *hayiti* [wainscoting] from Meknès?" A black velvet material, imprinted with a repeating pattern of slender Moorish arches, surrounded the bed's occupants with trompe l'oeil doorways. When given a choice, most of Dar Zitoun's overnight guests opted for the "Glaoui's room."

The *samsar* lifted a corner of fabric away from the wall. "Mildew," he complained, wrinkling his nose. Humidity was the principal enemy of the medina's antiquated structures. "It's a problem that you won't find in the new villas in town."

I threw open the shutters that faced the estuary.

"Yes, but their owners don't have this to look at," I reminded him.

Monsieur Know-It-All continued his unwelcome inspection. He tapped a damp patch of wall with his fingers, dislodging a piece of plaster, and was on the point of doing even more damage.

"*Arrêtez, monsieur* [Stop, sir]!" How dare he lift Dar Zitoun's skirts in such a disdainful way? For the first time, he looked at me with concern, realizing that he may have crossed the line with someone whose business he desperately sought.

"And I'll bet you know a good plasterer," I said rhetorically.

Hadj Moustapha was close on my heels as I headed for the kitchen, where Bouchaïb was blanching fava beans. I knew our invasion would displease him. "Never let a stranger into your kitchen," he once warned me, "for fear he will poison the food."

"Don't cook the beans too long," kibitzed the *samsar*. Bouchaïb's back stiffened. He cast an impatient look my way. Mercifully, the telephone came to our rescue.

Bouchaïb answered it. "*Allô. Oui, madame est là* [Yes, madame is here]."

The *samsar* pressed a business card into my hand. It read: *Hadj Mustapha, propriétaire* [owner]. *Propriétaire*, indeed! I showed him out.

"This house can fetch a lot of money. I am at your disposal," he said, keeping one foot in the doorway. "*Au revoir, mademoiselle.*"

I closed the door behind him and leaned back against its rough surface for a moment before rushing back to take the call. "*Allô.*"

"Hello, Kitty. My name is John Barnaby. I was a friend of your father's." I remembered Daddy speaking fondly of the gentleman.

"I've been out of the country and just learned of Clive's death. Please accept my condolences. I am attending a conference in El Jadida for a few days. Let me know if I can help in any way."

As he was just twenty minutes down the coast, I invited him for lunch the following day. The anticipation of cooking for so eminent a guest lifted Bouchaïb's spirits. To entertain a friend of my father's was to continue *comme avant*, as before.

The atmosphere in the kitchen provided relief from the stress of the previous hour. My irascible response to the *samsar*'s comments about Dar Zitoun's quaint idiosyncrasies, no matter how apt, was out of character for me. Whatever the cause, it was clear that dealing with Hadj Mustapha wasn't in my psychological best interest.

In an effort to make myself useful, I grabbed the brass *mehraz*, mortar and pestle, and began to pulverize the cumin seeds Bouchaïb had just toasted. Their beguiling aroma inveigled my senses and helped quell my conflicting thoughts.

Tomato, Fava Bean, and Preserved Lemon Salad

Serves 4

1 cup fresh fava beans, shelled
2 ripe tomatoes, peeled, seeded, and coarsely diced
¼ teaspoon salt
2 teaspoons seasoned rice vinegar
1 tablespoon olive oil
2 teaspoons ground cumin
2 teaspoons minced preserved lemon rind (see page 255)
5 sprigs cilantro, minced

In a medium saucepan, bring water to a boil and blanch fava beans for thirty seconds. Drain. Remove tough outer skins. Set aside.

In a bowl, combine beans, tomato, salt, vinegar, olive oil, cumin, and preserved lemon rind. Sprinkle with cilantro and serve.

7

Bouchaïb Entertains

"Dar Zitoun!" called out the plump-cheeked *fonctionnaire*, government employee. I'd gone to the *municipalité*, town hall, to amend the power of attorney that Daddy had granted Bouchaïb in matters concerning the *riad*. The time had come to draw up a new agreement with my name in the place of my father's.

I broke away from the scrum of petitioners to stand before the panel of three clerks in hijab scarves — typist, scribe, and custodian of official stamp and inked pad.

"*C'est à vous?*" asked the woman at the antique typewriter, waving my document. It had languished on the front edge of her desk for the better part of an hour. She gave it a cursory examination before typing something onto a blank card, which she passed to a timid young woman for entry into the official register.

The Zemmouris that crowded around me at the counter seemed keenly interested in the proceedings. There was no such thing as a line on the floor behind which one had to stand until one's name was called. I hadn't expected privacy. Everyone watched the registrar draw letters in flowing longhand, from right to left, connecting the Arabic characters *ba, waw, sheen, ayn, ya* and *ba* — our *gardien's* given name. The completed document moved on to the applier-of-the-official-seal. *Thump, thwak*, she stamped the paper with *Président de la Délégation*.

"Five dirhams, please," she requested before handing me a couple of adhesive-backed stamps to affix to it as proof of my payment of the tax.

Fortunately, Bouchaïb required no proxy certificate for his work in the kitchen. He could do as he pleased with the *ashabel*, one of the world's boniest fish and among the most difficult to fillet. On that day, there was no cheery "*Bonjour*, Katy" when I returned from the *municipalité*. He was too engrossed in the meticulous task of cleaning the fish. Few chefs had the skill to remove the four rows of curved bones without making a mess of things and sacrificing soft rich meat in the process. The shad met its match in our *cuisinier*, who used to while away countless hours along the river with his fishing net. "When I was younger, I could clean an *ashabel* with my eyes closed," he bragged.

The kitchen was Dar Zitoun's nerve center. Aromas from Bouchaïb's bubbling concoctions spread like neurons to every corner of the *riad*. The space was small, but functional. Glazed green and white tiles covered the lower half of the walls. The upper half was painted canary yellow.

"Monsieur Changler let me choose the colors," Bouchaïb boasted to his friends. He applied the same decorative sense to the floor, surrounding a patch of original zillij mosaic with drab concrete tiles. The dysfunctional sink and gas stove had even less aesthetic qualities.

"You know," Bouchaïb reflected, looking down at the *ashabel's* opaque white flesh. "I'm not as fast as I used to be."

The species of shad was Azemmour's gastronomic claim to fame, and for hundreds of years, provided Zemmouris with their livelihood. In the early 1500s, the King of Portugal exacted the fish as tribute. Its oil lit the lamps of Lisbon.

Catching one had become a rare event, due to the destruction of the Oum er-Rbia's reproductive nooks. Still, the delicacy suited the occasion, with John Barnaby coming for lunch. Though I didn't know the British diplomat, I wanted to treat him royally in honor of his friendship with my father.

I looked around at the already prepared side dishes. "Bouchaïb, there're just the three of us. You've made enough for a soccer team!" I scolded, knowing full well that he, like all Moroccans, considered a bountiful platter a measure of hospitality. Besides, leftovers never went to waste. Bouchaïb made sure of that.

"Perhaps Monsieur Barnaby will bring his driver and a bodyguard," he reasoned. "And *le commissaire de police* [police superintendent] may show up unannounced, with a guest or two of his own."

Le commissaire! I had completely overlooked the issue of security. Surely Mr. Barnaby's staff would have seen to such matters. Maybe I should have hired a *chabakouni*. The term amused me because of its etymology — born of the French, *ça va cogner* (it is going to hit) an expression used by Morocco's paramilitary police in reference to the stout government-issue club they carried. Over time, the officers themselves came to be known by the eponymous expression, or rather, its pidgin cognate, *cha-ba-kouni*. The idiom struck fear into the hearts of juvenile miscreants throughout the land. Anyway, if we included a *chabakouni* and a few uninvited guests, Bouchaïb's calculations may not have been far off the mark. I eased into a chair to watch our culinary Merlin work his magic.

"Katy, would you mind putting together the *ras el hanoot* [top-of-the-shop] spice blend?"

I jumped up to organize the diverse ingredients on the kitchen table in preparation for toasting. Bouchaïb freed up a burner so we could stand shoulder-to-shoulder at the stove. To the kitchen gods I toasted my offerings – whole cumin and cardamom seeds, saffron, dried ginger, and turmeric roots. The heady fragrance swirled around us like a *jinn* released from its bottle.

"What's happened to the *mehraz*?" I asked. "It was here on the counter yesterday."

He pointed to the faded kilim rug spread out near the fountain. Like generations of women within these walls, I sat cross-legged and poured the whole spices into the heavy implement. Each strike of the pestle strengthened my bond with the sisterhood of Dar Zitoun *dadas*.

Bouchaïb sifted impurities from the sienna-colored powder and then sprinkled a couple of perfumed teaspoons over the tagine. He nestled the *ashabel* into the tangled bed of caramelized onions and raisins, called *t'faya*, a spoonful of which he tasted before setting the dish on a charcoal brazier. "*Très bon.*" He smacked his lips.

"*Et moi?* [What about me]?" I pouted. He dipped a second spoon into the sauce and handed it to me.

"*Tu aimes* [You like it]?" he asked, eyes glistening like ripe olives.

The two of us had always been each other's toughest critics . . . and biggest fans. I'd lost count of the hours we'd spent collaborating in the kitchen. I nodded my approval.

"This tagine, I made it for your father when I first came to work here. *Il aimait beaucoup, beaucoup* [He liked it a lot]!" He smiled wistfully.

Twenty-five years earlier, a friend had informed him that an *Inglizi*, an Englishman, was restoring a *riad* in the Azemmour medina.

"I came to see your father immediately. I told him, '*Moi, je peux faire le nécessaire*

[Me, I can do whatever is necessary].' He hired me without even asking for references. *Allah.* What a gentleman."

My father soon realized that, like an accomplished musician, his new caretaker/ *cuisinier* was blessed with perfect pitch when it came to cooking. Tasting the symphony of flavors in his *t'faya* reinforced my own appreciation for his talent.

How far he had come from a poverty-stricken childhood, scurrying about the medina, running errands for a few centimes. As a teenager, Bouchaïb sought employment in Casablanca to support his parents. He caught the attention of a French couple that introduced him to *la bonne cuisine française*, to which he took like a duck to orange sauce. He thrived under their tutelage.

After his mentors' return to France, his gastronomic savoir-faire would bring many lucrative offers of employment from *caïds* to CEOs, all of whom had dined at the home of his former patrons. But he was never tempted. Despite his style and perfectionism, he was a country boy at heart, with an overwhelming desire to return to the calm of his native medina. An arranged marriage with young Leila brought him back to his hometown. This was my father's great good fortune.

I watched our kitchen maestro adjust the *t'faya*'s seasoning. Was it my imagination, or had his height diminished under life's hardships? A photograph of a handsome young fellow in tie and cardigan, looking for-all-the-world like a fraternity man of the 1960s, hung on a bubblegum-pink wall of Bouchaïb's apartment. Comparing that picture with my kitchen companion tugged at my heart. How many more years would we be able to cook

together like this? The authoritative relationship between employers and *domestiques*, like the one I witnessed at Manou's when I was a girl, was more relaxed, at least among my contemporaries.

"Your father, he was like my father. So me, I am like your brother," he joked. He wasn't far from the truth. We argued like siblings to prove it, reconciling ten minutes after a spat. I dreaded the idea that, one day, he too would be gone from my life.

Bouchaïb sported a Charlie Chaplin mustache and went toothless, relegating to a drawer a pair of dentures my father paid an El Jadida dentist to fabricate. He was uncertain of his age because his parents hadn't formally recorded his date of birth.

"My father told me I was born in 1942, the year the Allies attacked the Vichy French

government," he recalled. "But I think I was born earlier because I remember my mother coming back from the market with a leaflet that had rained down from an airplane. It bore a photograph of President Roosevelt." I had one of the fliers too, given to me by my mother, who'd come across thousands like it on a Casablanca street when she was in her twenties.

Though Bouchaïb didn't know his age, he dealt with other numbers at record speed. In that respect, he had a mind like an abacus. Six decades hadn't slowed him down. The same was true when it came to cooking. I stole a second spoonful of t'faya. Bliss lingered on my palate as I headed upstairs to prepare for our guest.

Then disaster struck. Loud curses in Arabic brought me back to the kitchen. Bouchaïb was already on the phone with Ouadoudi, a local jack-of-all-trades, a man intimately acquainted with the quirks of our antiquated plumbing. We needed that outdated web of pipes to oblige us today, not undermine Bouchaïb's lovely lunch.

A feeling of utter helplessness, magnified by anxiety skating on adrenaline, had come over me by the time our Lancelot appeared at the door. Ouadoudi looked like a disheveled bear in his brown woolen djellabah. He came armed with only a couple of miserable wrenches, a screwdriver, and a length of wire — a far cry from an American plumber with his van full of fixes. Because Ouadoudi had saved the day for my father so many times before, the stolid workman inspired confidence. Years of auscultating the corroded pipes had taught him just which one required attention. I hoped to hurry things along, but there was no getting around the obligatory glass of mint tea.

"Bismillah," prayed Ouadoudi before his first loud sip. "The sink again. These old riads, they are all the same."

"Maybe you can hammer on the drain like you did last time?" suggested Bouchaïb. Ouadoudi said nothing. He took his time finishing the tea and then lit a cigarette before acting on the suggestion. Non-smoker that I was, I felt like lighting up too, to allay my apprehension. Bang! Bang! Bang! The house shuddered. After two hundred years, Dar Zitoun was a living thing, every strainer and drain line as interconnected as hipbone to thighbone.

"Hit it here!" coached Bouchaïb. Ouadoudi did as directed. Nothing happened. As time ticked away, I began to panic. Our plombier left us for several minutes before returning with a plunger. The first attempt yielded nothing but a sickly gurgle. The second brought forth a slurry of disgusting liquid that splashed over the front of the sink and onto his plastic sandals. Maledictions in Arabic followed. The drain stared at us like the evil eye.

Our problem would require more improvisational measures. Ouadoudi fashioned a hook at one end of the length of wire he'd brought and thrust it as far down the trapless drain as he could. Bouchaïb and I stood by in silent supplication.

In answer to our prayers, Ouadoudi reeled in an amorphous black glob and then opened the faucet. When he heard the triumphant trickle of grey water in the garden, our taciturn plumber uttered but a single word, "Safee [Finished]."

"Shokran, Ouadoudi," I said with an audible sigh of relief.

The price of his service call, twenty dirhams, about two dollars.

Many Zemmouri households obtained their potable water from a public fountain. I reminded myself that we were the lucky ones with our running water and the means to employ men like Ouadoudi, masters of the jury-rig, who, with limited resources, were able to wheedle water lines under historic zillij floors or within thick stone walls.

The corrosive influence of our riverfront location ensured our home's gradual decline. The decades-old plumbing and infrastructure functioned on borrowed time.

As Ouadoudi shuffled out, Bouchaïb lamented, "Every time he fixes one thing, something else goes wrong. It's always been like this, even when your father was alive."

My father accepted that Dar Zitoun was a "money pit." On the other hand, unrelenting repairs brought colorful characters like Ouadoudi into our lives. One day we would have to undertake a comprehensive overhaul, but not until after we entertained John Barnaby.

The curtain had barely lowered on our household melodrama when there came a loud knocking at the door. I shot a worried look at Bouchaïb, who was still cleaning sludge from the sink. Our guest wasn't due for half an hour. Who could it be?

Neighborhood children delighted in banging the knocker for no reason at all. To deprive the *petits merdeux*, little shits, of the satisfaction of knowing they'd tricked us, Bouchaïb and I adopted a rule: Open only to those who identify themselves. So I went to the door and bellowed, "*Shkoon* [Who is it]?"

"It's John Barnaby," replied my father's distinguished friend, the British consul general to Morocco. I felt my face flush. I knew what protocol was. *Shkoon*, it wasn't.

The bespectacled diplomat smiled from under his floppy cloth hat. He'd negotiated the medina unaccompanied, leaving his car and driver at the *place centrale*. He bantered in Arabic with several small boys around him, but quickly sent them packing with a couple of choice phrases I didn't catch when the oldest among them tugged at his jacket and begged, "*Un* dirham, *un* dirham!"

Even though I'd never met the consul before, the recent extra-culinary challenge weakened my normal reserve, and I had to restrain the impulse to throw myself into his arms like a little girl. If Sir John was amused by his unceremonious reception, he never let on.

We climbed to the terrace and settled into the corner banquette to watch a regatta of kayakers zigzag their way upriver. The Mother of Spring seemed to hold its breath between tides. The blindfolded dromedary that once padded in endless circles around a water wheel on the opposite shore was gone, replaced by a pump and one-cylinder engine. Its dull, asthmatic chugging drifted across to where we sat.

I related my recent run-in with the *samsar*, the call from the Casablanca notary, and my overall reluctance to tackle Daddy's probate. "Unfortunately, the British government can't get involved in private legal matters," stated my guest. Unofficially, he advised me to retain the services of a lawyer as well as a notary to shepherd me through Morocco's arcane bureaucracy. "And you should consider using a local *adoul*, a notary versed in Islamic law, to discourage false claimants."

"False claimants?" I gasped.

"In Morocco, anyone can claim ownership to real estate."

Sir John paused then spoke deliberately: "Be forewarned, probate in this country is an ulcer-inducing affair. Arm yourself with patience. And try to keep the proceedings out of the courts."

I shot him a pained look.

"*Le déjeuner est prêt* [Lunch is ready]," Bouchaïb announced. No ringing of the dinner bell for the consul general. Bouchaïb was resplendent in the starched chef's coat he reserved for special occasions. He dressed the way he cooked — intuitively. Working attire normally consisted of a sleeveless, ankle-length *gandoora* and sandals, but for the consul's luncheon he chose to wear the chef's jacket my father bought for him in London. Perfectly creased black pants and black dancing slippers, probably acquired during a junket into the flea market in Casablanca, completed his ensemble.

The plumbing setback hadn't fazed him. He floated between kitchen and atrium in a one-man choreography of haute cuisine, delivering the tagine and removing its conical lid with theatrical flourish to release the heady aroma all at once. "*T'faya de Poisson aux Amandes Grillées,*" he announced.

"Bouchaïb, I've never seen such a beautiful presentation," exclaimed Sir John.

"*Merci, monsieur.* It's not every day that we come across *ashabel.*" He spooned a generous portion onto each of our plates and wished us "Bon appétit," before heading back to the stove.

I'd already had a sneak preview of our plat du jour, so I fiddled with my silverware in order to observe our guest's reaction to the dish.

"My word! Simply brilliant!" gushed Sir John. "I'd love to get this recipe into the hands of our cook in Casablanca. What are the chances of that?"

Although Bouchaïb's grasp of English was rudimentary, I suspected that behind the kitchen door, one supremely talented *cuisinier* basked in the consul general's compliments.

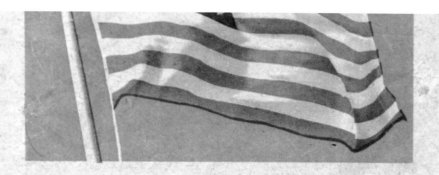

Message du Président des Etats Unis

Le Président des Etats Unis m'a chargé comme Général Commandant en Chef des Forces Expéditionnaires Américaines de faire parvenir aux peuples de l'Afrique française du Nord le message suivant:

Aucune nation n'est plus intimement liée, tant par l'histoire que par l'amitié profonde, au peuple de France et à ses amis que ne le sont les Etats Unis d'Amérique.

Les Américains luttent actuellement, non seulement pour assurer leur avenir, mais pour restituer les libertés et les principes démocratiques de tous ceux qui ont vécu sous le drapeau tricolore.

Nous venons chez vous pour vous libérer des conquérants qui ne désirent que vous priver à tout jamais de vos droits souverains, de votre droit à la liberté du culte, de votre droit de mener votre train de vie en paix.

Nous venons chez vous uniquement pour anéantir vos ennemis — nous ne voulons pas vous faire de mal.

Nous venons chez vous en vous assurant que nous partirons dès que la menace de l'Allemagne et de l'Italie aura été dissipée.

Je fais appel à votre sens des réalités ainsi qu'à votre idéalisme.

Ne faites rien pour entraver l'accomplissement de ce grand dessein.

Aidez-nous, et l'avènement du jour de la paix universelle sera hâté.

Dwight D. Eisenhower

DWIGHT D. EISENHOWER
Lieutenant Général, Commandant en Chef
des Forces Expéditionnaires Américaines.

رسـالة من رئيس حكومة الولايات المتحـدة

ان رئيس حكومة الولايات المتحدة قد طلب مني بصفتي القائد الحاكم للقوات التجريدية الأمريكية ان أبلغ شعوب أفريقية الفرنساوية الشمالية الرسالة الآتية :

لاترتبط أية أمة مع الشعب الفرنساوي واصدقائه بروابط التأريخ والمحبة الصميمة أوثق منها بالولايات المتحدة الأمريكية .

ان ما يسعى اليه الأمريكيون ليست سلامتهم في المستقبل فقط بل أيضا لأن يردوا على كل من عاش تحت علم التريكلور مثلهم العليا وحرياتهم وديموقراطيتهم :

انا نجيء، بينكم لننقذكم من قاهرين مقصودهم ابادة حقوقكم للحكومة الذاتية وحقوقكم الحرية الدينية وحقوقكم لحياة مطمئنة تعيشونها لأنفسكم ابادة مطلقة أبدية .

نجيء بينكم ليس لنضر بكم بل لكي نهلك أعداءكم فقط .

نجيء بينكم ونحن نؤكد لكم اننا سننسحب فوراً بعد ما أزيل عنكم ما يهددكم من المانيا وايطاليا .

انى أدعو الى احساسكم بالحقائق والى مصالحكم والى مثلكم العليا .

لا تعترضوا لهذا القصد السامي .

أعينونا يعجل يوم السلام للدنيا .

Dwight D. Eisenhower

دويت د. ايزنهاور

السرعكر في جيش الولايات المتحدة
قائد القوات التجريدية الامريكية

Fish Tagine with T'faya

Serves 6

2 tablespoons vegetable oil
½ cup whole blanched almonds
2 tablespoons olive oil
2 tablespoons butter
5 teaspoons *ras el hanoot* spice blend (see page 156)
6 large onions, thinly sliced
1 tablespoon sugar
½ cup raisins, soaked for 10 minutes and drained
6 (4-ounce) boneless, white fish fillets such as halibut or sea bass
1 cup water
Salt and pepper, to taste

In a skillet, heat vegetable oil over medium high heat. Add almonds and fry until golden. Drain on paper towels. Set aside.

In a medium tagine pot or Dutch oven, heat olive oil and butter over medium heat. Add *ras el hanoot*. Cook, stirring, until spices start to foam. Add onions, sugar, and raisins. Cook, stirring occasionally, until onions turn a light caramel color, 20 to 25 minutes. Nestle fish in the onion mixture and add water. Cover and cook until fish is tender, 15 to 20 minutes. Season with salt and pepper.

Spoon *t'faya* sauce over the fish and garnish with almonds. Serve with crusty bread.

8

The Notary

Sir John's advice underscored the perils of delay and stirred me from my procrastinations. I needed to commence the process of proving my father's testament as soon as possible. If not, I risked forfeiting our inheritance through any number of nefarious schemes. Probate horror stories abounded of real estate tied up for years while corrupt forces conspired to maneuver titles away from rightful heirs and into the market as hot commodities.

I was personally aware of one such instance. An American friend lost his beachfront cottage to a squatter who sold the property to a well-connected buyer without producing a single document as proof of ownership. Recalling the story was unsettling and inspired me to get the ball rolling with Maître Tanja, the Casablanca notary who'd phoned the week before.

I was about to pull out of Messaoud's parking lot, when Bouchaïb set two bottles of water on the passenger seat of the old Peugeot. "Your father always carried water for the radiator," he reminded me. He'd already cleaned the windshield and made sure the trunk was locked. I knew he would fret like a mother hen until I returned.

"Fold in your side-view mirror when you drive in Casablanca," he cautioned.

I dreaded the trip, primarily because a vague mercenary guilt hung over the formal appropriation of Daddy's assets — an irrational concern I would have to overcome. My brothers and I *were* Daddy's legal beneficiaries. His testament was proof of that. I was also reluctant to get involved with anyone in the legal business, including those lowest in its pecking order — notaries. To make matters worse, I would have to brave Casablanca's notoriously anarchic traffic to do so.

Over the decades, my native Dar Beida had been transformed from a picturesque port into a metropolis of densely populated *quartiers* linked by wide, congested boulevards of honking taxis, diesel trucks, and overcrowded buses belching yellow-brown exhaust. I had not experienced worse in Bangkok or Cairo. No wonder the distinctive colonial architecture had lost some of its luster. What a few thousand gallons of whitewash wouldn't do to help my hometown live up to its name.

Driving in Casablanca was akin to a game of chicken. A car in the center of town came so close I could have rapped on its fender with my knuckles. In the oncoming traffic, a reckless moped operator latched on to the side of a pickup truck like a pilot fish, a common though risky method for operators of two-wheeled conveyances to economize on fuel. Everywhere, jaywalkers tempted fate like athletic *razeteurs*, bullfighters from Provence, sidestepping bulls. "Pretend not to notice pedestrians when you're behind the wheel," was Daddy's advice. "Otherwise you'll never get through town."

I continued along one of the city's main arteries, Boulevard Mohammed V, and parked on a littered side street. Gone were the days when fresh water spewed from apertures in the curbs to flush the gutters clean each morning.

I left the Peugeot in the care of a blue-jacketed *gardien* and entered a Moorish art deco building. Tears of grime streaked the façade as if the building were mourning faded glories. The vintage elevator was out of service, so I climbed the stairs to the top floor. Halfway down a gloomy corridor, a tarnished plaque read, "Maître Tanja, *Notaire.*" On the second ring of the doorbell, a stylishly dressed young woman appeared. "You have an appointment?" she asked.

"*Oui. Je suis* Madame Morse." The secretary showed me to a cell-like waiting room and then disappeared down the hall. A pallid light fell onto a lugubrious couple seated on straight back chairs. The slight man in wrinkled suit and plastic sandals barely looked up. I claimed a seat across from him and the fleshy, djellabah-clad woman I assumed to be his wife. The office was completely silent — no ringing phones, no typing, nothing.

"Have you been waiting long?" I asked.

"About two hours," replied the man, without a hint of impatience. His stoicism and humble demeanor told me that he was from the provinces.

"You're from Casablanca?" I asked, knowing that he was not.

"No. Bir Jdid," the little town on the way to Azemmour where my father used to stop for *kefta* sandwiches. No wonder the notary's clients were so resigned. Waiting was a way of life for Bir Jdidis, not to mention the inhabitants of Azemmour. Of that I had firsthand knowledge as a veteran of the queue at the *municipalité*.

Just then a frenzy of drums and metal castañets erupted in the courtyard below. *Gnawas!* I sprang to the open window.

* * *

The moment took me back to happier days when another troop of itinerant percussionists performed in the sheltered quadrangle of our old apartment building to solicit tips from tenants. My brother Philippe and I did not disappoint those we affectionately dubbed *Les Mohammed Boum Boum*, as embarrassingly insensitive as the term would later sound. But we were just kids. Our ears pulsated to the rhythm as we watched dancers in vermillion pantaloons leap in the air and twirl the black braids on their skullcaps. The traveling musicians filled our heads with dreams of the jungle.

The word "*Gnawa*" was a distortion of "Guinea," the sub-Saharan country from which the musicians' ancestors had come. *Gnawas* entertained nightly on the famed Jmaa el Fna, Square of the Dead, in Marrakech, along with fire-eaters, acrobats, and snake charmers. I'd even read of jet-setting *gnawas* doing gigs with Mick Jagger.

* * *

Maître Tanja's jaded secretary leaned from a window of the next room. It was time to get reacquainted. I stole down the hall and peeked into her workspace. "Excuse me, but is Maître Tanja actually in the building?" I inquired.

At that very moment, the notary hurried past me clutching an attaché case in one hand and a croissant in the other. A trail of florid cologne floated in his wake. The rural couple soon disappeared into his private office — "private" in the sense that Maître Tanja was the room's sole occupant, not because it offered privacy to his clients. I heard every word of his conversation with the Bir Jdidis through the open doorway.

"I can't notarize this paper! You've forgotten the stamps!" scolded Maître Tanja. "Come back after you've bought them at the *bureau de tabac*." He marched the bewildered couple down the hall to hasten their unceremonious exit.

"Mademoiselle Chandler?" he asked, suddenly in front of me. I held out my hand. Before I knew what was happening, he lifted it to his lips.

"*Mes hommages.*"

His hand kissing left me with the same feeling of unpleasantness I experienced the week before during our brief telephone conversation.

A glistening layer of pomade kept my advisor's dyed, jet-black hair close to his scalp, though a few renegade strands curled jauntily over the collar of his shirt. He invited me to his office, where I handed over the dossier I'd compiled at Dar Zitoun.

"I knew your father well, God rest his soul," he said, his gaze lingering on my bust. "And how are the young Chandlers holding up?"

"As well as can be expected, maître."

His gold-link bracelet clinked against the desktop as he shuffled my documents. "This will take at least six months to process," he warned, looking at me over the top of his reading glasses. Never had I met a man with such long eyelashes. I imagined he could still bat them shamelessly.

"You've brought the notarized documents from your brothers?" he asked.

"They should be in there with the others," I said of the papers Nigel and Philippe had signed in the presence of Moroccan consular officials in England and Canada respectively. I leaned across the desk to help him locate the documents in question. "Here they are!"

"Now, all we have to do is prepare a document for *you* — to prove to the bank that you are your father's daughter. And, to expedite things tomorrow with the clerks, I will need a little cash. You understand, mademoiselle?" he said, staring at me with myopic eyes. I did indeed. "B & C," as my father referred to bribery and corruption, worked wonders when strategically dispensed.

"A thousand dirhams [about $120] ought to cover it," he continued, visually assessing my reaction to the charge. I could have bargained for a lesser amount, but thought better of it.

"You'll need a lawyer to get this done. Let me call someone for you." He picked up his phone and dialed without waiting for my answer. "Maître Tanja here. I'd like to make an appointment for one of my clients." He placed his hand over the receiver. "Ten o'clock tomorrow?" he asked looking over at me. I nodded.

I saw no harm in meeting with the lawyer Maître Tanja recommended. Since I had to stay in the city for my appointment with the bankers, I might as well get started on the legal front as well.

Friends Roselyne and Abderrahmane Rahoule had invited me for lunch. I'd take them up on their standing offer to let me spend the night rather than risk the dangerous evening commute along the coastal road, with pedestrians in dark clothing and unlit horse carts blithely encroaching on the tarmac.

"You're planning to sell Dar Zitoun, mademoiselle?" asked Maître Tanja. "For the right price, a friend of mine can take it off your hands."

Another wily professional to beware of! He'd have to get in line with the *samsar*.

"I must first consult with my brothers, maître."

"Well, just let me know. And your husband, he isn't with you on this trip?"

My brilliantined interlocutor removed his glasses. "If you get lonely, it would be my pleasure to show you around Casablanca. Or if you prefer, I could come to Azemmour."

"*Merci beaucoup*, but my husband is arriving in two days," I lied.

"Lucky man," said the *notaire*.

I bolted from his office without giving him the chance to escort me to the door. His *au revoir* slithered behind me as I fled down the stairs to the lobby. The smell of urine hadn't been there on arrival. With few public toilets, Casa's older structures occasionally fell victim to wandering *pisseurs*. I emerged onto the busy boulevard gasping for fresh air. Luckily, I'd be able to decompress at Rose and Abder's over lunch, for which I'd promised to bring dessert.

The delicacies I was after resided at Le Trianon, a pâtisserie I frequented forty years earlier with my genteel grandmother, who rarely ventured outside her apartment without hat and gloves. Le Trianon's decor was unchanged. The little girl who once stocked pastries on weekends, the daughter of the shop's owner, was now its matronly *caissière*. A smile from her confirmed our mutual recognition. In confronting the expansive array of goodies, I recalled Mémé's standard admonition: "Katy, you may have only one. So choose carefully."

Through force of habit, I scrutinized every offering from one end of the display case to the other, then back again. What would it be? Spongy *babas au rum*, *mille feuilles* oozing crème anglaise, or sinful *puits d'amour* filled with *mousse au café*? I settled on a perennial favorite, lovely, tempting *choux à la crème*, cream puffs. Mémé used to gild the lily by filling those she made at home with a combination of whipped cream and chocolate buttercream.

"*Une douzaine, s'il vous plaît*," I told the clerk.

Mémé's Choux au Chocolat

(Cream Puffs with Chocolate)

Makes 8

Choux:
4 tablespoons butter
½ cup water
¼ teaspoon salt
½ cup all-purpose flour
⅛ teaspoon baking powder
1½ teaspoons granulated sugar
2 eggs

Filling:
4 tablespoons butter
3 ounces bittersweet chocolate, broken up
2 egg yolks
1 tablespoon powdered sugar
⅛ teaspoon cinnamon
⅛ teaspoon salt
1½ tablespoons Amaretto
1 tablespoon warm water
1 cup (½ pint) heavy whipping cream
2 tablespoons granulated sugar
Powdered sugar, for garnish

In a saucepan over medium heat, melt butter in water. Set aside.

In a bowl, whisk together salt, flour, baking powder, and sugar. Add dry ingredients all at once to the saucepan. Return to the stove and stir mixture with a wooden spoon until dough no longer sticks to pan. Transfer to mixing bowl to cool. Add eggs. Blend until smooth. Refrigerate dough for 30 minutes.

Preheat oven to 425 degrees F.

Place a heaping tablespoon of dough on a large, non-stick baking sheet. Continue in this manner with the rest of the dough, keeping *choux* two inches apart. Bake until golden, 12 to 14 minutes. Lower heat to 375 degrees F and bake another 6 to 8 minutes, until crisp. Turn the oven off. Poke a hole in each *chou* with a toothpick and return baking sheet to the oven, leaving door ajar, for another 10 to 15 minutes. Let *choux* cool.

Meanwhile, prepare filling. Bring water to a boil in double boiler. Remove from heat. Add butter and chocolate. Stir until smooth. Set aside.

Whisk together egg yolks, powdered sugar, cinnamon, salt, liqueur, and water. Continue stirring this mixture while slowly adding molten chocolate. Set aside.

In a mixing bowl, whip cream and granulated sugar until soft peaks form.

Slice *choux* in half, horizontally. Fill bottom halves with chocolate and top halves with whipped cream. Cap the tops to the bottoms and serve.

9

Lunch with Friends

A gleaming black SUV tried to wedge in front of my car near the snarled intersection. The bullying tactic elicited a predictable chorus of horns.

"*Et alors* [What do you think you're doing]?" I sounded off, my grip tightening on the steering wheel. I inched forward in an attempt to thwart the encroachment and laid on my own horn. How easily I adopted the prickly temperament of the local drivers.

A cabbie making rude gestures in my rear-view mirror got out of his vehicle and walked past me to tap on the SUV's window. Its *conducteur* ignored him. The standoff resolved when the light turned green. The confrontation on Casablanca's Boulevard Hassan II was a far cry from what I remembered in my youth, when more courteous drivers had to share the streets with horse-drawn wagons and an occasional camel caravan.

The all-male clientele at the sidewalk café in front of the Hôtel Excelsior sipped mint tea or demitasses around small, marble-top tables. The absence of women underscored their unequal status in society. Those who frequented cafés were considered to be of easy virtue. Moroccan men, by contrast, risked nothing by downing a beer or nursing a glass of wine in the recesses of the hotel's smoke-filled bar, despite Islam's prohibition against the consumption of alcohol.

The Excelsior's instantly recognizable Hispano-Moorish façade became a city landmark as soon as it was completed in 1912. My grandfather Pépé, then a newly appointed *inspecteur* in the French colonial government, was an Excelsior habitué.

"I was there on August 1, 1914, when Lyautey stood on a table to announce the outbreak of World War I," Pépé used to recount, in the reverential tone he adopted whenever speaking of his former boss, Morocco's first *Résident Général*. "Everyone rose to sing *La Marseillaise*. *Le général, quel personnage* [The general, what a personage]!" My grandfather's reminiscence mirrored so closely the scene in the movie *Casablanca* that I suspected him of embellishing the account.

A policeman's whistle, followed by "*Allez-y* [Move it]!" forced me to step on the gas. I circled the familiar roundabout and headed up the avenue toward the apartment building where I'd lived during my teenage years. The sprawling edifice took up an entire city block. For decades, it reflected the height of colonial elegance with its symmetrically curved façade and wrought-iron balconies. Alas, a garish neon sign had sprouted on the green-tiled cupola roof above our former living room. I longed to fling open its lifeless, grey shutters to take in the view of the park once more.

As I approached Roselyne and Abder's, I prepared to squeeze into the first open space on that rare city street not yet invaded by meters. As luck would have it, I found a spot in front of the *quincaillerie* that my father nicknamed "Ali Baba's Cave" because it always had in stock whatever miscellaneous item our family happened to need.

The hardware store's owner, Monsieur Djilali, was a Shleuh Berber from southern Morocco. He and his fellow tribesmen practically monopolize that kind of trade in Casablanca. He lived with his wife and sons behind the shop, but spent most of his waking hours at work

— on a ladder — in search of knitting needles, light bulbs, or dog collars. I couldn't recall a single instance when "Ali Baba's" was *not* open for business.

Monsieur Djilali was memorable for his solicitude and also for his frequent use of the word "*carrément* [basically]." My brother Philippe and I jokingly referred to him as "Monsieur Carrément" behind his back. Grey-haired now, he was still at the helm of his emporium, amidst hairnets, mousetraps, and bug sprays. He recognized me immediately, even though it had been many years since our last meeting. From the way he greeted me, I could tell that, in his mind, I had never stopped belonging to the *quartier*.

"Basically, your father was a fine man. Allah is sure to take care of him. Basically, I know He will." Monsieur Djilali's emotion was touching. It also made me feel somewhat remorseful about the puerile nickname my brother and I had given him.

"*Viiyeeeeeh* [a contraction of the French, *vieux habits*, old clothes]!" came a ragman's ear-piercing cry. One like it used to rouse me from the deepest sleep, even with the windows and shutters of my bedroom sealed tight. I stepped outside the *quincaillerie* as an old man walked past pushing his over-loaded bicycle. "*Viiyeeeeh!*" Never before had I been so close to the source of the sound. The unnaturally strident call, with an intensity that is impossible to mimic, almost lifted me out of my shoes. No other human utterance was quite like it.

Roselyne and Abder had been my father's neighbors in Casablanca, but also in Azemmour where they'd restored a *riad* of their own. They kept close tabs on Daddy during the last year of his life until he flew off to London for "medical consultations." Roselyne was waiting for me on the second floor landing.

"*La voilà, l'américaine!*"

I flopped into an easy chair in their salon to regale my friends with the morning's adventure. The usually reserved Abder laughed out loud.

"I'll bet Maître Tanja puts the moves on all his female clients," teased Rose.

"*Et toi*, Katy, you must have worked up quite an appetite keeping away from him," added Abder.

"That's all behind you now," Rose reassured me, pulling me into the kitchen where their housekeeper was adjusting the seasonings in a tagine. "Can you believe it? Rajja stumbled upon the first fennel of the season at the market this morning." The section of crisp, leftover stalk I pinched from the housekeeper's cutting board as I walked by possessed a flavor more assertive than that of its California counterpart.

After lunch, I was sipping an espresso and quizzing Rajja about her unusual tagine when Roselyne announced, "Katy, you've had such a stressful morning that Abder and I thought you'd enjoy a pleasant diversion."

The surprise was off-premises, they informed me, within walking distance of their apartment. So out the door we went, across the Boulevard Hassan II, through the park, and along the familiar grimy wall surrounding what was formerly called Lycée de Jeunes Filles, the largest girls' high school in the city — the one I attended for five memorable years.

"*La directrice* intimidated everyone, including my parents," I told Roselyne, who was not an alumna of the landmark institution. I was sure that the headmistress's uncompromising approach to rules and discipline had much to do with the lycée's top-notch reputation. She was less particular when it came to the school's gloomy *réfectoire*, dining hall. Neither I, nor any of my fellow *demi-pensionnaires*, half-board students, were likely to forget the luncheon platters of soggy couscous, stale baguettes, and mucilaginous mashed potatoes that we could wash down with the astringent red wine the school provided — a convention that seemed at cross-purposes with the posters of cirrhotic livers that hung on the walls of our science laboratory. The lycée's bizarre message to its impressionable girls: Drink wine, but in moderation. Small wonder the *gros rouge* and diseased livers didn't turn me into a teetotaler.

"Our destination's just around the corner," Abder informed me.

"Where are we going, Abder? Please don't keep me in suspense," I pleaded.

The newly appointed director of Casablanca's Ecole Nationale Supérieure des Beaux-Arts finally relented.

"Chaïbia asked me to bring you by," he said, before checking his watch. "Two o'clock, we're right on time."

10

Morocco's Matisse

Everyone recognized Chaïbia, a woman of my father's generation, doyenne of Morocco's modern art scene, and one of the country's leading feminists. Fellow Beidaouis waved and called her name whenever she made one of her rare public appearances.

At Abder's request, I had done a favor for the celebrity the year before by collecting and shipping via courier a portfolio of her unsold canvases from a gallery in Beverly Hills. She telephoned the moment the precious shipment arrived to express her gratitude and to extend an invitation to visit her home on my next trip to Morocco.

I'd long been an admirer, both of Chaïbia's art and her involvement in Morocco's fledgling women's movement. Her dedication to the latter meant even more to me given my current jousting with the country's male-dominated bureaucracy. In breaking cultural taboos, she'd become a role model in the Arab world.

Roselyne and Abder left me at the tumble of bougainvillea that hid the artist's home from the street. I infiltrated the flowery curtain and rang the bell. A waif of a girl in billowy pantaloons unlocked the gate in the garden wall. The heels of her *baboosh* slippers spanked the bricks as she ushered me down the walkway into Chaïbia's modest villa. I hadn't expected French colonial furnishings, from pendulum clock, permanently frozen on VII, to oversized armchair large enough to accommodate my famously ample hostess. I would learn later that she had inherited the house years before from her French employer and never bothered to redecorate, save for adorning the walls with her exuberant paintings.

The maidservant left me alone in the room, but returned shortly with a tray containing several glasses and pitcher of chilled juice. She struggled with its weight.

Financially strapped families, mostly from the countryside, were forced to indenture their daughters with prosperous households like Chaïbia's in return for a small stipend. An adolescent nanny one encountered on the street usually wasn't much bigger than the infant she propped up on her narrow hip. Leading newspapers ran exposés on abused *petites bonnes*, little maids, while billboards raised public awareness of their plight. On a personal level, I had to admit that their servitude tarnished the exoticism of Dar Zitoun's bygone *dadas*.

"Chaïbia will be in shortly," the girl announced in a wispy voice. She handed me a glass of what I guessed was a blend of pureed strawberries and orange juice.

"*Mezzian* [Delicious]," I complimented her. I should have known that orange blossom water was in the cocktail. Its fragrance was unmistakable.

I asked if she spoke French.

"*Nekdar n'gool* [I can say], '*Je m'appelle* Zarah [My name is Zarah],'" she replied.

With my urging, she brought over a pen and sheet of paper. I wrote, "*Je m'appelle* Zarah" and asked her to copy it. She backed away, waving her hands back and forth. "*Manqdarsh* [I can't]," she insisted, too embarrassed to even try.

She shared her illiteracy with forty percent of the country's female population, including her mistress, who could write only the block letters of her signature. I'd finally succeeded at getting young Zarah to have a go at Latin letters when our impromptu lesson was cut short. Chaïbia arrived with a Yorkshire terrier tucked under her arm. She seemed pleased that I'd taken an interest in the girl.

"You know, she's quite a clever little thing," bragged Chaïbia. "She begins school in October." This *petite bonne* was one of the lucky ones.

"We'll have our tea now," directed Chaïbia with softness in her tone. I reached out to pet her Yorkie, but received only a snarl and bared teeth for my effort.

"He's always like this with strangers," my hostess apologized.

Chaïbia was dressed in a magnificent, and voluminous, burgundy kaftan. Dark eyes matched her raven hair, which she wore tied back. A faint, Berber tribal tattoo ran from the middle of her lower lip to her chin.

"I was born near Azemmour. Did you know?" Abder must have given her some background information about me.

"You must stop by Dar Zitoun next time you are down our way."

"*Insh'Allah*," she replied, adjusting the cuff of gold bangles on her wrist. She sank into a sturdy sofa, and almost immediately, reached for a box of chocolate truffles.

"Have one," she urged me. I avoided the ones that were half-eaten. My hostess took time to study her options. She bit into one, but set it back in its fluted paper cup with a mischievous wink. The second and third selections were more to her liking.

"Talal!" she called.

A middle-aged man with shoulder-length hair soon appeared.

"*Enchanté* [Happy to meet you]," he said with Parisian elegance. "Since Chaïbia's French is a little rusty, she prefers that I do the talking for her," he explained. I thought it unusual that he referred to his mother by her given name.

He was several shades darker than she and had the mournful eyes of one who'd experienced many hardships. Smudged oil paint on his fingers reminded me that he was a well-known artist in his own right, though he hadn't attained his mother's level of commercial success. Talal propped himself on an arm of the sofa.

"When did your mother begin painting?" I asked. He prefaced his reply with a concise account of her girlhood, if one could call it that: a bride at thirteen, a mother at fourteen, and a widow at fifteen.

"Her parents were poor farmers who couldn't afford to send her to school," he backtracked. "So they sent her to Casablanca to work as a domestic and later arranged a marriage to a man fifty years her senior. That man would become my father. When he died, she supported both of us by taking a job as a *femme de ménage* [cleaning lady] in this very house." The biographical information gave me insight into Zahra's situation and also explained Chaïbia's manifest kindness toward the girl.

"She discovered her passion by helping me with assignments from my fine arts class at the lycée," added Talal.

Chaïbia poked her son in the thigh. "Tell her about the wild flowers," she prompted in Arabic.

"When Chaïbia was a girl, before her marriage to my father, she used to adorn herself with crowns of poppies and daisies. Since no other children behaved in that manner, the villagers thought she was crazy." Chaïbia smiled at me.

She poked her son again. "And my dream!"

"Chaïbia believes in the power of dreams," said Talal. "When she was twenty-five, she had a vision: of a blue sky filled with colorful banners . . . of a door opening from out of nowhere . . . and of old men dressed in white robes who showered her with canvases and brushes."

My hostess nodded and pointed to the ceiling as if to corroborate her son's account.

"Chaïbia took the dream as a prophetic sign. The next day, she bought ordinary house paint. She couldn't afford commercial art supplies," Talal continued. He saw me admiring some of his mother's framed gouaches on the wall. "Do you notice Chaïbia's penchant for primary colors? They remind her of the flowers she loved as a child."

"When I opened my first studio in Casablanca, an art dealer from Paris paid me a visit," Talal went on. "Chaïbia invited him for lunch, hoping to win him over with her cooking. But he couldn't concentrate on the *poulet au citron* after he saw her unframed paintings, which he said showed the influence of Matisse and Rouault."

Chaïbia's work created quite a sensation in Parisian art circles. In the estimation of some critics, her distinctive style placed her in the same league as her more established French contemporaries. By doing what she loved — following her bliss — she broke the Muslim taboo that forbade representation of the human form. It took uncommon courage for a woman who could barely sign her name to buck the mores of Arab society.

Talal and I helped Chaïbia to her feet and escorted her to the patio, where murals, portraits, and stylized *khmissas* (hands of Fatima, symbols of good luck) covered every square centimeter of wall. The eruption of color in her inimitable, naïve realism, vibrated with the passion of one set free from cultural constraints. My hostess pulled me toward a framed gouache, drawn in broad strokes of red, yellow, and blue — her interpretation of a woman. I wondered if Chaïbia'd made a conscious decision to hang it above her washing machine?

"Do you remember this one?" she asked. "It was in the exhibit in Beverly Hills. I want you to have it."

"But Chaïbia, I never expected anything for . . ."

"Katy, my mind is made up!"

I looked to Talal for solidarity, but found none.

"Take her! She's yours!" he said with finality.

Chaïbia and I moved to another sofa in front of a riotously painted wall just as the Yorkie reappeared in the company of a large, blonde-haired retriever. The former jumped into its mistress's lap and the latter squeezed in beside her. At the tinkling of a silver bell, Zahra delivered a pot of mint tea and a shallow bowl of *mulhalbiya* custard.

"Let me have a look at your hand while the tea is steeping," said Chaïbia. Palm readers practiced their art at the Azemmour souk, but I never availed myself of their services. For the famous artist, however, I was willing to make an exception.

She studied the intersecting creases of the "life," "head," and "heart" before running her index finger from the distal end of my palm to my wrist. "Your line of destiny reveals obstacles ahead," she told me, "but your heart line tells me a dark-haired stranger will come to your rescue."

Her prophecy elicited a disquieting vision of Maître Tanja.

"Events will turn your way by the end of the summer. Now, let's have our tea."

My clairvoyant's earnestness captivated me more than her message. I hadn't been brought up to believe in Morocco's pervasive metaphysics. Nevertheless, I was grateful to Chaïbia for her words of encouragement.

She plucked a candied almond from the *mulhalbiya* and crunched it between her teeth.

"Abder told me that there is a *marabout* buried at Dar Zitoun," she said, shifting to another paranormal topic.

"Yes, Sidi Makhfi's remains lie under our stairs, or so we are told," I answered.

"You must look to him for protection," she suggested.

Clearly, she presumed that my beliefs were in consonance with hers. Intellectually, I appreciated the role of the supernatural in the Maghreb. Deep down, however, my faith in the spiritual presence of Sidi Makhfi was uncertain at best.

Talal hadn't sat idly by during the palm reading. He'd taken the opportunity to unframe "my" gouache portrait, roll it up, and was about to slide it into a poster tube when the doorbell rang. It was Abder come to fetch me. Chaïbia kissed me on both cheeks. "Remember, *Allah eeshoof* [God watches]," she reassured me.

Orange Blossom Mulhalbiya with Pomegranate Seeds and Honeyed Almonds

Serves 6

Honeyed Almonds:
2 tablespoons plus 2 teaspoons honey
¼ teaspoon salt
⅛ teaspoon cinnamon
2 tablespoons plus 2 teaspoons sugar
1 cup sliced almonds

Custard:
2½ cups whole milk
¼ cup cornstarch
4 tablespoons sugar
1 cinnamon stick
2 tablespoons orange blossom water
Ground cinnamon for garnish
½ cup pomegranate seeds
Mint leaves, for garnish

Preheat oven to 325 degrees F.

For the honeyed almonds: In a saucepan, lightly warm honey. Transfer to a mixing bowl. Add salt, cinnamon, and sugar. Blend thoroughly. Add almonds and mix to coat. Spread nuts on a lightly oiled, non-stick baking sheet. Bake until nuts are lightly golden and sugar coating bubbles, 8 to 9 minutes. Do not over bake, or almonds will become bitter. Cool and break up.

For the custard: In a small bowl, blend ½ cup milk with cornstarch. Set aside.

Place remaining 2 cups milk, sugar, and cinnamon stick in a saucepan over medium heat. Bring to a simmer. Whisk cornstarch mixture into the simmering milk. Add orange blossom water. Cook, stirring until custard thickens. Discard cinnamon stick. Set aside for 5 minutes, stirring occasionally to prevent a skin from forming.

Divide custard among 6 shallow bowls. Sprinkle with candied almonds, cinnamon, and pomegranate seeds. Garnish with mint. Serve warm.

11

King Tut

I took Roselyne's advice and wore my jacket over my shoulder bag on the walk to Maître Drissi's law office. It was located in the former *quartier juif*, Jewish quarter, a section of town become notorious for pickpockets. By the mid 1960s, most Moroccan Jews had pulled up stakes. Their emigration to Israel, Canada, France, and the United States changed forever the ambiance of the *quartier*.

Even as I was growing up, Casablanca was a heterogeneous metropolis, a racial, religious, and cultural mosaic reflected in my own hybrid descent by way of a British Anglican father and French mother of Sephardic ancestry. Maternal forebears fled Spain at the time of the Inquisition to seek asylum in Algeria, the country of my grandfather's birth. All were tossed together in Muslim North Africa.

Since I was early for my appointment, I took a circuitous route through the city's central plaza, formerly called Place de France. The keyhole archway on its northern boundary led into the old medina, the one we Beidaouis dubbed "Chicago" because of its thriving black market.

Farther west, the welcoming steeple of St. John the Evangelist peeked from a cluster of palms. When completed in 1906, the Anglican chapel lay just outside city limits. General George Patton worshipped there following the Allied invasion of World War II, and, in gratitude for church support to American troops, he donated a pulpit and a carved oak frontispiece for the altar. My brothers and I contributed an engraved silver chalice in memory of my father who'd once served as St. John's warden. The vessel was in good company with the general's pulpit.

I was baptized at St. John's, and at the age of thirteen, studied my catechism there under the direction of the Reverend Cecil B. Green, the same pastor who married my parents and interred my godmother, Kathaleen Patton-Bethune, in the churchyard's quaint cemetery. The kindly parson would bless my own civil union years later. The sanctuary's continued existence was remarkable, considering its location on so choice a parcel of commercial real estate.

My legal advisor's office was just around the corner, between Café Zanzi-Bar and Glacier La Floride, an ice cream parlor. The serendipitous location made the impending session with my lawyer more palatable. I could treat myself to a gelato when it was over.

Maître Drissi's secretary wasn't concerned with *la dernière mode*, the latest fashion. Her long-sleeve dress with high collar and hijab demonstrated her devotion to the dictates of her faith, notably, to Sura XXIV, Aya 31 of the Qur'an: ". . . [Tell] believing women . . . to cast down their looks and guard their private parts and . . . not display their ornaments except what appears thereof, and . . . wear their head-coverings over their bosoms, and not display their ornaments except to their husbands . . ."

I waited, as ordered, and took stock of my surroundings. The railing of a potbellied balcony was visible through French doors. I hadn't seen such artistic ironwork since I was a girl at Madame Simone's grandiose apartment overlooking the Place de France.

* * *

As a family, we spent many a New Year's Day at her seamlessly orchestrated dinner parties. She was far and away the most impeccable hostess within my parents' circle of friends. Madame Simone left no detail to chance when she entertained. That made more humiliating an incident when my slightly tipsy father shattered a few crystals in a chandelier with an errant cork he launched from a bottle of Veuve Clicquot champagne.

The food was always *trois étoiles*, three star, at Madame Simone's, even to my then unsophisticated palate. But what I marveled at most was the artistry with which she blindly applied her carmine lipstick. I had plenty of opportunity to study her meticulous technique as she recoated her lips with *rouge à lèvres* almost as often as we changed plates during the multi-course banquet. While the adults sipped champagne and debated political issues around the starched-linen tablecloth laid with monogrammed cutlery, antique candelabras, and sparkling *crystal de Bohème*, my brother and I diverted ourselves with the fun-house reflections our faces made in our hostess's polished silver goblets.

Cheeks flushed from a fingerbreadth ration of chilled Vouvray wine, we savored plump Belon oysters abducted from their beds in the Oualidia lagoon four hours south of town. Like seasoned gastronomes, we devoured *dinde aux marrons*, roast turkey with chestnuts, and made piglets of ourselves with the perfectly ripened *fromages*, cheeses, and *salade d'endives aux noix*, Belgian endives with walnuts.

* * *

Musing on the lavish spread at Madame Simone's stirred my already growling stomach. Unfortunately, satiety would have to wait until I completed my business. Precisely one hour to the minute from the time I arrived, Maître Drissi's secretary announced, "*Il est prêt a vous recevoir* [He is ready to receive you]."

She led the way to a claustrophobic office stacked floor to ceiling with musty dossiers. A reed-thin, sallow-featured man in a dark business suit sat behind an oak table with his back to the window. The harsh glare hurt my eyes. I took a seat across from him. The gentleman reminded me of someone. The cogs rolled into position. I *had* indeed come across his look-alike — in Los Angeles in the late 1970s, at a traveling exhibition of the Treasures of King Tutankhamun. Who'd brought my counselor to mind? The mummy!

Maître Drissi wore the same timeless look. I examined his countenance more carefully. Experience was an admirable quality to have in one's legal representative, up to a point.

"Maître Tanja has already briefed me on your case," he said in a voice as feeble as his frame. "And he asked me to convey his apologies."

"Apologies?"

"Yes. He had urgent business in Rabat. You'll have to reschedule your appointment at the bank. Call him next week." One step forward, two steps back, just as Sir John predicted.

"I'll need a power of attorney from you, Nigel, and Philippe," my new counselor informed me.

With palsied hand, Maître Drissi took several minutes to scratch something onto a pad of paper using a fountain pen. I hadn't seen one since my years at the lycée.

"You've brought your father's testament?" I slid the document across to him. His eyes grew noticeably wider.

"But this, this is in English!" he stammered.

"My father *was* English, so he wrote his testament *in* English."

"But I must have an original in Arabic!"

"There is none, maître."

"Hmmmm," he pondered.

He again hunched over his writing pad to concentrate on his spidery scrawl. The walls of documents around us had an unintended and eerie acoustical effect, dampening the sound pressure to intensify the office's tomb-like quality. I heard every tick of the wall clock and every stroke of Maître Drissi's antique writing implement. I didn't dare fidget or clear my throat for fear of distracting him from his composition.

"I have drafted a letter to the chief clerk at the tribunal annex to request he translate your father's testament into French and Arabic," he informed me. "Of course, your *notaire* Maître Tanja will have to oversee the work in order to testify as to its authenticity before the magistrate."

"Magistrate? Isn't there an easier way to get a certified translation?" I asked. "Must we involve the court?"

"Madame, this is the way it is done," he said.

"But I am only in the country for a few more weeks, maître."

"Time is not the tribunal's concern, Madame Morse. *La procédure* [The process] must be followed." With that, he lifted a meaty file from the cabinet behind his desk. "Twenty-five years, madame! Twenty-five years it has taken me to resolve *this* case!"

I slumped in my chair. Morocco's mongrelized legal system — part Napoleonic code and part Islamic law — was like a rip-tide pulling me into the open ocean, away from my comfort zone near the shore.

"Can we communicate by e-mail?" I asked.

"*Jamais, madame. Je n'ai pas confiance* [Never, madame. I don't trust it]," he proffered. Instead, we exchanged phone numbers.

"This first step in the *procédure* takes time," he cautioned. "I will call you in due course."

The door to his office groaned shut behind me, my future sealed in his "mausoleum." Morocco's arcane web of statutory law had already pinned my wings. This ominous sense of victimhood didn't suit me. Rather than fall into the tragic disillusionment of a Miss Havisham, I wanted to emulate the optimism of a Scarlet O'Hara. The news would surely be more encouraging in two weeks, I told myself.

I pointed my car in the direction of the ocean and cruised through the opulent suburb of Anfa, past the historic Hôtel d'Anfa, site of the 1943 Casablanca Conference, where Churchill and Roosevelt planned their strategy against the Axis alliance.

I was admiring the architecture of the upper class *arrondissement*, urban subdivision, when a familiar image came into view, one that I wasn't expecting — the Golden Arches — set against a backdrop of the cerulean Atlantic. Maybe a taste of home was what I needed.

McDo was *the* hot spot on Casablanca's *Corniche*, oceanfront boulevard; the fast food restaurant was jammed with a well-heeled clientele to prove it. I rolled into the parking lot overlooking the beach. "*Bienvenue à* McDo," said a smiling greeter in her crisp uniform. The menu at the franchise, the first on the African continent, was almost identical to that in San Diego, Sydney, or Paris.

I ordered a Middle Eastern specialty not on other menus — a McArabia sandwich, featuring two juicy, cumin flavored beef patties, lettuce, tomato, onion, and a dollop of garlicky mayonnaise. It was on my tray within a minute.

I continued along the glamorous boulevard in front of the salt-water swimming pools where, during *les grandes vacances*, summer vacation, my girlfriends and I once perfected our tans and shared confidences about Pierre, Gérard, Jean-Claude, and the other muscular young men who showed off on the volleyball court.

On the way out of town, pilgrims clambered over the rocks surrounding the shrine of Sidi Abderrahmane, a scaled-down version of Brittany's Mont Saint Michel. They hurried to reach the *marabout* of Casablanca's patron saint before the incoming tide washed over the isthmus, leaving them stranded. I identified with their sense of urgency.

Sidi Abderrahmane was said to have performed miracles. Belief systems — in saints like him — take over when hope is lost, and the supernatural becomes the only option. Had I reached that point? I didn't think so. At that moment, there was at least one thing that remained under my control . . . and under my right foot. I stepped on the Peugeot's accelerator.

Salade d'Endives aux Noix
(Belgian Endive Salad with Walnuts)

Serves 4

2 teaspoons Dijon mustard
2 tablespoons white wine vinegar
3 tablespoons walnut oil
¼ teaspoon salt
Freshly ground pepper, to taste
2 teaspoons minced tarragon leaves, or 1 teaspoon dried, crushed
4 Belgian endives
¼ cup walnut pieces, toasted
¼ cup crumbled Blue cheese or Roquefort
½ cup bacon bits

Whisk mustard with vinegar until smooth. Continue to whisk while adding oil in a stream, until sauce emulsifies. Stir in salt, pepper, and tarragon. Set aside.

Wipe endives with a damp paper towel. Trim and discard ¼ inch from stumps. Cut 1½ inches from tips and set aside.

Cut what remains of endives into ½-inch-wide slices. Arrange in the center of a serving platter and surround with separated leaves from the tips. Drizzle with dressing and sprinkle with toasted walnuts, Roquefort, and bacon bits.

12

A Tagine As History

Roselyne and Abder phoned as soon as they arrived in Azemmour the following weekend. Our *riad*s were so close to one another that, had we been on our respective rooftops, we could have communicated using two tin cans and some fishing line.

"*J'arrive* [I'll be right over]!" I told Roselyne. From Dar Zitoun, my crooked route to their place would take me right — left — dogleg left —dogleg right — and dogleg left again.

Three teenage girls, arms interlocked, dawdled in the lane ahead. Getting around them would have required a bit of maneuvering. But since I was in no hurry, I simply fell into step behind them. Their interplay reminded me of my own adolescent to-and-fros with Joëlle, Lisbeth, and Chantal during my lycée years. The Zemmouri girls tacked onto an intersecting lane when they reached the public fountain — my destination, more or less, in that it lay directly across from my friends' striking, petroleum blue door.

Abder had a sense for color. An attribute one would expect in an artist. He also knew his way around the kitchen. That day, without Roselyne's help, he was putting together his grandmother's *tangia*, a recipe I'd long coveted. Fortunately, Abder had no qualms about betraying a family secret. He was compounding his sin by preparing the so-called "bachelor's stew" on Friday, the day for which couscous was the national *plat du jour*. Its heady, saffron aroma drifted from the doorways of most other households in the medina.

The small footprint of the Rahoules' three-story *riad* gave it a feel that was more vertical than horizontal. Part home, part gallery, it was a place for Abder to display many of his modernistic paintings and more modest ceramic works. His larger sculptures and murals adorned urban sites throughout the country.

On three sides the *riad* shared walls with other structures. The kitchen and dual staircases were adjacent to the lane. They helped to insulate the living quarters from activity associated with the public fountain. Occasionally, Abder had to poke his head from the second-floor window to glower at a particularly boisterous gaggle of youngsters. My physically imposing friend was soft-spoken, not given to anger or raised voice. A menacing look from him was usually all that was necessary to quash a disturbance.

Roselyne let me in. Even though I'm not much over five feet, I had to duck to avoid hitting my head on the hand-hewn lintel. Inside, the lush canopy of a rubber tree filled the atrium.

For his weekend attire "chef" Rahoule preferred a light-grey *gandoora*, like the ones favored by men of the Sahara. He'd already taken care of the *tangia's* mise en place. A small armada of bowls held turmeric, cinnamon, mace, ground ginger, black pepper, nutmeg, cumin, garlic, chunks of lamb shoulder, and several pounds of onions.

"Shall I trim the fat?" I teased, knowing full well the Moroccan love affair with fatty meats.

"Absolutely not. Fat gives the sauce its depth of flavor," he chided. "But I'll let you peel the onions." Meanwhile, Abder blended the ingredients for his marinade. It didn't take him long to massage the ochre-hued mixture into the meat.

"*Tangia*," he ordered, like a surgeon to his operating-room assistant. I rinsed my hands, splashed water on my face, and delivered the amphora to the prepping table.

"Do me a favor, Katy, pour some olive oil into the bottom," he directed. "Don't measure. Just pour." I was lucky not to have bungled the assignment following my bleary-eyed encounter with the onions. Abder soon had them tumbling through the narrow isthmus of the amphora while I held fast to its handles.

Logically, one would have expected a Zemmouri like Abder to confine his talent to regional fare rather than the specialty of Marrakech bachelors. For hundreds of years, unmarried laborers from the Pink City delivered their "loaded" amphora to a neighborhood *ferran* before heading off to work. Slow cooking in a wood-fired oven improved the texture and taste of cheaper cuts of meat favored by men of their station, transforming collagen in the fat, cartilage, and bone into silken liquid gelatin, in which the lamb and onions would braise until reclaimed by their owners.

"As you can see, Katy, *tangia*'s not difficult to prepare. No expensive or exotic ingredients. I don't know why restaurants charge so much for it," said Abder. Indeed. High-end eateries in Marrakech required two days' advance notice for the dish.

Abder covered the mouth of the amphora with a piece of heavy butcher paper, which I helped him secure to the vessel's narrow neck with a length of string.

"*Yallah*. We're ready for the *ferran*." Rather than cooking the dish over a charcoal brazier, he chose to follow bachelor tradition by using the public oven. Abder took hold of the amphora with both hands and headed down the stairs, with me close on his heels.

We interrupted several aspiring soccer stars as we stepped outside. Although Dar Zitoun's door was a favorite goal for local *footballeurs* because it lay at the end of a long alley, the more confined area in front of Rose and Abder's was better suited to perfecting dribbling and heading techniques.

The baker we sought had kindled and stoked a fire an hour before our arrival in order to bring his kiln to temperature. After banishing embers to the oven's perimeter, he'd gotten about the business of baking bread. A half-dozen unclaimed loaves of *khobz* awaited the hungry passerby. I bought two.

We entrusted the *tangia* into this man's care. As we were leaving, a woman arrived with a tray of unbaked *feqqas*, anise-flavored biscotti. The good-natured exchange between patron and owner crystallized my theory that frequenting the public oven did something to reinforce one's sense of community, even for intermittent medina dwellers like me.

Since Abder and I both had errands to run, we agreed to rendezvous at the *ferran*'s at six that evening.

On my way home, I heard a familiar voice: "Madame, it's me."

Living in a fortified enclave like the Azemmour medina, with only a handful of gateways, increased the probability of bumping into sticky characters like the *samsar* on a daily basis. He again had me cornered.

"Madame, I have a Frenchman interested in purchasing a *riad*, one with a view of the river. May I bring him by?"

"I've got to run, Hadj. I'm expecting an important call from the United States," I said to put him off. There would be time later to craft a more nuanced excuse for not receiving him, but I wasn't feeling particularly fast-on-my-feet at that moment. What was more, the warm *khobz* I clutched to my breast was begging to be slathered in butter and honey.

Abder and I rejoined forces at the appointed hour to begin our victory march. Once safely behind the petroleum-blue door, he removed the amphora's scorched seal and upended the vessel over an earthenware platter. The steam-shrouded, lava-like flow of *tangia* sauce, lamb, and braised onions sent my salivary glands into overdrive.

With a full stomach and a calm produced by several infusions of lemon verbena, I mentioned my recent encounter with the *samsar*. "Hadj Mustapha is wearing me down," I complained to my ever-supportive friend.

"Don't take it personally," advised Abder. "Like most Muslims, he believes that the time of death is predestined. The Qur'an requires a decedent's family to get on with their daily activities as soon as possible. The *samsar* just isn't attuned to the Western concept of grief."

I appreciated his explanation — from an intellectual standpoint. But Abder could see I was of two minds.

"The country is experiencing tough economic times. The *samsar* knows there will be other suitors for your business, so he must be persistent. Remember, he has two households to support," he continued.

"On top of that, he is after all, a *samsar*," Abder concluded with a wink.

"Well, then I'll just have to get used to it," I lamented.

"Katy, we have a saying, 'If you can learn to live for a year on onions, your whole life will be filled with honey.'"

How Abder's proverb applied to my situation, I wasn't quite sure. But I found it as delectable as his *tangia*.

Tangia (Bachelor's Stew)

Serves 6

Since amphorae and public ovens are difficult to come by in the United States, I use a slow cooker to prepare *tangia*.

2 tablespoons ground ginger
1 teaspoon freshly ground black pepper
1 teaspoon sweet Hungarian paprika
2 teaspoons ground turmeric
1 teaspoon freshly grated nutmeg
2 teaspoons ground cumin
2 teaspoons salt
¾ cup olive oil
3 pounds lamb shoulder, cut in chunks
8 garlic cloves, peeled
3 pounds yellow or white onions (no larger than a golf ball), peeled
1 cup beef broth
2 red bell peppers
Crusty bread, for serving

In a medium bowl, combine ginger, pepper, paprika, turmeric, nutmeg, cumin, salt, and ½ cup oil. Stir to blend. Coat each piece of lamb with this mixture. Set aside. Swirl the broth in the bowl that held the spices. Set aside.

Place garlic and onions in a slow cooker. Top with pieces of meat and reserved broth. Cover tightly. Cook on low setting until meat falls off the bones, 7 to 8 hours. Skim off fat.

Meanwhile, preheat oven to 425 degrees F. Cut peppers into wedges and remove seeds and ribs. Place wedges in baking pan and sprinkle with remaining olive oil. Roast until skin is evenly blistered, 25 to 30 minutes. Reserve for garnish.

Transfer *tangia* to a shallow bowl and garnish with peppers. Serve with crusty bread.

13

Pilgrimage

Joyous exclamations rebounded through the twin foyers and atrium to the salon where I was reading. I hurried downstairs to discover the source of Bouchaïb's merriment.

"*C'est ma cousine* [This is my cousin] Kenza," he said, proudly introducing me to the sturdy, rosy-cheeked young woman beside him. She was cradling a newborn in her arms. Bouchaïb pulled back the soft blanket that partly obscured the baby's face. "*Et ça, c'est son fils* [And this is her son] Mehdi."

I was well acquainted with our caretaker's immediate family — wife Leila, son Omar, and daughter Alia. His mother I'd met only once. He also had an uncle living somewhere in the Middle East. That was the extent of my knowledge concerning the Melhaj family tree.

Thus, Kenza's visit was an occasion quite out of the ordinary. I was delighted to learn from the little I caught of the rapid-fire Arabic that passed between her and Bouchaïb that she planned to spend several days in Azemmour. She'd stopped by Dar Zitoun only long enough to surprise her cousin. With Leila and Alia waiting for her at their apartment, she didn't stay long. She bent forward at the waist, and as a juggler would, flipped tiny Mehdi onto her back and secured him with a cotton shawl. Bouchaïb escorted her to the door.

"*Tiens* [Well, I'll be]!" he said when he returned. "We've had no news from that girl in over three years, ever since her husband repudiated her and sent her away."

"What?"

"Her husband Larbi, he wanted a son. And since Kenza couldn't give him any children, he simply *cassé la carte* [tore up their marriage contract]," recounted Bouchaïb. In a society obsessed with a bride's virginity and her ability to bear children (especially a male heir) there was no fate worse than infertility. I'd heard of fathers refusing to provide sanctuary to a repudiated and barren daughter whose future prospects for remarriage were nil. After all, what self-respecting man would take a once-married infertile woman for his wife? By tradition, declaring, "I repudiate you" three times was all that was necessary for a husband to divorce his wife. Upon ratification in 2004, reforms to the Mudawana (family code) initiated by King Mohammed VI began to curtail the summary practice.

"Isn't it wonderful? Larbi has taken her back," gushed Bouchaïb, assuming I was in agreement.

"Sure, now that her 'shortcomings' were no longer an issue," I thought.

"And Larbi has his son," Bouchaïb went on.

"*His* son? Wait a minute. You just told me that Kenza had been away for three years?"

"Yeesss," said Bouchaïb, not quite clear on the point I was trying to make.

"But how *can* that be?"

"But the baby is *his*, Katy! My mother, she told me that once a woman conceives, she is able to carry her baby for as long as she likes before giving birth," he explained.

My lifelong immersion in Morocco had not prepared me for this. I wondered how many other once-repudiated wives had redeemed themselves in this manner.

It was pointless to argue. For Moroccans like Bouchaïb, the myth surrounding extended gestation, dubbed *l'enfant endormi* (sleeping baby) by cultural anthropologists, is a tenet of Islamic law intended to protect the honor of a young mother and secure the patrilineage of her children. According to my calculations, Mehdi must have "slept" for a little more than two years before being born. But why upset Kenza and Larbi's amicable resolution for the sake of science? What mattered was that father, mother, and son were reunited.

"Tomorrow Kenza wants to visit the shrine of Lalla Bahria to give thanks for her good fortune," Bouchaïb informed me.

"Do you think she'd take me with her?" I asked.

For years, I'd watched carriages rumble along the beaten path on the opposite side of the river carrying pilgrims to the shrine of Lalla Bahria by the Sea. I often wondered about the goings-on at the holy site, but never took the initiative to go there on my own.

"*Mais oui, bien sûr* [Yes, of course]," Bouchaïb answered on his cousin's behalf.

"It wouldn't be an imposition?"

"*Mais non!*" he insisted.

"Tell her I'll drive."

Kenza arrived promptly at seven the following morning with chestnut-haired Mehdi gurgling contentedly on her back.

I had great faith in Daddy's old Peugeot — until the first hundred meters on the sandy, rutted *piste*, unpaved road. I parked a safe distance away from the river's tidal range and mud flats to consider my options. The medina's reflection in the Mother of Spring was particularly lovely that morning. How fortunate I was to live there!

Kenza flagged down a *calèche*. We hoisted ourselves onto the wagon's flat bed and dangled our legs over the side like the other passengers. But the mule wouldn't budge. After a few slaps from the driver's whip elicited no response, a barefooted lad was dragooned into tugging on the stubborn animal's halter.

I'd worn a light peach djellabah in order to make myself less conspicuous. Fellow pilgrims were wrapped in more colorful cotton haiks that made them look like exotic birds.

"Lalla Bahria will help me find a husband, *Insh'Allah*," a passenger confided to Kenza.

Every shrine was reputed to be particularly effective in setting right a specific malady or problem. For many supplicants, a visit to a mystical *marabout* may have been as effective as an hour of psychotherapy. Sufferers of unrequited love or infertility held no shrine in higher esteem than Lalla Bahria by the Sea.

"I'm going to give thanks for my little boy," replied Kenza. "I will say a prayer at the *marabout*."

Another member of our sorority of hope glanced quizzically at me, no doubt intrigued by a *nesraniya*'s visit to the shrine of a Moroccan saint. I was well past my childbearing years and recently celebrated my thirtieth wedding anniversary with my first and only husband. How could I explain my fact-finding excursion — my snooping — in a diplomatic way? Kenza read the woman's mind, and with a sweet smile, said simply, "She's with me."

The shadow play of my legs upon the trail, the sway of the *calèche*, and the clip-clop of the mule's hooves, had an almost hypnotic effect upon me. I roused myself just in time to keep my open-heel *baboosh* from slipping off my feet. We passed another carriage idling alongside the *piste*. The embroidered hem of a pantaloon peeked coquettishly from under the haik of one of its passengers.

"Isn't that considered *h'shooma* [shameful]?" I asked Kenza.

"If a man sees the hem of a *sarwal* [pantaloons] it drives him wild," she replied. "Women everywhere, they have their secrets, you know."

We made way for a *grand taxi* that came up suddenly behind us. The packed Mercedes roared by, leaving us in a wake of dust and diesel fumes. Its thoughtless driver was indifferent to our discomfort, and apparently, to the welfare of his axle. We caught up with him not far from the shrine, his feet sticking out from beneath the disabled vehicle as he assessed the damage.

The taxi's noxious cloud didn't dampen the enthusiasm aboard our *calèche*, nor did it give me second thoughts about abandoning the comfort of the Peugeot. There was something more soulful about traveling to the shrine of a saint by animal-powered conveyance.

The sight of the white-domed shrine sent my fellow passengers into a frenzy of uninhibited singing, ululating, and synchronized clapping. Kenza, coming under the spell of this contagion, joined the chorus, her tongue fluttering like the wing of a hummingbird.

Our driver parked his *calèche* near a cluster of pack animals. The sorrowful creatures inspired me to renew a promise: If reincarnated, I would never, ever return to earth as a Moroccan burro! I wasn't the first American to be affected by the pack animal's inhumane treatment. In the late 1920s, a wealthy New Yorker felt so compelled by the plight of abused donkeys that she established a veterinary clinic in Fez specifically for their care.

Eddies of litter swirled erratically in front of Lalla Bahria's *marabout*. It was an unsettling sight in such a sacred place. So was the boy with outstretched palm demanding, "*Un* dirham, *un* dirham." Kenza cut him short. "*See'eer* [Go away]!" she scolded, before turning to me.

"If you give him something, you won't have a moment's peace," she warned.

We joined the stream of pilgrims, whose emerald, turquoise, and tangerine haiks billowed in the light ocean breeze. Snug as an Australian joey in its mother's pouch, serene Mehdi bounced in time to his mother's steps. Kenza took the opportunity to fill me in on the story of the venerated saint:

"Many years ago, Lalla Bahria helped her teacher, the sheik of Baghdad, with his ablutions. A ray of light, the spirit of his most famous protégé, Moulay Bouchaïb of Azemmour, followed him everywhere. Its sudden disappearance devastated the holy man and his disciples, including Lalla Bahria. Grief-stricken, she threw her prayer rug upon the water and willed it to carry her across the sea. But she never reached the tomb of Moulay Bouchaïb. She collapsed and died on the very spot where her *marabout* now stands."

In some respects, Kenza's mythical tale agreed with the historical account I later read regarding the twelfth century noblewoman who studied under a renowned Sufi mystic in Baghdad, at that time the center of Arabic learning and culture. She began a passionate, lifelong correspondence with fellow disciple, Moulay Bouchaïb. Over the years, word of the Zemmouri's erudition and spiritual insight spread throughout the Islamic world, with his fame eclipsing that of his Baghdadi mentor. Moulay Bouchaïb's death brought despair to Lalla Bahria and impelled her to begin an arduous journey to the Maghreb. Sadly, she succumbed to its rigors on the northern bank of the Oum er-Rbia, within sight of the object of her devotion, the tomb of Azemmour's patron saint.

Centuries later, Lalla Bahria's ill-fated odyssey and untimely death still drew lovelorn pilgrims to seek her guidance in resolving their affairs of the heart. "Lalla Bahria died of a broken heart," Kenza said solemnly. "That's why she understands women."

Kenza and I parted company at the entrance to the shrine, which was restricted to Muslims. Luckily, I had no romantic issues to iron out. While I waited for my friend to perform her ceremonial washing, I sought out the shrine's resident *neqqasha*, henna artist. My companion had sung the praises of the natural dye, telling me how: "Henna, *nor n-nbi*, ensures *baraka* [good fortune] and keeps the evil eye at bay." A prior experience with the colorant proved disastrous. The gray strands of hair I'd hoped to tint a warm auburn turned carrot-orange. But an ephemeral tattoo for my hand posed little risk.

I infiltrated the huddle of women watching the *neqqasha* practice her trade. Using a syringe, she expressed tendrils of henna paste to create whimsical designs on a customer's palm. Once the artist became aware of my presence, she beckoned to me. "*Ajee, gelsee* [Come and sit down]," coaxed the ample-bosomed woman, patting the stool in front of her. I'd expected to wait my turn, but she insisted that I be next. The other women seemed to champion my preferential treatment, too.

"One hand, twenty dirhams."

I presented my right palm.

On the *neqqasha*'s left, a wooden crate held the medium and paraphernalia of her art — a bowl of clove-scented henna paste the consistency and color of pureed spinach, a box of cotton balls, a saucer of sweet garlic water, a plastic syringe, and a blunt-tipped (though still fearsome) needle.

The *neqqasha* drew some paste into a syringe, expelled the trapped air and affixed the grim needle. Our knees touched as she gripped the back of my hand to study her new "canvas" more closely.

Instinctively, my heart skipped a beat when needle met skin — an irrational fear in the bloodless process. The henna design felt cool at first, but after several minutes, elicited a slight burning sensation thanks to a modern additive, kerosene, used to expedite drying. Nevertheless, I felt at ease in our clove and garlic-tinged intimacy with my hand the center of the artist's creative thoughts.

In the space of five minutes she produced a design as intricate as Belgian lace, which she fixed with a dab of garlic water. The decorations were my talismans. My fate was in my hands, literally, if not in Lalla Bahria's.

"Let it dry. Don't touch," she warned. I felt my skin tighten under the crusting paste.

"*Zoueen* [Beautiful]," the onlookers agreed.

Upwind from the *marabout* and *neqqasha*, an enterprising *sfenj* vendor had strategically positioned his doughnut cart and canvas canopy on the leeward side of a dune. His business needed no advertisement other than the fragrant smoke that wafted over hungry pilgrims. Strutting pigeons played their part in the entrepreneur's operation by policing the area for tidbits.

The baker adroitly fashioned soft rings of dough, which he dropped into the roiling oil of an adjacent cauldron. Next to it, several cooling, golden bracelets awaited nothing more than a customer and a sprinkling of granulated sugar. Mouthwatering. From experience, however, I knew the sizzling pastries, concocted simply from flour, salt, yeast, and water, to be relatively tasteless and tough. I never understood why Moroccan beachgoers were so taken with the popular fare. Nevertheless, I asked the man to prepare a dozen for the road — a treat for my traveling companions on our return to Azemmour. The vendor strung my take-away order on a slender leaflet of palm frond.

From time to time, when the spirit moved him, Bouchaïb was known to whip up a batch of a tastier, more chewable variation of the time-honored recipe, one that was more suitable for edentulous consumers like him.

Just offshore from the shrine, the surf battered the rusted shipwreck locals called *Le Titanic*. The carcass of the Portuguese dredging ship, which had foundered on a sandbar a decade before, partially obstructed the Oum er-Rbia's estuary. Maybe the developers of the beachfront resort being planned just south of town would deal with the eyesore as part of an overall campaign against litter. I had mixed feelings about a spic and span Azemmour overrun with tourists. On the positive side, the new venture held out the promise of jobs to a woefully underemployed population.

Kenza emerged from the shrine doing up a scarf around her wet hair. She noticed how I protected my hand. "*Baraka*," she wished me.

I couldn't help but envy the serenity she found in her belief. Reason and practicality didn't rule her mind. At that moment, her life seemed more filled with poetry than mine.

By the time we got home, most of the henna paste had dried and flaked away, leaving behind a rust-colored decoupage. Bouchaïb inspected the *neqqasha*'s work.

"I hope it makes the bureaucrats nervous," he said with a chuckle.

Bouchaïb's Sfenj (Doughnuts)

Makes about one dozen

½ cup lukewarm water (100-110 F)
2 teaspoons active dry yeast (see note)
3 cups flour
¼ cup sugar
½ teaspoon salt
¾ cup *Iben* (buttermilk)
¼ cup melted butter
4 to 6 cups vegetable oil, for frying
Granulated sugar, for sprinkling
Fruit preserves and honey, optional

In a bowl, combine water and yeast. Stir. Set aside until the mixture starts to bubble, 10 to 12 minutes.

In a large bowl, whisk together flour, sugar, and salt. Make a well in the center. Add yeast mixture, buttermilk, and melted butter. Mix with your hands for 2 to 3 minutes and form dough into a ball. Cover and set aside in warm place for 3 to 4 hours. Dough should double in size.

Pour oil to a depth of 3 inches into a heavy pan or deep skillet. Set heat to medium high. Oil is ready when a test-piece of dough sizzles instantly and floats to the surface.

Wet hands and pinch off a piece of dough the size of an egg. Poke a hole in the center and shape into a rough bracelet, 3 to 3½ inches in diameter. Carefully drop into the hot oil. Fry until golden brown, 1 to 1½ minutes on each side. Transfer to a paper towel to drain. Continue in this manner with the remaining dough. Sprinkle with sugar. Serve warm with fruit preserves and honey on the side.

Note: Moroccan cooks use *hamira*, baker's yeast, when preparing *sfenj*.

14

The Registrar Of Deeds

After months of living day-to-day, coddling my grief while trying to walk in my father's shoes, the time had come to try on my inheritance in earnest. In order to do that, I needed to make progress on the legal front. But as my former Latin teacher would have put it, *omnii augurii mali erant* — all the omens were bad. Weeks passed since I'd had news from Maître Drissi. From the very first he seemed unconcerned about getting the show on the road. Commitments in California weren't closing in on *him*. Age was also a consideration. His days of burning the candle at both ends were over. I was beginning to fear the worst when at last he telephoned.

"Madame, I am happy to inform you that we have received the Arabic translation of your father's testament."

Finally some progress! Next stop, *la conservation foncière*, the office of registrar of deeds, in El Jadida. My elation lasted only until the implications of a meeting with the *conservateur*, the registrar, hit home. Such an audience involved an inordinately powerful and unaccommodating official, one with whom my father experienced unpleasant dealings that left him considerably lighter in the pocketbook. Yet there was no way of getting around the fact that the *conservation foncière* was the shallow strait through which the Dar Zitoun title would have to sail en route to transfer. To be sure, moments of propriety would punctuate the professional charade, but somewhere in the tortured process, there would also be the need for cash. I would have preferred a session with the Grand Inquisitor.

Maître Drissi's determination to sally forth from his dreary office in Casablanca *was* good news. Since his feeble condition precluded his driving, he decided to come by train.

"Why not get off at Azemmour?" I suggested. "That will give you the opportunity to see the house. We can share a taxi to El Jadida after lunch."

He arrived on time at the Halte d'Azemmour station, one kilometer south of the ramparts. I hurried to the railroad car dedicated to *non-fumeurs* in order to assist him with the last precipitous step onto the crushed rock rail bed.

Maître Drissi seemed more agile and upbeat than at our previous meeting. I hoped to keep him that way by not wearing him out. To that end, I agreed to quadruple the *petit taxi* driver's fare if he delivered my fragile charge as close to Dar Zitoun as possible. One didn't often come across automobiles within the ramparts due to the narrowness of the streets. Mopeds, occasionally; cars, almost never, although they weren't strictly forbidden.

The driver carefully negotiated through the Sidi Makhfi archway to link up with the medina's main artery — an exaggerated term for the twisted alleyway of irregular width that in places was barely wide enough to accommodate a sub-compact vehicle. From my vantage point in the passenger seat, there were times when I felt I was inside a tiny store rather than in a vehicle rolling past it.

Although there were dozens of contiguous shops, none was larger than a breakfast nook, and none stocked more than thirty items. Unfortunately, we had no "Ali Baba's cave" to fall back on. Our corridor of industrious entrepreneurs would have been reduced to obsolescence in America's big-box store economy, devoid of the personal touch between vendor and buyer. *Zemmouri* shops had character.

A seasoned urbanite, Maître Drissi had never visited Azemmour and gawked like a tourist. Had he been more robust, I would have shown him the Portuguese fortress complete with portcullis, crenellated ramparts, and bronze cannon embossed with the words *Poderoso es Dios*, Powerful is God. And I would have led him through the abandoned *mellah*, a term derived from the Arabic *mel'ha*, salt, because of the historic proximity of most Jewish quarters to the salt market. In Azemmour, the *quartier* was once the nucleus for gold dealers, silversmiths, tailors, and metal workers, many of them, descendants of Sephardim from Al Andalus. All had contributed to the town's reputation as a *centre artisanal*.

"When I was a boy, I had many Jewish friends," claimed Bouchaïb. "I'd play in their homes and eat in their kitchens. I am sorry they left." He'd once pointed out a molded-plaster Star of David above the entryway to the home of Madame Rachel, one of the town's Jewish residents, whom he referred to as his "surrogate mother."

"Madame Rachel, she was a wonderful lady. She used to buy all the fish I could catch," he told me. "And when she cooked them on the *canoon*, she'd set a plate for me."

Muslims and Jews still visited the grotto-cum-synagogue that sheltered the tomb of Rabbi Abraham Moul Niss, "Author of Miracles," according to the sign in Hebrew above the entrance. An annual religious festival in his honor attracted pilgrims from all over the world, when Zemmouri émigrés, their children, and grandchildren returned to search for their roots in the Jewish cemetery outside the ramparts. My father and I used to pass its northern limits on our late afternoon strolls along the river.

* * *

I wondered if a lonely tortoise still grazed on the thick vegetation that surrounded the untended stone sarcophagi. A kind-hearted, but somewhat naïve passenger on one of my tours had purchased the reptile at a Saharan souk for fear that a tagine pot lay in its future. Later, I learned that the woman's original plan had been more ambitious — to rescue and export a Moroccan donkey. Without my knowledge, the tortoise stowed away on our bus all the way to Azemmour, spending its nights installed in five-star bidets upholstered in lettuce.

Second thoughts about the tortoise adoption crept into the woman's mind during the farewell dinner at Dar Zitoun, although she remained determined to find her traveling companion a good home. My husband Owen hit upon the idea of the cemetery. The task of explaining the bizarre plan to Bouchaïb fell to me. His "*Quoi* [What]?" reminded me of the Spanish waiter in the British television series *Fawlty Towers*, who often responded to his employer's requests by uttering, "*Qué* [What]?" in the same tone of utter incomprehension.

* * *

The driver of the taxi I'd engaged for Maître Drissi set his parking brake not fifty feet from Dar Zitoun's front door.

For the second time in a month, Bouchaïb had donned his starched white jacket. I marveled at his adherence to the rules of etiquette. The longer-than-usual litany of salutations that he delivered with Shakespearean flair was, no doubt, in deference to our guest's advanced age and social status. Bouchaïb might have thrived on stage if his family's economic circumstances hadn't forced him to cut short his schooling after only *cours élémentaire.*

Maître Drissi contented himself with a once-around the atrium since climbing to the terrace was beyond his capacity. No two of the twenty-four irregularly constructed stairs had the same rise, making their ascent difficult, even for the able-bodied.

"*C'est un vrai petit bijou* [It's a real jewel]," he marveled. "My family owned a *riad* in the Fez medina," he continued. "Like yours, it was filled with history. I was sad when infirmity forced my grandparents to abandon it for an apartment in the *ville nouvelle* [new town, lying outside the medina]."

By that time, Bouchaïb had set before us three dishes, each styled with the eye of an artist: cooked carrots and raisins flavored with orange juice and cinnamon; a salad of fennel, grapefruit, and black olives doused with garlic infused vinaigrette; and a tagine of lamb meatballs in tomato *chermoula* sauce.

"*Tbarka llah lek* [Well done], Bouchaïb," praised Maître Drissi. "I wish my wife were here. She comes from a long line of outstanding cooks."

Bouchaïb bowed modestly.

"*Vous êtes très gentil* [You are most kind] maître."

My lawyer suddenly became remote, as if he were about to lose an important thought, something he wanted me to know. No more compliments about Bouchaïb's prowess in the kitchen. "Madame, let me do the talking when we are at the *conservateur*'s. We must remain respectful, never questioning or impatient. We have to walk a fine line with this man. I've followed *la procédure* to the letter, but I am afraid it is personality upon which our success now rests."

We arrived in El Jadida a bit early. Most government offices were still closed for lunch. Better to hit town during the midday torpor rather than during the rush hour bedlam, especially in the summer months when the population of the resort city swelled with vacationers.

Portuguese colonizers occupied Mazagan, later renamed El Jadida, from 1486 to 1769. We skirted their oceanfront citadel, La Cité Portugaise, a World Heritage site. Orson Welles' movie classic, *Othello*, made famous its most popular attraction, the fortification's cavernous cistern. Local authorities recently dedicated an adjoining space as a municipal art gallery to showcase the country's most prominent artists, Chaïbia and Rahoule among them.

Our driver doubled back to drop us in front of the *conservation foncière* at precisely two o'clock, just as guards unlocked the iron gates that held back the petitioners who'd gathered on the sidewalk. The way my bony lawyer sprang into action took me by surprise. He wasn't shy about using a combination of sharp elbows and old age to get us into the reception hall ahead of the others in order to stake out a position along the forty-foot counter. An unsmiling *fonctionnaire* turned into Mr. Sunshine when he spotted the envelope making its way from Maître Drissi's coat pocket to the wooden counter. In short order, we were headed up a flight of terrazzo stairs as well as up the chain of command.

Officious underlings in the *conservateur*'s department assiduously recorded documents in antiquated ledgers. I took note of the slowly turning ceiling fan and manual typewriter. They seemed more suited to Sam Spade's office than that of the twenty-first century executive who was about to summon us into his presence. I raised my hand when I heard my name, but otherwise kept silent, as I'd been directed. Case files covered every square inch of the bureaucrat's desk. The burnt-orange henna designs on my palm, a soul-stirring reminder of my trip to Lalla Bahria's, had faded to a soft pastel. Would they bring me luck?

My counselor fumbled through his briefcase and offered up my dossier to the *conservateur*, who studied it in silence for a full five minutes before speaking.

"And what do you do in America, Madame Morse?" So much for Maître Drissi's gag order.

"I write Moroccan cookbooks." My interrogator's steely demeanor seemed to thaw.

"Americans, they like Moroccan food?" he asked, with a mixture of astonishment and pride.

"Yes. Moroccan cuisine is quite à la mode," I replied.

Dar Zitoun's riverside location must have spawned his next question.

"You know about *ashabel?*"

"*Oui, bien sûr.* I was lucky to find one at the souk recently. We prepared it with *t'faya* sauce."

The look the *conservateur* shot toward Maître Drissi was unmistakable. She knows more than I thought, it said. My lawyer appeared relieved. However, his optimism would be short lived.

The registrar, we were about to learn, was a man of mercurial disposition. His mood became somber as he turned his attention to my sheaf of documents. Several agonizing minutes elapsed before he spoke. "You've given me certified copies of a testament in English and Arabic, but where is the original?" He waved the certified copies in front of Maître Drissi to reinforce the point.

"The original, *Sidi*," my advocate replied defensively, "my client turned it over to the tribunal archivist in Casablanca, since that was Monsieur Chandler's city of residence. I assumed that a copy, certified by the British consulate, would be sufficient for the purpose of transferring title."

"You assumed wrong, maître," countered the stone-faced official. "We can't proceed until I have the original in front of me."

Before I realized what was happening, he was on his feet, shaking my hand and that of my lawyer with grotesque geniality. "I'd love to have one of your cookbooks for my wife."

I knew I would hate myself later for replying, "I'd be happy to bring one for her on my next trip."

Outside, Maître Drissi and I stood in a daze beside the congested avenue, our efforts wasted. My counselor looked exhausted after the rough treatment he'd received. Dueling with an official as arrogant as the *conservateur* was sport for younger men.

"I'm sorry. The requirements in El Jadida are not what I am used to," he said. "I will get an appointment with the clerk of the court in Casablanca to see what can be done about procuring the original testament. We can try our luck again in a couple of weeks."

"But maître, I fly home to California in ten days."

"I'm sorry, madame, I had forgotten," he replied sheepishly. "We'll have to take care of it on your next trip." I remembered his account of a client's twenty-five year quagmire. In another quarter of a century, would Maître Drissi's junior partner hold up the Chandler/Morse dossier as an example of hamstrung probate? Like two wounded warriors, we repaired to a pastry shop down the street for mint tea and gazelle horns before our retreat to Azemmour.

Cornes de Gazelles (Gazelle Horns)

Makes about 40 pastries

Almond Paste:
1 pound slivered blanched almonds
¼ cup water
¾ cup powdered sugar
3½ tablespoons unsalted butter
⅛ teaspoon almond extract
2 tablespoons orange blossom water

Dough:
2 cups all-purpose flour
½ teaspoon salt
4 tablespoons unsalted butter, melted
½ cup orange blossom water
1 egg, beaten with 1 tablespoon water, for egg wash
Powdered sugar, for garnish

For the Almond Paste: Spread almonds over a lightly oiled baking sheet. Toast until lightly browned, 12 to 15 minutes. Cool. In increments, reduce almonds to a paste using a spice grinder or mortar and pestle. Alternatively, run almonds through a food grinder fitted with a coarse grinding plate and then process three or four times using a fine grinding plate in order to achieve a smooth paste.

In a medium saucepan, combine water and sugar over medium-low heat. Cook, stirring, until mixture begins to foam. Remove from heat. Add butter and stir until melted. Add almond paste, almond extract, and orange blossom water. Stir vigorously until paste separates from sides of pan. Set aside to cool.

For the Dough: In a large mixing bowl, sift flour and salt. Make a well in the center. Stir in melted butter and orange blossom water. Using a mixer fitted with a dough hook, process until dough is smooth and elastic, 4 to 5 minutes. Set aside to rest for 15 minutes.

Preheat oven to 325 degrees F.

Divide dough into 4 equal parts. Between two sheets of parchment paper dusted with flour, roll each dough ball to approximately 9 inches in diameter. Cut into rectangular pieces measuring about 2¼ x 4¼ inches. Form a half-tablespoon of almond paste into a 3-inch-long spindle and center on a piece of dough. Using a pastry brush, paint dough's perimeter with egg wash. Fold over, seal, and form into a crescent shape. Trim excess dough with a pastry crimper. Prick pastry in 5 or 6 places with a toothpick. Continue in this manner until all pastries are assembled.

Set on a non-stick baking sheet. Bake on center rack of oven for 8 to 10 minutes. Cool. Dust with powdered sugar and serve. Gazelle horns will keep in the refrigerator for up to a month in a sealed container.

15

The Herbalist

I hadn't expected a metaphysical experience when, on the following morning, I accepted a mission from Bouchaïb that took me into the realm of a *fkih*, an herbalist and practitioner of native medicine. He was also the patron of an exotic emporium that handled, among other things, a unique combination of spices called *ras el hanoot*, top of the shop, a house blend for which he had acquired a certain celebrity in and around Azemmour.

Whether he could also resolve medical maladies from headaches to infertility, as many of my fellow Zemmouris believed, I had my doubts. Nevertheless, our neighborhood grocer sang his praises. So did Bouchaïb's wife, an ardent subscriber to the philosophy of alternative medicine, who applied hot spoons to the webs of her husband's toes when he suffered from athlete's foot and was known locally for having a calming effect on rabid animals. I never personally witnessed these bizarre ministrations, but heard about them second-hand through Bouchaïb's embellished accounts. Leila regularly sought the herbalist's guidance as well as his potions in her lifelong battle against the mischievous *jnoon*.

She wasn't the only one engaged in the struggle against them. Kebira, a Berber woman who worked in our home when I was a child, both fascinated and scared my brother and me with tales of *Al Jinn* of the Qur'an, supernatural creatures of free will, created from smokeless fire, that had the capacity to influence human affairs for good or ill — to keep one on the moral path or lead one astray. Especially frightening was the sinister sorceress of legend, creator of spiritual mayhem and caster of the evil eye, Aïsha Kandisha. Among other misdeeds, she turned normally faithful husbands into philanderers. As a child, I learned not to broach the subject of Moroccan occult practices with my parents as it only served to bring their displeasure upon Kebira for "filling my head with such nonsense."

They must have had a change of heart when they paid a visit to a French *fkih* in Marrakech to rid Philippe of tenacious warts. The treatment worked. On another occasion, I overheard my mother advising a friend to plant a white rosebush in her garden to improve the odds of having a baby with curly hair. Even at the tender age of twelve, I had trouble reconciling the ambivalent attitude toward things beyond scientific understanding.

For women with little or no education, like Kebira and Bouchaïb's wife, there was no such uncertainty. *Jnoon* manipulated their daily lives and had to be thwarted by all means possible. This belief inspired Leila to hang a stylized hand of Fatima, called a *khmissa*, on the wall of Dar Zitoun's atrium, with the absolute conviction that the symbol would ward off the evil eye. One found the same good-luck charms everywhere around town — in doorways, on the backs of trucks and buses, on the windshields of automobiles, and dangling from the rear-view mirrors of taxis. I didn't think the superstition had rubbed off on me, though I'd worn one of the engraved amulets around my neck for so long, more as a fashion statement than anything else, I felt almost naked without it.

The dusky interior of the herbalist's shop appeared deserted. "Exhilarated curiosity" best described my state of mind as I inched carefully toward the back of the surreal establishment, not wanting to entangle myself in the outlandish talismans suspended from fishing lines or disturb the items that jutted precariously from unsound shelving — the sloughed skin of a viper, an ostrich egg in custom leather pouch, or the horn of an antelope.

Votive candles cast ghostly shadows on the walls of the healer's low-ceilinged consultation chamber, where the man of mystery was huddled in hushed conversation with a troubled soul. That he understood which wild herb or natural remedy targeted a specific pathology, which incantation accompanied musk-infused charcoal, how to invoke a curse, or how to rescind one, was impressive enough in itself. I hadn't considered the possibility that he also served as de facto psychologist. Medical care in Morocco was cheap by Western standards, but still out of reach for many inhabitants, thereby creating a niche for a man of his many talents.

I poked my head through the doorway. The air inside was heavy with the scent of henna, cloves, and perspiration. The *fkih* raised his eyebrows and held up his index finger in a gesture I took to mean he would be with me presently.

Leila claimed he'd rid her of chronic headaches after Western medicine had failed. Several years earlier, a physician friend from California, travel bag well stocked with pharmaceuticals, spent a week as my father's guest at Dar Zitoun. According to Leila, the side effects of the drugs he'd given her were worse than the migraines from which she suffered. Not so the curative powder the herbalist subsequently prescribed as an additive to mint tea. I knew little of folk medicine, but had to admit that Leila's experience made me more receptive to its potential benefits, placebo or otherwise.

The *fkih*, in white skullcap and shabby *gandoora*, escorted a hunched client outside. Several women slipped into the shop while they were away.

"I am in no hurry sir," I said on the herbalist's return. "Look to these women's needs before mine." I did so partly because I wanted his undivided attention, but mostly because I hoped to eavesdrop on his consultations with other customers.

"How may I help you, *Lalla?*" he asked, turning to the veiled woman beside me.

The gauzy fabric that covered her face below the nose swelled and contracted in little puffs as she described the verbal abuse and humiliating treatment she received at the hands of her mother-in-law. Like all good Muslim wives, she had to submit not only to her husband's will, but also to that of his mother. "*Fkih*, what can I do to soften this old woman's heart?"

The healer moved directly to a glass jar that contained translucent crystals. To me, they looked like rock candy. Six he placed on the woman's hennaed palm. "Every afternoon, cast one of these onto the coals of your *canoon*. Capture the smoke in an inverted clay pitcher before filling it with cool water. Offer a glass to your mother-in-law. She will turn as sweet as a lamb."

The woman kissed the healer's hand. It was hard to understand her acceptance of a remedy so patently spurious. At the same time, I hoped that faith in the herbalist's magic would somehow bring her suffering to an end.

Another woman's tale of marital infidelity sent the herbalist rummaging through the shop's helter-skelter accumulation of oddities. From the sheer effort of his search, I imagined he was bringing up the heavy artillery. He was. "The next time your husband makes love to you," he whispered, "save some of his semen without his knowing. Rub it over the turnip seeds that are embedded on this ball of dried dung and throw it onto the fire." The *fkih* paused several seconds for dramatic effect and then stated, "Your husband will burn with desire — for you alone."

The bizarre object the size of a tennis ball quickly disappeared into the hood of the woman's djellabah. This exchange almost made me forget the purpose of my visit. I simply had to have one, not for any therapeutic reason, but for its unrivaled value as a conversation piece in my collection of Moroccan memorabilia.

"I'll have one of those, too," I interjected. My request elicited giggles from the others, but not from the *fkih*.

"It's much too powerful for a *nesraniya* [foreigner]," he said sternly. Just as well. U.S. Customs would have frowned on its importation. I was aware of government guidelines regulating foreign spices, listing allowable amounts of contaminants in each of several categories, among them, "mammalian excreta." A figure that came to mind was around one or two milligrams per pound of spice. If that was the case, government agents surely would have taken a dim view of my scheme to illegally import the antithesis — one pound of manure garnished with a measly gram of seeds.

"*Fkih*, my husband and I want to have a child. Can you help us?" pleaded the next despondent client. According to her, she had already seen the generalist at the Azemmour dispensary several times and made numerous day trips to Lalla Bahria's, with no results.

"*Meskeena* [Poor thing]," sang the sympathetic chorus.

"I will give you a strong potion," promised the healer. "But you must follow my instructions to the letter."

His concoction must have been powerful stuff judging by the strange potpourri of ingredients he collected on his brass tray — a section of dried umbilical cord of unknown origin, herbs picked by the light of the moon, the tip of an antelope horn, and the wing of a bat.

The healer turned suddenly secretive and whispered instructions in her ear.

"Yes, *fkih*, yes," she said earnestly. "I will do it today."

By being privy to the woman's desperation, we in her gallery of commiserative onlookers broke into smiles when we saw renewed hope in her eyes.

I spotted a jar of what looked like dried jujubes. On a whim, I asked for 100 grams. They were the primary component in the ointment the French herbalist had used on my brother's warts. I knew that Bouchaïb ate the fresh, mucilaginous drupes to soothe a sore throat and steeped the shrub's dried leaves to make tea whenever digestive disorders laid him low. Surely he or Leila would appreciate such a gift.

Finally we got around to the original purpose of my visit — *ras el hanoot*. This herbalist's blend was reputed to be one of the most elaborate, containing more than thirty ingredients: rhizomes, dried rose petals, cinnamon bark, whole nutmegs, pink blades of mace, belladonna berries, long pepper, and grains of paradise (Melegueta pepper), among others. When he could afford to splurge, Bouchaïb purchased a few grams to add to the broth of the Friday couscous.

There was no doubt that the herbalist's decision to add a special ingredient to the blend was triggered by my earlier interest in the aphrodisiacal ball of dung.

"*Abban elhand*," he declared, as several tiny, desiccated insects, commonly known as Spanish flies, tumbled from a biscuit tin into his palm. I had heard that the emerald-green, iridescent beetles (when ground and added to a spice blend in minute quantities) were rather innocuous, although sensitive individuals still faced the risk of priapism and urethral inflammation, unpleasant side effects that inspired another creative apothecary with a penchant for marketing to dub the additive "*la poudre qui fait monter au lustre* [the powder that makes you climb the chandelier]." I hoped the few specimens of *Lytta vesicatoria* I planned to smuggle back to California would keep dinner guests in their seats.

Ras el hanoot (Top of the Shop Spice Blend)

Makes about 3 tablespoons

1 teaspoon whole coriander seeds
½ teaspoon allspice berries
½ teaspoon anise seeds
3 shelled cardamom seeds
1 1-inch piece dried turmeric
1 1-inch piece stick cinnamon
½-inch piece blade mace
1 2-inch piece dried ginger root
½ teaspoon black peppercorns
2 teaspoons ground nutmeg
2 teaspoons salt

In a heavy skillet over medium high heat, combine coriander, allspice, anise, cardamom, turmeric, cinnamon, mace, ginger root, and peppercorns. Toast, while shaking pan back and forth, until spices release a fragrant aroma, 2 to 3 minutes. Do not let them burn. Cool.

Using a mortar and pestle or a spice grinder, grind toasted ingredients to a powder. Sift through a strainer to eliminate fibrous elements. Add nutmeg and salt. Store in a tightly sealed container.

16

A Cooking Lesson

What luck! *Tante* Suzanne would be visiting Morocco before my scheduled return to the United States. My maternal grandfather's sister Tita, as we called her, had left the country after her husband's death to live with a daughter in Venezuela. I was filled with happy anticipation at the prospect of seeing her again to catch up on the news of her far-flung family and to compare notes on an issue close to both our hearts — food. I also hoped to learn the secrets of her success as the driving force in settling her mother's estate in Casablanca.

Years before, in furtherance of my university major, I went to Caracas to study Spanish. My great-aunt proved to be my finest tutor, not only in language, but also in cooking *à la marocaine*. Our common passion strengthened the bond between us.

Tita's former next-door neighbor in downtown Casablanca had lent her his apartment while he was away in France. Two granite cherubs guarded the entrance to the building. Inside the lobby, a hint of bleach tickled my nostrils. The *concierge* must have given the smooth terrazzo floor a good drenching earlier that morning. I let my hand glide along the brass railing that wound up the helical staircase to the second floor. When I reached apartment #4, I gave three short rings, as I used to do in Caracas.

"*Bonjour madame,*" greeted the barefoot servant, baring a stunning arch of gold-capped teeth. Less exotic than her smile but equally welcoming were the familiar aromas coming from the kitchen. The silk panels of the maid's kaftan swelled to the rhythm of her wide hips as she led me down a long corridor past dozens of tightly arranged portraits from a bygone era. They gave the apartment a museum-like quality.

"*Bonjour, ma chérie!*" welcomed Tita. Her hair had become a snow-white halo since I'd last seen her, but the still vibrant pitch of her voice made her sound much younger than her seventy-eight years. "I am so happy to see you!"

I planted a sonorous kiss on her cheek. As a child, I feared that her skin, so delicate as to be almost transparent, would dissolve under the pressure of my lips. A soupçon of the gardenia perfume she favored carried me back to SMART, the elegant boutique she'd once owned on Casablanca's Rue de Foucauld.

* * *

Every afternoon, the usual clique gathered in the back of Tita's store for gossip, recipe exchange, and matchmaking for nieces, nephews, and grandchildren. My mother and I occasionally dropped by to soak up the ambiance.

"*Comment ça va mes chéries?*" Tita would welcome the ladies of a certain age who were fond of haute couture and socializing.

The striking Madame M., who hailed from the former Spanish protectorate in northern Morocco, was among them. She wore her hair in a tight chignon, like a flamenco dancer, and enough eyeliner to make a thespian envious. Her enchantingly theatrical manner of speaking caused words to flutter from her lips like butterflies. "*Rrrregarrrdes cette rrrrobe rrrouge* [Look at this red dress]," she'd say, trilling her Rs like a Spaniard instead of giving them the throaty delivery of a native French speaker.

"*Alors, ma chérrrrie*, how are you doing in school?" she'd always ask, patting me on the head as she would a lapdog.

None of the other ladies with roots in what had been Spanish Morocco could match Madame M.'s delivery. They peppered their sentences with *haquetiya*, the Sephardic dialect that was an amalgamation of Spanish, Arabic, and Hebrew, and retreated completely to its linguistic sanctuary in order to pass along a snide comment whenever an unsuspecting foreign customer wandered into the boutique. "Poor thing, that dress doesn't suit her," or "That one ought to lose a few pounds."

* * *

Tita always dressed impeccably. Even at the stove she wore a well-tailored black dress and a long string of pearls under her dainty, hand-embroidered apron.

I regretted never writing down her recipe for *pastelitos*, the fried pastries she served as appetizers at family gatherings in Caracas. Here was my opportunity, with the kitchen's leading lady taking me on as understudy.

She and Barka must have gone to the *marché* before I arrived, judging from the *couffin* that overflowed with bouquets of cilantro and parsley. On the table, a stack of *warka* pastry leaves was sealed tightly inside a plastic bag.

"I've brought some American measuring cups and spoons I keep on hand at Dar Zitoun," I announced up front, knowing how she eschewed the practice of measuring ingredients. She cast a contemptuous look at my implements. "I never use the things, you know."

"I am aware of that, Tita, but how will I make *pastelitos* as good as yours without exact measurements? Remember, I don't have the benefit of your vast experience," I told her, hoping a little flattery and self-deprecation would make the bridle more tolerable.

"Well, just for you, *ma chérie*," she relented.

Tita adhered to the time-honored principle of *eenek mi zanek*, let your eyes be your scales, a tradition and skill I respected, but did not employ. Nevertheless, in order to document an important family recipe, I had to slow her down enough to quantify "pinches" of paprika and "handfuls" of diced onions into conventional measurements.

Just then, the doorbell rang. "I hope it's not Leah," said Tita, rolling her eyes. "She is the *nosiest* woman!"

The sound of high heels confirmed her fears. A former acquaintance that lived in the same building appeared in the kitchen doorway. The aging diva was drenched in *Maja Myrurgia* perfume. Snowy bangs, smoothed just so above her eyebrows, set off haunting aquamarine eyes. Like Norma Desmond in *Sunset Boulevard*, she was always ready for a close-up. Leah, it was clear, relished the limelight.

Barka grabbed a bowl of garlic cloves and a paring knife and headed for a stool in the corner. Her facial expression warned of trouble ahead. Tita forced a smile.

"Leah, what a nice surprise," she said in a saccharine tone. "I'm showing my grand-niece Katy how to make *pastelitos.*"

"I've got a recipe she ought to try," countered Leah, a comment indicative of the rivalry between the two women. Intentional or not, her words had a predictably irksome effect on my great-aunt.

Sans permission, Leah removed the stack of *warka* from the plastic bag, peeled off a leaf with her crimson claws and held it up for inspection.

"Where did you get this?" she asked. "It doesn't seem thin enough."

These two women shouldn't have been in the same room together.

"I hired Asmah at the *marché*," Tita replied acidly.

"Well, she's losing her touch," continued Leah. "This one's no good. It's too thick. You should be able to read a newspaper headline through it."

Leah was being overly critical. The painstaking process of making the phyllo-like leaves on a traditional tin-coated *tobsil dial warka* took years of experience to perfect. *Warka* specialists deserve respect, not only for their high degree of skill, but also for the monotony of the work they perform — turning out one round after another over a sweltering *tobsil*, fingertips becoming calloused and inured to the intense heat after interminable hours of dabbing slippery dough against the implement's searing surface.

"It's thin enough for me," Tita shot back. The staccato of her blade intensified as she chopped a bundle of parsley. "Leah, why don't you make yourself useful," my great-aunt suggested, pushing her cutting board across the table.

I too tried to change the subject by inserting comic relief — through the narrative of my narrow escape from the notary's office.

"Maître Tanja. Isn't his office just around the corner?" asked Leah. "My, he's been at it a long time. Does he still dye his hair jet black?"

"I wouldn't care if he dyed it mauve, as long as he got the job done," I griped.

"Delays are a way of life here. The sooner you accept that, the better off you'll be. If you show impatience, the system will progress even more slowly, so try to maintain your composure," advised Tita.

"Easier said than done," I quipped.

"*Ma chérie*, it took me nine years and an audience with the minister of justice to settle my poor mother's affairs."

"My Yacov, God rest his soul; he used to tell me there was no problem a few hundred dirhams couldn't resolve," Leah chimed in.

"Perhaps, but I preferred to work *within* the law," snapped Tita.

"Come on, Suzanne," parried Leah, using Tita's given name. "*Ce n'était pas comme si Yacov avait défloré une vierge, mais simplement réglé un compte avec une fille de joie* [It wasn't as if Yakov deflowered a virgin, but simply settled an account with a trollop]."

The metaphor made me laugh despite the possibility that I could be facing the same predicament in the not too distant future. Nothing Leah had to say amused my great-aunt. Fate intervened before the need to smooth ruffled feathers. Our visitor sliced halfway through one of her long fingernails in the process of chopping parsley.

"My manicure! It is ruined!" she wailed. She dropped the knife, and without so much as an au revoir, disappeared down the hallway and out the door. We could hear the heels of her shoes clicking double-time up the marble stairs.

"Leah failed to mention that bribing an official at the tribunal almost landed Yacov in jail. Believe me *ma chérie*; it's best to follow the rules. Your father didn't approve of shady dealings. Sometimes bribery was unavoidable. But for the most part, he preferred to play by the rules. I'm sure he would want you to do the same."

"Thanks for the advice, Tita," I said as I gave her a hug.

"You can't have nails like Leah's and spend much time in the kitchen," Tita muttered as an afterthought, still miffed by the invasion of her workspace.

Leah's visit had *one* positive effect. It intensified my great-aunt's desire to see her recipe formally written down. Spleen vented, she refocused on the *pastelitos*.

"Barka, *touma!*"

The maid tossed a hillock of minced garlic on top of the ground meat.

"Katy, just write down two soup spoons," she ordered. "I can tell by looking. It's two soup spoons."

"*S'il te plaît*, Tita, as long as I'm making the effort, let me measure everything," I pleaded. She humored me and stood aside for a moment while I retrieved the garlic.

"Enough of measuring," Tita scolded. "Put your pen down and get your hands into the mix. It's the only way to incorporate the ingredients evenly." I relegated pen and notebook to the top of the refrigerator.

"I used to work like this alongside Mémé Luna, *my* grandmother, *your* great-great-grandmother," confided my culinary mentor while I mixed the ingredients into a homogeneous mass. "My brother and I used to stand on hassocks next to the counter so we could help." The "brother" she spoke of was my grandfather, a gourmet himself, who had gone so far as to request my mother deliver a platter of couscous to him during a short stay in hospital. Tita made me understand how he came by his discriminating palate.

"The aromas in Mémé Luna's kitchen were out of this world, especially before the feast of *La Mimouna*," Tita sighed.

She was referring to a Sephardic celebration to mark the end of Passover. For Tita, *La Mimouna* was emblematic of an idyllic childhood in Algeria, where her Spanish antecedents had sought refuge following Queen Isabella's Alhambra Decree (of 1492 CE) that ratified the Muslim surrender of Granada and forced Jews and Muslims to convert to Catholicism or leave the country.

"I wish you could have met Mémé Luna," said Tita. "Luna wasn't her real name. We called her that because her face was as round as the moon."

An antique photograph of the intimidating woman dressed in black from head to toe had hung on the wall of my grandfather's study.

"And could *she* cook! You should have seen the spread she laid on for *La Mimouna!*" raved Tita. "Pyramids of crisp *pastelitos*, clove-scented *moustiniz* macaroons, a stack of *moofleta* crêpes oozing melted butter and honey, and delicate candied figs. She prepared everything herself." I'd have to cajole those recipes out of her at my next lesson.

"Once, your grandfather and I ate so many of Mémé Luna's *pastelitos* that we caught an indigestion. Mother was so angry, she sent us to bed early."

Tita's reminiscences brought family genealogy to life. They also made me realize that the *pastelito* recipe didn't originate with her or even Mémé Luna, but in the kitchen of some unknown ancestor in Moorish Spain. My great-aunt cut short my musings. "Come on, Katy. Let's finish the job."

She coached me on handling the *warka* and taught me how to fill and fold each strip of dough into a perfect equilateral triangle.

"Look," she explained, pushing me gently aside. "Tuck in the tab like this."

I appreciated her dexterity all the more when it took me six tries to assemble a pastry correctly. I had to work quickly before extended contact with the air rendered the dough brittle and unworkable.

The burner on the stove whooshed to life at the strike of Barka's match. In minutes, pungent smoke from the skillet was swirling through the doorway to the rear terrace. Under my great-aunt's tutelage, I waited for each *pastelito* to turn amber before I rescued it from the hot oil and set it onto a rack to drain.

"*Coo-coo* [Yoo-hoo], Suzanne! *Oh, coo-coo!*" The sound of Leah's voice echoing through the inner courtyard caused Tita's face to drop.

"*Celle-là, elle me casse les pieds* [That woman is a pain in the butt]," she griped before stepping from her aromatic haven onto the terrace. From a balcony across the quadrangle, Leah was waving a dishtowel. Once she'd caught my great-aunt's eye, she cupped her hands to create a megaphone to broadcast her request.

"The *pastelitos* smell divine. Would you mind saving a few for me?"

Tita waved to indicate that the request would be granted. What else could she have done, with hot oil bubbling away on the stove?

"What chutzpah!" sputtered my great-aunt, as she reentered the kitchen.

"Madame Leah *matbreesh teyaab* [she doesn't like to cook]," declared Barka matter-of-factly. Tita and I burst out laughing.

My great-aunt assessed her latest culinary performance with the objectivity of a food critic. "Maybe I was a bit heavy-handed with the garlic," she admitted. "It must be these old eyes of mine." I should have known what was coming next.

"What are the chances of your leaving the measuring spoons with me?" she asked.

Tita's Pastelitos (Auntie's Little Pastries)

Makes about 30

1 pound ground beef
½ onion, finely diced
1 medium carrot, coarsely grated
2 garlic cloves, minced
1 tablespoon minced fresh mint leaves
2 tablespoons minced flat-leaf parsley
1 teaspoon ground cumin
1 teaspoon cinnamon
½ cup golden raisins, plumped in warm water and drained
1 egg, lightly beaten
2 teaspoons salt
Freshly ground pepper to taste
10 sheets phyllo dough, thawed
Vegetable oil for frying
Lemon wedges, for serving

In a large skillet, cook beef over medium high heat, breaking up lumps with a fork. Add onion, carrot, and garlic. Cook, stirring, until mixture is almost dry, 10 to 12 minutes. Let cool. In a medium bowl, combine meat with mint, parsley, cumin, cinnamon, raisins, egg, salt, and pepper. Set aside.

To assemble: Set phyllo stack on a work surface. With long side of phyllo facing you and using a sharp knife, cut through stack to create 3-inch-wide strips. Keep dough covered with a damp towel until ready to assemble *pastelitos*.

With the short side of a phyllo strip facing you, place 1 tablespoon of filling about ½ inch from the bottom. Fold lower-right corner halfway to the left side of strip. Then fold the new, diagonal edge at the bottom up and over until it is flush with the right side. Continue folding in this manner, as you would a flag. Tuck leftover phyllo tab inside final fold.

To freeze: Place uncooked *pastelitos* in a single layer on a baking sheet lined with wax paper. Freeze and transfer to an airtight container. Separate layers with wax paper. Freeze for up to 2 months. Do not thaw before frying.

To fry: In a heavy, medium saucepan, pour oil to a depth of 2 inches. Heat over medium high heat until a test-piece of phyllo sizzles instantly. Fry pastries in batches until golden, 6 to 8 minutes. Transfer to paper towels to drain. Serve with lemon wedges.

17

Locusts

Si le bonheur pouvait se planter avec des rejets de plante,
J'aurais planté cent boutures de verveine pour moi seul;
J'aurais entouré ma plantation d'une clôture et j'aurais invoqué Dieu en Lui criant:
"Ô redresseur suprême des destinées, redresse la mienne!"

If happiness could be sown with the shoots of plants,
I would have sown one hundred verbena cuttings for myself;
I would have surrounded my garden with a fence and I would have invoked God by crying out to Him:
"Oh, supreme Redresser of destinies, redress mine!"

— from *Chansons de l'Escarpolette à Fès et Rabat-Salé*
(Songs of the Swing in Fez and Rabat-Salê)
French translation by Jeanne Jouin

I couldn't believe that a single insect had devoured all the leaves from a branch of the potted lemon verbena bush on Dar Zitoun's terrace and was poised to do the same to the lancet-shaped leaves of another. I moved closer to examine the voracious creature's green, armor-plated body, coffee-bean eyes, and quivering antennae, seemingly attuned to the evil secrets of the universe. How I hated locusts!

* * *

The unpleasant confrontation brought to mind a more harrowing experience with a swarm of acridians in the summer before my enrollment at the Lycée de Jeunes Filles in Casablanca. My eight-year-old brother Philippe and I, just turned ten, were blissfully dunking our flaky croissants into the bowls of the café au lait that our housekeeper had enriched with dollops of sweet butter, when Kebira brought a finger to her lips. "*Skoot* [Quiet]!" she ordered. "The air is too still. The *jnoon* are behind this." Philippe and I froze in ominous expectation. To the dismay of my parents, Kebira filled our heads with tales of the misbehaving spirits. She found evidence of their handiwork in every inexplicable phenomenon.

Gossamer pink bracts of bougainvillea outside the kitchen window that normally trembled at the slightest breeze were motionless. The stillness of the air also intensified the fragrance of the flowering acacias.

"*Ah williwilli!*" wailed our housekeeper with the widespread Moroccan exclamation of helplessness. She ran into the garden, with my brother and me close behind. We were soon joined by my mother, still in her bathrobe, and my father, face lathered in shaving cream. When Kebira scanned the southern sky, the rest of us did likewise, out of reflex, without knowing what we were looking for. "Locusts. *Ah williwilli!*"

A low-lying band on the horizon looked at first like drifting smoke, but turned strangely fluid and grainy the closer it got to our idyllic *Val Fleuri*, Flowering Vale.

Only days earlier had my parents commented on the fickle weather patterns, comparing the wetter-than-normal rainy season of the year before with the drought conditions of the previous eight months. The wet/dry scenario led to cramped quarters for the thriving population of desert locusts and triggered in them metabolic changes (including the release of pheromones) that transformed the solitary, mild-mannered foragers into the gregarious marauders that headed our way on a sirocco.

"Get the potted plants into the shed!" ordered my father as the leading edge of the "cloud" whipped against our house with the terrifying swiftness and ferocity of a brushfire and the sound of a million frenzied castañets.

"Close the windows and shutters!"

I'd like to report that Philippe and I performed above and beyond the call of duty. In truth, we were the most hopeless of subordinates, too frozen by fear to follow Daddy's orders, too busy screaming and extricating spiny-legged invaders from our hair. My father armed himself with the garden hose, but his weapon of choice had no effect on the arthropods that blighted our once lush garden and settled in a thick, heaving blanket over the lawn. My mother needn't have closed the windows. Disoriented insects must have stormed down the chimney, we realized later, when we discovered their yellow-and-black carcasses scattered across beds, rugs, tables, and countertops.

In the midst of the most terrifying twenty minutes of my life, I was too petrified to be of help to anyone. The attack was so acute, so overwhelming, that it short-circuited my instinctive urge to seek parental protection. The eighth plague of Exodus became real to me that morning. Why Pharaoh hadn't thrown in the towel when faced with it would forever remain a mystery.

The swarm completed its destruction in minutes. With nothing left to devour, the insects surged aloft like one roiling organism, leaving thousands of straggling overeaters behind. Kebira appeared with a large glass jar and enlisted our help in gleaning the yard of the wretched pests. What was she up to? To Philippe, who was stomping around on their little bodies like a winemaker trampling on vintage grapes, capturing his victims alive seemed like better sport. He was more enthusiastic about it than I.

"Katy is a chic-ken! Katy is chic-ken!" taunted my suddenly valiant brother. Defiance, and a desire to prove him wrong, compelled me to join in the roundup. Kebira's motives became clear when she returned with a *canoon* and several sticks of charcoal. The locusts cooked up quickly. Kebira hot-fingered them into a bowl for seasoning with salt and cumin. I admit to being caught up in the exoticism of her entrée — until she passed the delicacy my way. With me, she had no taker. Understandable for a girl of my age — given the macabre crackling sound of roasting exoskeletons and the sickening crunch coming from between Kebira's molars. Ironically, years later, I grew addicted to the locusts' diminutive Mexican cousins, *chapulines*, flavored with hot chiles and lime.

* * *

I wasn't about to let Dar Zitoun's lemon verbena suffer the same fate as the vegetation in *Val Fleuri*. I whacked at the insect with a bamboo rod to send it zigzagging over the parapet and across the water.

"*Va t'en* [Get lost]!" I cursed. Our winded *guardien* appeared on the terrace soon thereafter.

"Katy, are you all right?"

"I'm fine, Bouchaïb." I didn't want to get into the psychology of my confrontation with the locust. "Really, Bouchaïb, *ce n'est rien* [it's nothing]."

My fit of rage did more damage to the poor bush than it had to the locust. Chastened, I collected the fallen and mutilated verbena leaves to brew a pot of *luisa*, a soothing remedy for frayed nerves.

 Luisa (Lemon Verbena Tea)

Makes 3 cups

Luisa is the Arabic word for *Aloysia citrodora,* which the French call *verveine* and the English "lemon verbena." It is reputed to be a remedy for insomnia.

3½ cups boiling water
8 large leaves lemon verbena, fresh or dried
Sugar to taste

Rinse a teapot with ½ cup of the boiling water. Add verbena and remaining water. Steep for 5 minutes. Sweeten to taste.

18

Trials and Tribulations

It had been a long time since my father's death; and little by little, the rediscovered pleasures of Moroccan life had helped break the siege of slow mourning. Sure, there were occasional relapses, which usually related to probate, the *samsar*, or a stress-inducing phone call from Philippe to remind me of the purpose of my extended stay.

I'd give my brother a rundown of my accomplishments — whether they pertained to repairs to the house or matters of probate. As to my tense encounters with the *samsar*, I led Philippe to believe that I was the initiating party instead of the other way around. That bit of news seemed to please him most.

Truth be told, I had the sense that I was treading water rather than freestyling toward divestment. In an effort to mask my apprehension I'd inject local color into the conversations: "The *muezzin* has developed a case of post-nasal drip," I informed my brother. "What a way to wake up at 5:30 a.m. — with the poor fellow clearing his throat over the loudspeaker."

Philippe wasn't amused. He pressed me to get the house on the market as quickly as possible. I didn't fault him, or Nigel, for their emotional detachment from Azemmour. Spending the odd holiday there, as they had done in previous years, made them appreciate its unique charm. But long absences while they raised their families had estranged them from the medina's daily enticements. I, on the other hand, was becoming reinfatuated.

Whether I was cooking in the kitchen with Bouchaïb, reading in the atrium, or trimming the rosebush on the terrace, Dar Zitoun's walls wrapped me in a proprietary embrace, and like Daddy's arms, made me feel like I belonged. The unambiguous emotion exposed a deepening commitment. Would I be able to walk away?

I kept my brothers in the dark about my new "romance" for fear they'd use it as a pretext to complain about my handling of the estate. My conscience was clear, however. I'd made some progress with the dossier, despite not being much closer to securing title than when I began.

The slow going of the *procédure* made it clear that the conveyance of title, not to mention the sale of the property, would not be finalized on my first visit. I succumbed quite willingly to the protracted course of events.

More than the fate of Dar Zitoun hung in the balance. There was our *gardien*'s future to consider. Would a new *propriétaire* overlook Bouchaïb's eccentricities and keep him on? Or would our loyal servant be forced to join the ranks of the unemployed? It was a little late in life for that.

As I was pondering the issue, the man in question returned from a shopping excursion. He was conversing with someone in Arabic. My stomach tightened as soon as I recognized the voice of his interlocutor.

The *samsar* made me feel like a cornered animal. On that day, Hadj Mustapha brought with him a prospective buyer, a Frenchman from Toulouse, who was in the market for a place to retire. From the enraptured look on the gentleman's face, I felt sure he would have moved into Dar Zitoun that afternoon had the papers been in order.

"*Quelle maison extraordinaire. J'en ai la chair de poule* [What an extraordinary house. It gives me goose bumps]!" he raved. To prove it, he rolled up his sleeve to show me his stippled forearm. The slow going at the *conservation foncière* didn't concern him.

"I won't retire for another two years," he insisted. "I can wait."

I liked him. He was mellow and understanding, not crafty in any way. He certainly laid his cards on the table with his comment about *chair de poule*. His flexible timetable would give me cover for a more deliberate transition. The Toulousain and I exchanged cards in front of the self-satisfied *samsar*, who observed the convivial encounter with obvious pleasure. I almost felt like a traitor conducting such business in front of Bouchaïb, though he wouldn't have seen it in that light. Fatalism, an important tenet of Islam, made him more accepting of life's ups and downs.

He showed our visitors to the door.

Confusion. Weak rationalizations. Homesickness. A jumble of sentiments swept over me. I hadn't made a commitment to the Frenchman, formal or informal. So why then did I feel so torn? That first unofficial "showing" was but a baby step on the road to divestment. I wondered if the one-who-no-longer-was, who wanted Dar Zitoun kept in the family, would have seen it as disloyal.

I headed upstairs with the intention of sinking into the cushioned *banquette*, but on a whim, turned into the salon, where a wooden cabinet held my father's cache of booze. Bottles of duty-free liquor from around world, courtesy of Daddy's many international visitors, had come to rest in the "bar." Among its offerings was a thirty-year-old bottle of Glenffidich scotch, a liter of Pimms No. 3 Cup brandy, and a fifth of Stolichnaya vodka. I seldom drank hard liquor, preferring an occasional glass of red wine, but I craved something stronger than domestic *cabernet*. I stared at the iconic labels. Like a nun with shaken faith, I reached for the Pimms. Alcoholic content: "25% vol." Just what the doctor ordered for the lazy afternoon I planned to spend in the shady corner of the terrace.

Across the river laborers were harvesting wheat in the timeless ritual of summer. The resident heron that waded through the shallows in search of prey became still as a Giacometti sculpture when a green-hulled skiff ran ashore to take on passengers. The breeze carried their voices up and over the wall to where I sat.

A furious batting of wings on the terrace aroused my Pimms-dulled senses and drew me to the watering can beneath a dripping spigot. A dove, driven there by thirst, was trapped inside. I would have freed it immediately had Hitchcock's *The Birds* not rendered me permanently ornithophobic.

"Bouchaïb, *il y a une colombe dans l'arrosoir* [there's a dove in the watering can]!" I screamed. "*Viens vite* [Come quickly]!"

Our *cuisinier* ascended the stairs with surprising alacrity, wearing a wild-eyed look more predatory than compassionate. He extracted the dove from the can and before I could stop him, twisted its neck.

"*Tagine*," was all he said. He knew my fondness for *pigeon aux amandes* [pigeon with almonds] and must have assumed that *colombe aux amandes* [dove with almonds] would be equally well received. Quite the contrary.

The dove's demise, Philippe's phone call, the *samsar*'s unsettling visit, my quasi-disloyal understanding with the Tolousain, and my sentimental tipsiness created the atmosphere for a perfect storm. It rained tears. I ran downstairs to phone home, leaving Bouchaïb behind to wonder about my mental health.

On the other side of the world, Owen must have understood my state of mind when I didn't come up for air for five minutes in relating the events of the day. When I complained about Philippe, he interrupted. "Why don't you buy him out?"

"What do you mean?" I asked.

"You and Nigel can buy Philippe's one-third interest in the property," he explained. "Look," he continued. "You're at a standstill there. The guy from Toulouse is in no hurry. Why don't you come home this week as planned? You need a break!"

Bouchaïb joined me downstairs, looking like the cat that ate the canary, to use an unfortunate idiom. There was no sign of the dove. I later learned he had whisked it down the lane to his apartment. He seemed eager to talk to my husband.

"Monsieur Owen!" he yelled into the mouthpiece. "*Labass . . . Oui . . . Oui . . . Je ne sais pas . . . Oui . . . Oui . . . Oui . . . D'accord . . . Très bien . . . Il'alleka* [How are you . . . Yes . . . Yes . . . Yes . . . OK . . . Very well . . . Until we meet again]."

Bouchaïb was smiling broadly by the time he handed the phone back to me.

"What was that all about?" I asked Owen.

"I told Bouchaïb I'd bring a few tools when I come with you next summer," he replied. *La mémoire de Dar Zitoun* must have taken that to mean that things would be continuing *comme avant*, as before. Until then, the House of the Olive Tree would remain in the family.

Pigeon with Almonds

Serves 4

Pigeon is marketed as "squab" in the United States. It's available from specialty butchers. Substitute quail or Cornish hens if you prefer.

¼ cup olive oil
⅛ teaspoon Spanish saffron, crushed
1 teaspoon turmeric
4 squabs, rinsed and patted dry
2 medium onions, thinly sliced
½ cup chopped parsley
1 cup whole blanched almonds
1 tablespoon *smen* (see page 268)
Salt to taste
1 teaspoon freshly ground pepper
Chopped parsley, for garnish

Preheat oven to 375 degrees F.

In a bowl, mix olive oil with saffron and turmeric. Coat the squabs with this mixture. In a Dutch oven over medium heat, brown squabs on all sides. Add onions, parsley, almonds, *smen*, salt, and pepper. Nestle squabs, breast side up, in the onion mixture. Cover and bake squabs until tender, 45 to 50 minutes. Garnish with chopped parsley and serve.

19

A Moroccan Holiday

And so I put aside the filial responsibilities I'd shouldered over the past several months and retreated to my life in California. Frequent calls to Bouchaïb kept me abreast of events in Azemmour. Again and again, our loyal caretaker demonstrated his ability to *faire le nécessaire*, doing whatever was necessary. Back home, I'd reflect on legal strategy, Daddy's life, and my sustained connection to Dar Zitoun. In one moment I'd convince myself of the complete lunacy of maintaining a *riad* a continent and an ocean away. In the next, after being swept by a wave of nostalgia, I'd resolve to hang on to what had belonged to my father in the way Scarlett clung to Tara. My only communication with Maître Drissi, whom, I feared, was closer to the grave than to sorting out our case, did not inspire optimism.

"The lower court has discovered an irregularity with one of your documents," read a fax from his office six months after my return to the States, without specifying the anomaly in question.

I should have been glum, but managed to remain upbeat — until the following week, when a garbled call caught me in the middle of a symposium sponsored by the California Farm Bureau. "Katy . . . *grand problème* . . . rain . . . stone wall . . . collapse!" came the broken-up message.

"*Attends une minute*, Bouchaïb," I yelled, hurrying out the door of the conference center in hope of improved reception.

Bouchaïb repeated the bad news — of torrential rains that lead to the collapse of the retaining wall above the river.

"We *must* do something *tout de suite*, or our house, it could be next," he continued at fever pitch. His use of the word *our* demonstrated an owner's concern.

"I've already hired a mason," he informed me.

Two weeks later, a French neighbor emailed photos of the reconstruction. I gasped at both the enormity and the charmlessness of the gray concrete where a vast tangle of geraniums and bougainvillea once flourished.

The mason took it upon himself to add three laughably small buttresses to the base of the *riad*'s thirty-foot façade. I didn't need a degree in structural engineering to realize that the woefully inadequate reinforcements hadn't a prayer of doing what their name implied. The workmen also poured in place, at the foot of the garden steps, a concrete pedestal, tabletop, and three cubical stools. I quickly deduced the purpose of the new patio set — to serve as a sanctuary where Bouchaïb could savor a bottle of *vin de table* and have a Casa Sport cigarette without fear of discovery.

Owen was more resigned than I to the fact that deterioration and repair are part of life for owners of historic *riad*s. "Just be thankful you're paying Moroccan prices for reconstruction," he reminded me.

No sooner had I wired money to the bank in Azemmour to cover costs than the next disaster struck. It too was related to the unusually wet winter. Since our foyer and atrium lay below the level of the lane outside the front door, we should have expected the worst when an obstruction occured in the sewer main. "Katy!" Bouchaïb was on the line again. "The atrium, it is flooded!"

After determining that the source of the problem lay on city property, he marched off to demand restitution. Workmen dispatched by the *municipalité* acted quickly, motivated in part by our *cuisinier*'s largesse of soft drinks from Zora's *épicerie*. A day later, Bouchaïb called to tell me that a ram's horn, of all things, had been the cause of the mysterious blockage. A victorious supervisor held the "trophy" aloft and bellowed: "Whoever managed to get this into the sewer . . . if you are listening . . . you're an ABSOLUTE GENIUS!"

The adage, "*Jamais deux sans trois* [Never two without three]," helped me take the next emergency in stride — Philippe's pecuniary difficulties.

"I need the money now!" he told me over the phone.

The "money" he referred to was tied up in Dar Zitoun, which was still in my father's name. Nigel, Owen, and I had already considered the possibility of a buyout and resolved to purchase Philippe's share. In accordance with Maître Drissi's advice, we drew up an *acte de donation*, in which Philippe agreed to relinquish his one-third interest in Dar Zitoun in return for cash. Submitting the signed *acte* to the *conservation foncière* in El Jadida proved to be a monumental mistake.

The *conservateur* must have rubbed his hands together in anticipation of the red tape such a document would unleash. "And where is your *acte d'exequatur?*" came the official's faxed message.

My what?

The meaning of the word *exequatur* eluded me until I put my nose into a voluminous French/English dictionary. The archaic noun's overly broad definition — *authorization* — did nothing, however, to enlighten me as to what it was the *conservateur* needed. So I wrote to him for clarification.

"*Chère madame, je me permets de vous signaler* [permit me to inform you] . . . " began his condescending reply. An *acte d'exequatur*, he explained, was a legal instrument used to ensure that our *acte de donation* conformed, not only to Moroccan law, but also, to the law of the countries in which my brothers and I held citizenship, i.e., Canada, the United Kingdom, and the United States. Hence, he would require notarized letters from lawyers in all three countries to certify the legality of Philippe's two-paragraph document. I remember thinking, "Houston, we have a problem," one that would take five long years and two rulings by a Moroccan court of appeals to resolve.

Meanwhile, I continued to lead gastronomic tours to Morocco as I had done for almost two decades. Each excursion culminated in a cooking demonstration and a seven-course gala in Dar Zitoun's atrium. I thought my father's death would put an end to this aspect of my professional life, but I needed only one tour to realize the emotional benefits of staying connected to the Maghreb.

Thus, a year after Daddy's demise, Owen and I were on our way back to North Africa. Among the sundry items we carried were copies of my latest Moroccan cookbook (to present to the members of my group), a pool cue Bouchaïb had requested, two electric blankets, four pounds of corn tortillas, a half-dozen boxes of brownie mix, and an assortment of Owen's hand and power tools. We were lucky to be traveling in the pre-9/11 era. A porter at Kennedy International hit me up for ten dollars to transfer our hernia-inducing suitcases from the trunk of our cab to the Royal Air Maroc carousel. "Lady, what the hell you got in here?" he grumbled. He wouldn't have believed me.

We were loaded down like nomads. How I envied friends who traveled the world with only carry-on luggage. But they weren't living on two continents, with heart, head, and possessions divided.

On this trip the customs officer at Mohammed V Airport cast only a casual glance in our direction before waving us through. Within fifteen minutes we were seated in a taxi speeding toward Azemmour. The venerable Mercedes had seen better days. The upholstery was lumpy from underlying springs; window handles were gone; wires stuck out like wild hairs from the slot that once housed a radio.

Our driver dropped us at the Azemmour ramparts. We normally employed a hand-drawn *carossa* to transport our luggage to Dar Zitoun. That day, however, we required something larger. Owen went in search of a donkey cart while the cabbie piled our bags on the sidewalk. My resourceful husband soon returned with a *charrette* and its operator in tow.

"*Makaeen mooshkeel* [No problem]," commented the old man with burnished face as he sized up the load. Easy for him to say. I looked to the spindly-legged donkey hitched to the heavy vehicle cobbled together with a bit of salvaged lumber, an automobile axle, and a pair of bald tires. I appeased my conscience by telling myself that ours was a relatively light burden for the pitiful animal when compared to the concrete blocks, sand, and gravel it normally hauled to construction sites around the medina.

We'd left California almost twenty-two hours earlier. Owen was beginning to show the strain of the trip. "Transporting tortillas and brownie mix half-way around the world doesn't make much sense!" he snapped. He was right about the food. No more *crêpes méxicaines* for Roselyne or brownies for Alia, I vowed, knowing full well I would abandon my resolution before the next trip.

The donkey momentarily lost traction going down a steep and particularly treacherous stretch of cobblestones just before we reached Dar Zitoun. We all grabbed the sides of the cart and dug in our heels in order to avert disaster.

What was that thumping? The realization that it arose from a corps of children playing *derboukas*, clay goblet drums, eliminated any hope of turning in early that evening.

I had difficulty keeping up with the dates of Moroccan holidays because of the eleven-day differential between the Muslim and Gregorian calendars. We'd arrived on Ashurah, the tenth day of the Islamic New Year, a major religious event, when Morocco's Sunni population celebrates the birth of the Prophet Ibrahim, Abraham. On that day, revelry was de rigueur, especially among the younger set. Playing *derboukas* and squirting water pistols at unsuspecting passersby were two Ashurah traditions. So were late-night bonfires.

"One dirham for Baba Ashur," demanded Rashid, the boy whose father owned the public oven. He'd grown a head taller since I last saw him. Owen gave in to the Moroccan-style trick-or-treater and dropped a coin into his inverted *derbouka*.

"*Merci m'sieur. Merci madame.*" Rashid rewarded us with a demonstration of his musical talent. Little did we know that a whole corps of drummers and squirt-gun-toting youngsters lay in wait at Dar Zitoun.

"One dirham, one dirham for Baba Ashur!" came the raucous demand from our welcoming committee. Owen was out of coins, and we were in trouble.

"Keep them occupied while I get change!" he shouted to me. The dispassionate owner of the *charrette* ignored the urgency of our predicament. He and his equally emotionless burro stood by patiently to watch events unfold.

Owen ran to the neighborhood *épicière* for assistance. Zora accommodated him with a handful of dirhams she kept in a cigar box under the counter. Unfortunately, several youngsters were witness to the transaction. My husband returned with the money, but also with reinforcements for the already formidable gang outside our front door. As soon as he dug into his pocket, the children lurched forward en masse with a combined strength and ferocity that both surprised and alarmed us — Westerners, for whom a dirham meant nothing. To kids from the medina however, even a lowly one-dirham coin was worth fighting for, especially when there might not be enough of them to go around.

"This isn't going to work!" yelled Owen as the delirious children drove him up against the door. Much to our relief, Zora's daughter came to the rescue.

"Salmia! Can you help Owen dole out dirhams so the big kids don't get everything?" I pleaded. I should have added, " . . . and so they don't kill my husband."

Short and square of stature, like her mother, she was the eldest of Zora's daughters. Her thick, black eyebrows gathered ominously across her forehead.

"Small ones in front, big ones in the back. *Dabba* [Now]!" she barked. Waiting in line was counterintuitive for them. Nevertheless, in order to get their hands on the dirhams, they quickly scrabbled into a compressed and tortured row. Owen pacified each one with a coin.

Bouchaïb, away at the market during the excitement, arrived with Alia, who struggled to uphold her side of the bulging *couffin*. I ran to embrace them. Our delight in reconnecting was obvious. "Katy, you are here! And Monsieur Owen, how are you? Your health? Your family? . . . ," he rattled on excitedly. His doe-eyed daughter Alia kissed me on each cheek. I detected the earthy fragrance of henna in her tousled curls.

While the men unloaded the *charrette*, I hustled through the twin foyers to kick off my shoes in the atrium. An ethereal feeling always swept over me on entering that mystical space with its harmony of squares, Moorish arches, and zillij-lined columns. I gave silent thanks to its unknown Arab architect before heading to the garden to evaluate firsthand our new retaining wall. Bouchaïb drew up behind me.

The masons' accomplishment was technically impressive, but all that concrete left me aesthetically numb. I'd have to make restoration of the garden a priority, a commitment reinforced by a trip to the terrace, where the pink geraniums I'd transplanted the year before billowed from a dozen terra cotta amphorae.

Afternoon dissolved into dusk, the time of day the French poetically call *entre chien et loup*, between dog and wolf. Owen and I scaled the ladder to the roof for a view of the medina. I reminded him of the Christmas when he descended the same ladder dressed as Santa Claus, hoping to surprise some British and American guests who were having eggnog and champagne punch on the terrace. His performance took a comedic turn when one of the ladder's vertical stringers slipped under his red djellabah, halting his descent, thus delaying the distribution of toys.

When it came to Ashurah, Owen, Bouchaïb, and I were observers rather than participants. We watched the noisy festivities from the rooftop. But not for long. A few thoughtless revelers stoked bonfires with anything that would burn, from paper, plastic, and cardboard to old tires.

Bouchaïb had no patience for such inconsiderate merrymaking. "What does polluting the air have to do with Ibrahim's birth?" he grumbled, rubbing his eyes. The acrid fumes drove us indoors.

184

"Almost worse than cigarette smoke," I pointed out. He took my sisterly teasing in stride.

"*J'allais oublier, le dîner est prêt* [I almost forgot, dinner's ready]," he informed us.

I wasn't aware of anything on the stove when I arrived. We could have made do with a simple egg tagine. But Bouchaïb's wife Leila had spent the better part of the day in her kitchen preparing *kuskusoo b'qaddid*, a special dish reserved for Ashurah. She'd just delivered a generous platter of leftovers.

Each year Zemmouri housewives set aside a joint from the sacrificial lamb of Aïd el Kebir for processing into *qaddid*. The meat is sliced into thin strips, rubbed with salt, spices, and garlic and hung in the sun to dry. Leila's favored spot for dehydration was the clothesline on Dar Zitoun's terrace. Following tradition, she stored the finished product in a crock of lamb fat.

The jerked meat was an acquired taste. American chef, Andrew Zimmern, globe-trotting host of the popular television series, *Bizarre Foods*, relished almost every international delicacy he tried, from roasted grubs to whole, deep fried bats, but turned up his nose when confronted with Moroccan *qaddid*. But I loved it, especially in scrambled eggs, or as we were about to have it that evening, incorporated into a steaming mound of couscous.

"*Kul, kul* [Eat, eat]," coaxed Bouchaïb. Owen, already hooked on the meat's intense saltiness, needed no encouragement. "My husband sprinkles salt on anchovy pizza," I'd often joked to friends.

"Did Leila hide the lamb's tail in your couscous?" I asked with a wink.

"*Bien sûr* [Of course]!"

"And I suppose you found it?" My question made Bouchaïb chuckle. By tradition, a husband's fidelity was ensured for one year by the simple act of consuming the fatty morsel.

Jetlag and our hearty repast did us in. We bid Bouchaïb goodnight and dragged ourselves to bed. But the cacophony of *derboukas* and the whooping of revelers made sleep elusive. Well past midnight, just as the street noise was abating, a high-pitched chirp, more intense than the low-battery warning on a smoke detector, emanated from the atrium. "What was that?" I sat up in bed with a start.

"It's a damned cricket!" griped Owen. The second chirp made him throw off his sheet and blanket, grab a flashlight, and storm downstairs in the altogether. My husband was singled-minded when it came to troubleshooting. The success of his mission was never in doubt. I pulled the covers over my head. However, the sound of breaking pottery followed by a string of expletives gave me a change of heart. I grudgingly joined in the hunt.

All the commotion caused the cricket to temporarily suspend its courting song. Owen put his finger to his lips. He and I stood motionless in the semi-dark atrium — until the next strident call reverberated around us.

"He's near the kitchen," I whispered. The acoustics made it hard to judge. Another chirp drew my husband to the base of the fountain. He dropped down on elbows and knees with hind-end elevated, unmindful of the absurdity of this scene.

"Flashlight!" he hissed. I illuminated the pearly chamber of a conch shell, the suspected hideout of our nemesis. Owen dislodged the offending insect and sent it off to visit its ancestors with a sharp slap of his hand and then immediately trudged back upstairs.

"That *qaddid*'s not easy to digest," groaned Owen. "I tried to be reasonable, but still my stomach's working overtime."

Dyspepsia didn't prevent him from falling asleep as soon as his head hit the pillow. I, on the other hand, remained strangely alert. I wandered onto the terrace, intrigued by a subtle white noise in the still night air. A school of fish splashing in the moon's reflection in the Oum er-Rbia brought me an intense feeling of peace. I returned to bed next to my gently snoring husband. Concerns over lawyers, concrete, gardening, and crickets dissolved in a haze of slumber.

Egg Tagine with Olives

Serves 4

2 tablespoons olive oil
2 medium onions, very finely diced
1 (14¼-ounce) can diced tomatoes, drained
½ teaspoon sugar
10 green or purple olives, rinsed, pitted, and coarsely chopped
2 garlic cloves, minced
1 bay leaf
8 eggs
1 tablespoon chopped cilantro
2 teaspoons ground cumin
1 tablespoon mashed preserved lemon pulp (see page 255)
Freshly ground pepper
Fresh cilantro leaves for garnish

In a tagine or medium skillet, heat olive oil over medium heat. Cook onions, stirring occasionally, until light brown, 8 to 10 minutes. Add tomatoes, sugar, olives, garlic, and bay leaf. Mash lightly with a fork. Reduce heat to low and simmer until tomatoes thicken somewhat, 15 to 20 minutes. Discard bay leaf. Set aside half of this mixture for garnish.

In a bowl, beat eggs, cilantro, cumin, preserved lemon pulp, and pepper. Add to tomato mixture. Cook, stirring gently, until eggs are not quite set. Garnish with the reserved tomato mixture and cilantro. Serve immediately with crusty bread.

20

Feathered Invaders

The bombardier wasn't far off target. His haphazard dropping landed on the white tablecloth just a few inches from Owen's bowl of *harira*, the quintessential Moroccan soup. "That's it! I've had enough!" declared my husband as the attacker took shelter in one of the hanging ferns.

For as long as I could remember, Saharan Buntings lived the high-life in our atrium, feasting on the seeds scattered around the cage of Dar Zitoun's resident parakeets. A dozen feral birds bathed in the granite fountain and nested in the carved-plaster fenestrations that provided ventilation to the rooms on the first floor. We tolerated the interlopers during our many short visits to the *riad*. Long-term cohabitation was proving to be more problematic.

"How can you tell when a bunting has scored a direct hit on your *harira*?" quizzed Owen, leading me into his riddle. I shook my head.

"Answer: You can't!" said Owen.

With that, he bounded up the stairs to the library for a pad of graph paper to draw up plans for a screen that would block the skylight to the buntings. My husband was an accomplished handyman himself, but decided to hire a local carpenter to assist him in the screen's fabrication. A *menuisier* named Abdeslam came to mind. His workshop lay in the town's *zone industrielle*, outside the medina, within range of the medieval Portuguese fortress's rusty canon.

The workman was sanding a wooden cabinet when we entered. A few hand tools and a glass jar containing nails occupied a shelf on the back wall. Electric tools were luxuries few Zemmouri artisans could afford. No commercial signage identified his *menuiserie*. Indeed, there were no notices of any kind. Nothing like: *Our Insurance Carrier Prohibits Patrons From Entering the Workspace* or *The Price is Double if You Help*.

My husband showed Abdeslam his drawing. Not surprisingly, the workman expressed his willingness to join our team immediately. Owen loved this impromptu aspect of life in the small town. Tradesmen from ironworkers and glaziers to mechanics and carpenters would drop whatever they were doing whenever he showed up, knowing they would earn more than the going rate.

Owen was never happier than when he was engaged in a construction project. I loved to watch him, whether he was confronting a rusted lock at Dar Zitoun or installing a granite countertop in California. As an owner/builder, he spent five years transforming our one-bedroom farmhouse in Vista into a Dar Zitoun-inspired Moroccan villa.

"I'll be there after lunch," promised Abdeslam. He showed up wearing a T-shirt and a frayed sport coat that made him look oddly hip, in a *Miami Vice* sort of way. He brought along an apprentice, or perhaps the fellow was just a friend come to satisfy his curiosity about the *riad*. On the terrace, the carpenter produced a battered measuring tape.

"*Tleta metr oo jooj centimetr* [Three meters, two centimeters]," he dictated to his assistant, who scribbled on a torn piece of brown paper. After Abdeslam had called out the three remaining measurements, "*Tleta oo sta . . . tleta oo tmenia . . . tleta oo arba,*" he shot a knowing glance at Owen. No two dimensions were the same, a reality that made our project somewhat more challenging.

"Shall we buy the wood now?" asked Abdeslam.

"*Yallah* [Let's go]," replied Owen. We headed back to the *zone industrielle*. The lumber dealer's was no larger than a two-car garage, stacked from floor to sixteen-foot ceiling with rough timber. The proprietor didn't often have foreigners come his way.

There were no price lists, bar codes, or labels. The cost of lumber was whatever the market would bear. And businessmen understood that foreign customers would bear more than the locals. Owen hand-selected every stick of lumber when he built our home in California and was pleased that the Zemmouri merchant extended the same courtesy. My husband rifled through a stack of planks until he found a straight, untwisted one from which he could cut the members of the frame.

Abdeslam joined Bouchaïb near the entrance, away from the imminent bargaining. Unfortunately for us, Bouchaïb didn't consider himself to be the protector of his patrons' economic interests during shopping excursions. He was maddeningly aloof whenever it came to my cutting a deal with a local merchant or craftsman. His habit was often a cause of friction, especially when we learned that the cost of an item or service we paid for while in his company, was completely out of line. Perish the thought that he and Abdeslam would receive something later, a so-called *petit café*, from an appreciative merchant. This was just the way the system worked.

"*Besh'hal hadee* [How much for this one]?" I asked.

"One hundred dirhams."

Was that the friendly price? I looked in vain to Bouchaïb and Abdeslam for any subtle change in demeanor, like a poker player's tell, to provide some indication as to the fairness of the charge. Our companions remained expressionless. Had I come right out and asked Bouchaïb, I knew what his answer would have been: "How would I know the price? I never shop for wood."

Owen had a theory about Bouchaïb's reticence in money matters unrelated to his salary, expenses for household supplies, new year's bonus, Aïd el Kebir bonus (to cover the purchase of a lamb), and the Ashurah contribution we made, through him, to buy sugar and flour for the poor. My husband believed Bouchaïb's detached behavior, when it came to our expenditures, sprang from his unwillingness to jeopardize good relations with his fellow citizens, with whom he had to live year round. However, arguing against such reasoning was the inveterate system of kickbacks within the culture.

The merchant dropped his price by twenty dirhams after we spoke openly of our intention to visit a competitor down the street. While I settled accounts, Owen and Abdeslam carried the rough beam to a nearby milling shop for ripping and planing. Such division of labor appealed to my husband, who appreciated each step in a raw material's progression to finished product. For him the process was more exciting than perusing the aisles of a home improvement center in the U.S.

Patches of perspiration saturated the underarms of the machinist's shirt. The fact that he was missing half of the index finger of his right hand didn't appear to affect his dexterity. Owen and Abdeslam bathed in the fragrance of the wood shavings generated by the milling machine while Bouchaïb and I remained outside.

"What should we tip him?" I asked Bouchaïb when the operator finished. I don't know why I bothered.

"*Comme tu veux* [Whatever you want]," came his predictable reply.

Transporting the wood through the medina attracted attention. Thanks to *le téléphone arabe*, the rapid transmittal of local news by word of mouth, everyone in town would soon know of our project. My husband eased his pace near an untidy stall devoted to fishing equipment and supplies, where two weavers were repairing a net. Owen had walked past the place a thousand times before, but never paid much attention to it until that morning. After we delivered the lumber to Dar Zitoun, I was delegated to go back for nine square meters of netting. A boy of twelve or thirteen who was minding the store rooted through a jumble of open-mesh material before finding something with the requisite dimensions. A real bargain too, at twenty-five dirhams, about three dollars. I countered with twenty dirhams, a figure he accepted.

I set three five-dirham coins on the counter in front of him and was digging through my purse for a fourth, when I caught an almost imperceptible movement out of the corner of my eye.

"*Voilà*," I said, as I lay down the last coin on the counter, only to discover that one of the first three was no longer there. The boy was looking me straight in the eye, with lips tightly pursed. I was incredulous. "*Feen* dirham?" I asked him. He grinned widely.

"*Hal fommuk* [Open your mouth]!" I demanded, in a phrase I learned from my husband, a dentist by profession, who'd once volunteered at a local free clinic. The boy hesitated several seconds before producing the saliva-swathed coin. Far from being upset, I burst out laughing. The sheer audacity of the boy's attempt, as well as the timing and coordination it took to propel my coin, almost undetected, from the counter to his mouth, with just a flick of his wrist, was impressive. Nevertheless, I decided to keep the feckless act to myself. The shop's owner seemed to be of the old school. Had he learned of the mischief, the youngster surely would have suffered a thrashing.

Hadj Mustapha's voice boomed behind me as I was unlocking the door to Dar Zitoun. "Madame, you've returned. I came by earlier, but no one was home. I hear that you are making repairs."

"We're correcting a minor problem," I told him without going into detail.

"I've got another prospective buyer on the hook. One with lots of cash," the *samsar* informed me. "I'm sure he'll offer more than the Frenchman." The Hadj wouldn't let me go until I agreed to another showing.

On Dar Zitoun's terrace, Owen re-measured the skylight's dimensions and did so again after transferring them to the wood. *Measure twice, cut once*, was the carpenter's maxim. Abdeslam seemed puzzled by all the repetition. He was eager to get going with the saw.

The coworkers cut the members of the frame and laid them out for assembly. Abdeslam produced a handful of recycled nails from his pocket, which Owen trumped with a bag of galvanized metal L-angles and matching screws he'd come across in my father's hardware locker. It was time for Owen's cordless drill to make its debut. Working with such a tool was a luxury to which Abdeslam quickly adapted. "Next time," he asked, "could you bring one of these for me?" How quickly the heft of our next journey grew.

Abdeslam and Owen assembled the frame and attached screw eyes and chains to lower it into the well of the skylight. It fit perfectly.

Early the next morning, a young man appeared at the door with bristle brushes, orange-colored wood primer, and a can of Azemmour Blue paint. Owen, caught up with pruning the olive tree, made the mistake of setting our new assistant loose without supervision.

All this happened while Bouchaïb and I were in the kitchen rubbing a chicken with preserved lemon in preparation for roasting. An abrupt slamming of the screen's frame on the terrace brought us upstairs in a panic. The careless painter, having primed one side of the frame, simply flipped it over as one would a pancake. He'd apparently been equally slipshod with his brush, applying primer as lustily as a pastry chef buttering a pie tin. An orange galaxy of dabs and droplets outlined the frame's former position on the pavers. Bouchaïb stepped in before I burned the young man's ears. "Don't worry, Katy, *weet speereet* [white spirits, paint thinner] will get rid of everything," he assured me, before unceremoniously hustling the "painter" to the door. Owen applied the topcoat himself.

The following day the carpenter returned to inspect the job and help Owen tack netting onto the frame. They lifted the finished screen over the wrought iron balustrade and secured it into place.

"Saïd *a fait du bon travail, non* [Saïd did a good job, didn't he]?" asked Abdeslam. Not wanting to spoil the moment, Owen and I kept mum.

To be sure, we felt quite proud of our accomplishment. "Let's see the buntings get around this," Owen crowed.

We turned our attention to the few birds that were still cavorting in the atrium, harassing them with pieces of cloth tied to the ends of bamboo poles. Meanwhile, Bouchaïb stood by with a kitchen towel to throw over the exhausted buntings as they came to rest on the atrium floor, in the entrapment phase of our catch-and-release program.

It didn't take long for one of the evicted birds to outwit us. Within an hour of our declaring victory, the daredevil negotiated the three ninety-degree turns of the stairwell to alight on the fountain. We countered by installing, at the foot of the stairs, a pair of graying voile curtains, hems weighed down with lead sinkers from (where else) the local fishing supply shop.

The second round of evictions went more smoothly than the first. We were more skilled at grounding the buntings, and they more accustomed to the relocation exercise. Despite our best efforts, however, one or two of the cheeky buggers still managed to breach our defenses by slipping adroitly past the drapes whenever they billowed out in a stiff downdraft. Reluctantly, we decided to accept a 10-2 win rather than pursue a 12-0 shutout. We'd been outsmarted.

Harira with Mint (Ramadan Soup)

Serves 6

2 tablespoons olive oil
2 medium onions, diced
3 ribs celery, sliced
1½ pounds lamb, trimmed of fat, and cut
into 1-inch cubes
½ cup wheat berries, rinsed and drained
½ cup dried fava beans, soaked overnight,
and drained (see note)
½ cup dried garbanzo beans,
soaked overnight, and drained (see note)
2 teaspoons ginger powder
1 teaspoon turmeric
8 threads Spanish saffron, crushed

6 cups water
1 stick cinnamon
½ cup lentils, rinsed, and picked over
5 medium tomatoes, peeled and diced, or
one (14¼-ounce) can diced tomatoes
3 tablespoons tomato paste
20 sprigs flat leaf parsley
2 teaspoons salt
1 teaspoon freshly ground pepper
1 cup water
½ cup flour
20 leaves fresh mint, chopped

In a soup pot, heat olive oil. Add onions and cook over medium high heat, 4 to 5 minutes. Add celery, lamb, wheat berries, fava beans, garbanzo beans, ginger, turmeric, saffron, water, and cinnamon. Cover tightly. Bring to a boil. Reduce heat to medium. Cook until beans are soft, about 1½ hours. Add lentils and cook for another 20 minutes, until they are tender.

Meanwhile, in blender, in increments, puree tomatoes, tomato paste, parsley, salt, and pepper. Add to soup pot. Cook until heated through. In a bowl, mix water and flour. Add in a steady stream to the simmering soup, stirring until *harira* thickens. Ladle into bowls and sprinkle with chopped mint.

Note: *Harira* can be made a day or two ahead and refrigerated. When substituting canned beans for the dried, add to the soup at the same time as the lentils.

Roast Chicken with Preserved Lemon and Braised Vegetables

Serves 4

1 4-pound roasting chicken, washed and patted dry
1 preserved lemon (see page 255)
1 bunch parsley, rinsed and tied with cotton string
Freshly ground pepper
1 onion, sliced
1 cup diced celery
1 cup diced butternut squash
2 zucchini, peeled and diced
1 rutabaga, peeled and diced
1 turnip, peeled and diced
12 baby carrots
1 cup chicken broth

Preheat oven to 325 degrees F.

Remove giblets and save for future use.

With a sharp knife, scrape pulp from preserved lemon. Dice and reserve rind.

Using your hands, coat chicken inside and out with lemon pulp. Stuff cavity with parsley. Sprinkle chicken liberally with pepper. Set aside.

Place onion, celery, squash, zucchini, rutabaga, turnip, and carrots on bottom of a medium baking dish or roasting pan. Sprinkle vegetables with half of the diced rind. Add broth. Set chicken on top of vegetables. Sprinkle remaining rind over the chicken. Insert a meat thermometer in thickest part of thigh, taking care not to contact the bone. Roast 2 to 2½ hours, basting with pan juices from time to time until thermometer registers 180 degrees.

Remove chicken from the oven and let it rest at least 15 minutes before carving. Discard parsley. Serve vegetables and pan juices in a separate bowl.

21

Tea at the Courthouse

Maître Drissi wasn't making much headway toward the recovery of my father's testament from the tribunal in Casablanca. I was able to reach him only twice from California for what Owen and I referred to as "impasse reports." I knew that my calls made my lawyer uncomfortable. They also kept him on his toes and forced him to be creative. His last extemporaneous story went something like this: "*Quelle coincidence* [What a coincidence]. Just this morning I tried to reach my contact at the tribunal to discuss your case, but unfortunately he is attending a conference in Spain and won't return until the end of the month, just before Ramadan."

I didn't believe a word. By alluding to the holy month, he clearly hoped to discourage my calling again until after the period of daily fasting, a time of the year when work slowed to a snail's pace. That was especially true in government offices, those models of false efficiency rendered even less productive by the diminished blood-sugar levels of their personnel.

I was caught in an endless shell game, one being conducted by my own lawyer. No wonder it had taken him over two decades to resolve a case similar to ours. Now that I was back in the country, however, I decided to visit the *greffier*, clerk of the court, at the Casablanca tribunal in order to get the ball rolling. I took a risk in confronting the high-ranking government official, a trained lawyer himself, without legal counsel by my side. I may also have violated the accepted rules of conduct. The *greffier*, no doubt, would ascribe my assertiveness to being *américaine*.

I dallied on the front steps of the building where my parents were married in 1946. Back home in my study, I kept a picture of them, Maman sporting the swept-back hairstyle of the day, Daddy in his dashing R.A.F uniform. My own life began on a cellular level not long after the photograph was taken.

The sirens in the adjoining clock tower had once regulated my daily schedule. They heralded the sacrosanct midday interlude so essential to the French way of life, and during Ramadan, signaled the precise moment of sunset when observant Muslims could suspend their daylong fast. My family took advantage of the early evening's deserted streets for a leisurely spin across town to visit friends, while Casablanca's Islamic inhabitants, for reasons of sustenance and tradition, were willing captives of their dining rooms.

The tribunal's clock tower, like the rest of the city, was in need of restoration. It displayed a different time of day on each of its four faces. The square it overlooked, formerly called Place Lyautey, spread out before me. Gone was the statue of my grandfather's boss, Morocco's first Résident Général, Maréchal Lyautey. Bronze horseman and steed had been relocated to the grounds of the French consulate.

Place Lyautey had undergone several name changes over the years to the consternation of a swelling cadre of authors of Moroccan guidebooks. Its most recent designation was Place Mohammed V. Pigeons scoured the square for breadcrumbs, while young mothers watched their children chase each other around beds of flame-colored canna flowers.

Once inside the tribunal, I followed an official doorman dressed in billowy red *sarwal* (pants), white shirt, tasseled fez, and yellow *baboosh* slippers down cool marble corridors and across several interior courtyards to the department of the *greffier*.

Maître Chentouf, the man I'd come to see, was most affable. His realm, unlike the governmental offices I was used to in Azemmour and El Jadida, seemed more reliant on computer technology. This gave me reason for hope. The *greffier*'s framed diploma testified to his graduation from the *Faculté de Droit* in Bordeaux, France. I introduced myself and briefed him on the reason for my visit.

"Madame, it is a pleasure to meet you. I was just about to order some mint tea. Why don't you join me?" With a nod from him, the doorman took his leave and returned several minutes later with a tea service. Maître Chentouf and I were soon clinking glasses and exchanging *bismillahs.*

"You said your father was the founder of Olive Branch Tours. I have heard of the company. It was the first, or one of the first, travel agencies in the country, *n'est-ce pas*?" It was heartening to hear at least one official acknowledge Daddy's contribution to the Moroccan economy.

"And you, Madame, what is your line of business?"

"I write Moroccan cookbooks." His eyes brightened. The nature of my work never failed to break the ice.

"You can find couscous in the United States?" he asked. I explained how the marketing of "instant couscous" had introduced American cooks to the Moroccan staple.

"But surely, couscous can never be instant, madame," he declared. " My mother spends a whole morning preparing couscous for the Friday meal."

"Maître, instant couscous isn't bad," I said in the product's defense. "And it saves time."

"Americans are always in a hurry, *non*?" the *greffier* opined. "Here, we don't rush when preparing meals." Nor when conducting probate, I was tempted to add.

"Couscous *instantané. Ces américains*," he muttered, shaking his head. He then addressed the legal problem at hand. "Let's try to locate your father's testament." He picked up the phone and issued a salvo of orders concerning the document, before returning to the subject of couscous.

"My mother comes from the little town of Ahfir on the Algerian border. Over there, they add meatballs to the broth. It's different from couscous beidaoui [Casablanca style]."

"Very original, too. I must try it," I replied. I hoped I wasn't too ingratiating in my praise.

"Maybe you could put her recipe in one of your cookbooks," he suggested. "Why not," I humored him. "I'll look into it when I return to the U.S."

A low-level employee drifted into the *greffier*'s office about a half-hour after my arrival. White-collar workers like him, on the bottom rung of the government service, dared not initiate action on their own, yet had the ability to wield inordinate control by impeding or promoting a cause, and in so doing, corrupting the system. I gave him the warmest of smiles.

Maître Chentouf excused himself before he undertook a rapid-fire debriefing of his subordinate. The *greffier* peeked in my direction before posing one final question: "*Vous êtes sûr* [Are you sure]?"

With the man's nod, the *greffier*'s expression darkened. "It seems your father's testament could not be found. It may have been misfiled or destroyed in the *inondation* [flood]."

"*Inondation?*" I mouthed in disbelief. The news was dumbfounding. "*Ce n'est pas possible* [It's not possible]," I stammered.

"*Hélas, madame, c'est possible.*" The *greffier* gave me a look of pained embarrassment. "Maybe your dossier was moved to another location for safekeeping following the disaster."

The tribunal was a good mile from the ocean, on high ground, miles away from the nearest river. Floods hit places like New Orleans, not Casablanca. Perhaps some interior water line had burst? In that case, surely word of the calamity would have filtered out to the legal community, and Maître Drissi would have got wind of it.

"Bbbbut the *conservateur* in El Jadida demands to see my father's testament. What am I to do?"

"Certainly you have a *copie conforme* [certified copy]?" he asked.

"I do, monsieur, but the *conservateur* insists upon seeing the original," I replied in a tone of desperation.

"I will assign two members of my staff to join in the search, day and night. There is nothing to do now but wait. *Je suis désolé* [I'm sorry]."

The unnerving turn of events called for appeasement, in the form of a half-dozen *sablés au beurre*, butter cookies, from La Normande, the pâtisserie across from the Marché Central. The moist fragrance of pastry settled over me in a buttery cloud and helped assuage my frustration. But my mind was too preoccupied to fully appreciate the baker's talent. Moroccans are compulsive record-keepers, like the French, I told myself. They place great value on legal documents. The testament would turn up, sooner or later.

The surfeit of La Normande carbohydrates brought on a carnivorous craving that drew me into the central market in search of charcuterie. I could almost taste the Armagnac-flavored pâté de campagne.

Bouchaïb longed to recreate *la bonne cuisine française* in the way he once did for my father. On the chance I would be similarly inclined, he had pressed a wish list into my hand before I left Azemmour. As much as I loved the variety of fresh seasonal produce our local souk had to offer, I too sometimes yearned for the ingredients of classical French cooking — crème fraîche, Belgian endives, foie gras, truffles, and *champignons de Paris*. The *greffier*'s maddening disclosure provided the perfect excuse for a shopping spree at the Marché.

I walked under the central market's arched entry past vibrant pyramids of sweet peppers, green-ribbed bouquets of Swiss chard, and crates of avocados. A score of Japanese shutterbugs, disembarked from the sleek Volvo bus parked outside the market, threw me off course. They were jostling for position in front of the tiny establishment that specialized in products derived from argan oil. A Berber employee in native dress demonstrated the technique for extracting it from roasted argan kernels using a stone quern, while the proprietor delivered a brief exposé on the exotic fruit. He told the tourists how, for centuries, women from the high plateau of southwestern Morocco made their living from the olive-like drupes of the thorny *Argania spinosa*, a tree so highly prized that it is listed among landowners' assets. I knew his monologue almost by heart. Like a contestant on *Name That Tune*, I could have completed any sentence in his spiel after only an introductory word or two, and added a few comments of my own.

I would have sung the praises of the Berber entrepreneurs who founded Morocco's first women's co-operative for the artisanal production of argan oil. Their mentor, an acquaintance of mine, Dr. Zoubida Charrouf, a noted economist from Mohammed V University, referred to these ladies as "the keepers of tradition."

Providing a simultaneous translation of the shopkeeper's monologue must have taken the starch out of the poor Japanese guide who, without warning, hustled his flock along to the next photo op. As the tourists made no purchases, I felt obligated to buy *something*. A colorful salad of roasted red bell peppers and anchovies dressed with argan oil and lemon juice would help Owen overlook the artery-clogging offerings from the charcuterie.

The products of my dreams awaited me in the market's central aisle where ducks and partridges flaunted their fleshy breasts. Glistening livers, sweetbreads, and other organ meats kept company with larded *rosbifs* while serpentine links of merguez, slices of pâté de campagne, *rillettes maison*, and *saucisson à l'ail* occupied the high rent district in the charcutier's luminous display case. My disposition lightened. Not so my suddenly leaden shopping basket.

I swung by Brahim's for some spices. His shop still displayed a washed-out sign that advertised *Poudre de Curry de* Madame P.B., a recipe the purveyor acquired decades before from my godmother, Kathaleen Patton-Bethune. A British expatriate, she had lived in India before settling in Casablanca at the end of World War II. The aroma of her legacy filled the car as I sped from town ahead of the frightful rush-hour traffic.

Red Bell Pepper and Anchovies with Argan Oil

Serves 4

2 red bell peppers
1 small can anchovies in oil, drained
1 lemon
Salt to taste
2 tablespoons argan oil
12 oil-cured black olives (for garnish)

Set oven to broil. Place peppers on a baking sheet lined with foil and grill, turning peppers with tongs until skins blister evenly, 8 to 10 minutes. Transfer to a bowl and seal. When cool, peel and seed. Transfer to a colander to drain.

Cut drained peppers into wide strips and arrange on a serving plate with whole anchovies. Lightly sprinkle with lemon juice and salt to taste. Drizzle with argan oil, garnish with lemon slices and black olives, and serve.

22

Turkey Couscous

The *Life and Opinions of Tristram Shandy, Gentleman* was a book I never expected to encounter at Azemmour's Café Etoile de l'Océan, where Owen and I had stopped for a pitcher of *limonade*.

The twenty-something patron seated next to us had his nose buried in the eighteenth century comic novel. I struck up a conversation in English. *Tristram Shandy* was his favorite book; one he had read many times. I noted his anachronistic diction. Had speaking in that manner become second nature, or was he making a conscious effort to mimic the Lawrence Sterne character with whom he was so obviously obsessed? To encounter an American who spoke English in this way would be remarkable. But a Zemmouri?

Our newfound acquaintance had a degree in English literature from the University of El Jadida. In a later reading of his erudite master's thesis on psycholinguistics, I was clearly out of my depth. Jamal had no steady job, a common predicament for Moroccan college graduates without connections. To make matters more difficult, he had assumed responsibility for three younger sisters after the death of his parents. Jamal's financial plight got Owen to thinking. He'd long wanted to have a proper course in darija, Moroccan Arabic — to learn to read and write it. Here was his opportunity. Jamal agreed to become his teacher and set up a meeting for the following day.

"And now, if you will excuse me, I am obliged to attend to a previous assignation," he said to break our hold on him at the café.

Over the next few weeks, we saw a lot of Jamal. Frequently, the subject of turkey couscous crept into the conversation.

"Katy, I am persuaded that you and Owen would profit greatly by a sojourn to my aunt Khadija's farm. She's widely celebrated for her couscous *bibi beldi* [of free range turkey]." We gave in to his dogged lobbying and accepted an invitation to dine on the regional specialty.

On the appointed day, Jamal, and Khadija's son Hamid waited for us at the west end of the ramparts. They were seated on a couple of duffle bags next to an array of *couffins* filled with bananas, apples, oranges, watermelons, and bottles of assorted soft drinks. Our friend directed us to pull our car into an adjacent space. When Owen pointed to the No Parking sign directly in front of us, Jamal moved to the driver's side window. "Do not concern yourself with that," he said. "My cousin is a constable from the municipality of Casablanca."

In other words, with an off-duty cop along for the ride, the chance of our getting a citation for any infraction of the motor vehicle code was nil. Our traveling companions took their time filling the trunk with the *couffins*. They pushed the duffle bag across the rear seat and squeezed into the tight space that remained, without complaint. In the land of the *grand taxi*, where drivers never leave the stand without a full complement of six passengers, the cousins didn't consider their close quarters a hardship.

The sheer quantity of stuff we were hauling made me suspect there may have been a secondary motive for Jamal's invitation. We were the most inexpensive way of getting everything to the farm. Rather than regard his roundabout stratagem as deceitful, I chose to see it as another lesson in the silent language of culture.

"*Yallah* [Let's go]," I urged Owen, and we set off.

"What a splendid motor car," said Jamal cheerily from his uncomfortable stowage. "Perhaps one day I shall be the owner of one like it, *Insh'Allah*."

The chance of that happening seemed unlikely. Full-time employment remained elusive despite his college degree and fluency in three languages — four, if one considered classical Arabic separate from darija.

I remembered the two bright young men who handled janitorial duties at the printing company where my first book was published. One of them held a Ph.D. in physics and the other the same degree in chemistry. A linguist like Jamal was lucky to have part-time work waiting tables (at the same café where we met) and tutoring the children of wealthy Zemmouris. Like so many of his generation, he dreamed of emigrating to Europe or North America.

The conversation en route to Hamid's farm inevitably turned to the Moroccan judicial system. Jamal was not a fan.

"Pray be vigilant," he warned. "When my mother departed this life, peace be upon her, a wealthy uncle, my mother's brother, defrauded my poor sisters and me by bribing someone in the court to purloin our inheritance." Tales like his I'd heard before. They'd come to have a visceral effect upon me.

"Have a favorite music channel, Jamal?" I asked as I switched on the transistor radio I'd brought along from Dar Zitoun.

"Please allow me," he said, reaching over the center console to take it out of my hands. "Let's try France Inter." Soon, notes of a Chopin piano concerto filled the passenger space. The clear reception didn't last. Fifteen seconds of crackling interference compelled Jamal to let down his hair and surf to a more powerful station, one that broadcast international pop music. As luck would have it, an American hit was playing. More improbable still, cousin Hamid knew the words — after a fashion.

"*Eelands een de strreen, dat eez vat vee arr,*" he sang along unabashedly to Kenny Rogers' and Dolly Parton's "Islands in the Stream" as we whizzed past a turbaned farmer plowing with a team of dromedaries.

Hamid was just getting warmed up. "Dream," by the Everly Brothers, was next on the countdown. It too was in his repertoire. "*Drree-ee-ee-ee-een, drreen drreen drree-een, drree-ee-ee-ee-een . . .*"

Owen, Jamal, and I couldn't suppress our laughter. Our hysterics dampened neither Hamid's enthusiasm nor his confidence. Once we regained our composure, we lent our voices to his, as our boom-car and dissonant quartet barreled across the Doukkala plain. Owen, normally a cautious driver, joined in the frivolity and momentarily lost his concentration.

"Watch out!" I screamed as he banked into a wide curve.

The traffic ahead of us came to a sudden stop. The cause: a collision involving a pickup truck and a moped. Miraculously the operator of the latter didn't appear to be seriously injured. He sat on the pavement nursing a bloodied knee. The police hadn't yet arrived on the scene. Or *had* they? But Hamid clearly wanted no part of a fracas that could have taken hours to resolve. He tapped Owen on the shoulder.

"À *gauche ici* [Take a left here] Monsieur Owen." His direction led us onto a road that cut through a field of garlic flowers. Soon, the air inside the car grew pungent with their scent.

"My father!" Hamid exclaimed, pointing to the horseman in hooded burnoose who cantered down a gentle hillside, scattering foraging turkeys in the process. He cut a swashbuckling figure on his Arabian stallion, despite riding roughshod through the poultry.

"Looks like our lunch may have just lost some weight," joked Owen.

My husband was four generations removed from his agrarian roots. I suspected he was using humor to come to terms with the grim reality that our meal would require a considerable sacrifice from one of the birds in our wake. I, on the other hand, had no such compunction. I relished the thought of sinking my teeth into a tender drumstick.

A silver dagger hung from a cord of braided silk across our imposing escort's chest. He rode alongside the car, probably being brought up to speed on his son's professional exploits in Casablanca. Ahead, other family members descended on the cluster of simple whitewashed structures. Several girls in white hijab crowded the doorway to the primary dwelling. Curiously, our hostess, whose couscous Jamal had praised so highly, was absent from the welcoming committee. Hamid invited us to enter. We no sooner kicked off our shoes than someone shouted, "Le foot!"

The effect was immediate and predictable. Every man, including my husband, bolted for the salon to watch the game. Owen never played soccer as a boy, but developed an appreciation for the sport while taking in other World Cup qualifying matches in a café off Azemmour's main square.

I peeked around the doorway. A pigtail of electrical wire connected an automobile battery to the flickering TV. Dar Zitoun had no such luxury. It also lacked the *baraboul*, satellite dish, that crowned most other Moroccan rooftops.

The outfit I was wearing, though appropriate for the relative cool of Azemmour, was unsuitable for the hot inland climate. Hamid's sister Atika noticed my discomfort and led me to the women's quarters where she opened a cedar trunk. "Try this, Katy," she said, holding up an embroidered kaftan.

"It's too elegant," I protested.

"You will honor me by wearing it."

I couldn't refuse. I wriggled out of my jeans and sweatshirt and slipped the loose fitting garment over my head. The lustrous silk settled on my shoulders as softly as a rose petal. Atika helped me fasten the row of frogs that ran down the front, attending me like a lady-in-waiting.

Once she had me properly dressed, an acolyte handed her a small vessel containing kohl, the powdered sulfide of antimony that adds such depth to the eyes of Arab women. Atika used a hand-carved wooden stylus to apply it in a thin black line along the inside of my lower lid. She added a unique touch to my makeover by brushing my cheeks and lips with a rouge that she and her sisters prepared from wild poppies. My cosmetician stepped back to evaluate her work and my transformation into a sort of retrograde *Pygmalion* — having made a proper country girl of her cosmopolitan visitor.

"*Daaba ntee maghrebiya* [Now you are a Moroccan woman]," she declared.

Her kid sister tugged at my sleeve and pulled me through the front door and across the farmyard to a detached structure, where her mother Khadija sat cross-legged in a sea of black feathers. In her lap was a half-plucked turkey.

"*Ah williwilli*," she joked, flailing her arms about as if she were drowning, not at all embarrassed at my having come upon her in such unflattering circumstances. It was hard to explain our instant rapport. I must have won points by donning her daughter's kaftan.

"Saïda Kitty Morse!" exclaimed Khadija before we were formally introduced.

"My mother remembers seeing you on television," Atika enlightened me. "She watched you prepare *sheelee amreki* [American chili]."

Khadija nodded her head and laughed some more. Several years earlier, she'd caught one of my guest appearances on Morocco's most watched program, *Maïda*, a cooking show that rocketed its ebullient host, Abderrahim Bargache, to national stardom. His fan base included almost every household in the country, Khadija's among them. For that particular taping, and at Bargache's request, I demonstrated an American specialty that could be easily recreated in Moroccan kitchens —Tex-Mex chili.

"My mother cooked *sheelee* every night for two weeks, until my father decreed, 'No more beans!'" said Atika.

Bargache would later film an episode of his show at Dar Zitoun to highlight Zemmouri cuisine, with none other than Bouchaïb Melhaj as his guest. The television trucks that descended on Azemmour set the whole medina aflutter.

Khadija finished depluming the carcass before carrying it to a terra cotta brazier. The featherless turkey didn't appear much larger than an American roasting chicken.

"Do you do it this way in America?" she asked as she rotated the turkey over glowing coals to singe its pinfeathers.

"The ones I buy are already plucked," I admitted. "They're raised by the thousands in enormous indoor shelters."

"*Bibi* from the Doukkala are the best," said my hostess, slapping her victim's thigh for emphasis. "It's because we feed them leftover couscous." Were I a turkey on her farm, nothing would have blunted my appetite more than the sight of the staple used for stuffing!

Khadija disjointed the drumsticks, thighs, and wings and cut up the breasts into chunks. The knife she used was one of her most extravagant utensils. She had few others — two or three wooden spoons, a gleaming *cocotte minute* (pressure cooker), a trio of *canoon*, and a shallow earthenware platter called a *g'saa*. I wondered how my hostess would react to my California kitchen, with its plethora of modern conveniences and superfluous gadgets.

An enormous amphora held water her girls had fetched that morning from the well. The cool glass Khadija offered me tasted faintly of clay.

Her choice of a *cocotte* over a *q'dra*, traditional aluminum soup pot, both surprised and concerned me. I'd always shied away from the *cocotte minute*, the cooking implement invented by a seventeenth century French physicist to increase the boiling point of liquids. To me, its use entailed an element of risk — of explosion — though I hadn't known anyone who'd experienced such misfortune.

"You don't use a *q'dra*?" I asked.

"Not any more," she replied. "A *cocotte* is much quicker. The vegetables and turkey are ready in thirty minutes instead of an hour and a half. That saves on fuel."

She set the turkey in the *cocotte*, added water, herbs, and vegetables and tossed in a few spices, before securing the lid and placing the pot over the single butane burner that served as kitchen stove. When steam began to whistle notes of ginger, cinnamon, and saffron, my hostess surprised me again, this time with a funnel-shaped implement filled with uncooked couscous. The opening at its apex married perfectly to the vent tube on the *cocotte*'s lid, an ingenious invention for channeling pressurized steam through the durum wheat semolina. In minutes, a cascade of plump steaming granules spilled onto the earthenware platter, ready for anointment with a pungent aged butter called *smen*.

My hostess raked a dollop of the homemade condiment through the hot couscous with her fingers. She shaped it into a steep mound and garnished the face with the saffron-tinted turnips, onions, celery, cabbage, and Mediterranean squash that she fished from the *cocotte*. I had the honor of drizzling the creation with aromatic broth.

The intermittent whooping that had been coming from the other side of the compound suddenly abated. One of the soccer devotees appeared in the kitchen doorway with the news: "Halftime, neither team has scored," he reported and then asked, "Where's lunch?"

Owen and the others were in high spirits when I joined them in the mint-colored salon. I was welcome at the men's table only because I was a foreigner. Khadija and the other women, when they weren't serving, confined themselves to the kitchen. Convention required them to tuck into a replenished platter only after the men had eaten their fill.

Hamid poured warm water from a copper kettle over our outstretched palms. It dribbled into a basin set in the center of the table. We were rubbing our hands with a ritual spritz of orange blossom water when Khadija delivered her pièce de résistance.

The *"bismillah,"* intoned by the family patriarch was our signal to attack. Khadija's *bibi beldi* tasted like no other turkey I'd eaten — like an entirely different species of fowl, one imbued with a hint of gaminess.

Hamid and the others dug into the semolina with the first three fingers of their right hand. Watching them made me think of my grandfather. As children, my brother and I marveled at the skill with which Pépé could shape a small piece of cooked vegetable and a little semolina into a tight ball that he deftly popped into his mouth with a flick of his thumb. But I was too clumsy. However hard I tried, most of the couscous ended up in my lap.

At the Doukkala farmhouse I was the first to surrender. I leaned back against the cushions of the divan to digest. One by one, Owen and the other men followed suit. While Atika replenished the *g'saa* before delivering it to the women's table, one of her sisters whisked our plastic tablecloth to the yard for a good shaking. Resident mongrels intercepted most of the table scraps and turkey bones before they hit the ground. Waiting nearby, maturing *bibi beldi* stood ready to glean any odd bits overlooked by the dogs.

As soon as the men turned up the volume on the television set for the second half of the game, I retreated to the bedroom to change back into my western attire. During the meal, I'd kept a bath towel in my lap to protect the borrowed kaftan. I was relieved to find the garment unsoiled.

The soccer match ended in Morocco's favor, without the maddening overtime I so dreaded in American sporting events. Hamid's decision to stay on for a few days with his family meant that Jamal would be able to stretch out in the back seat of the car on the drive home. The three of us piled in.

"B'lati [Wait]," yelled Khadija, in hot pursuit of a terrified bird. Why the evening roundup? A moment later she was at my window with a live, trussed up turkey — a going-away present.

"Tell her no!" groaned Owen emphatically. "Tell her we can't! The car belongs to a friend! Azemmour law forbids live turkeys in the medina after dark! Tell her anything!"

It was no use. The more we protested, the greater the laughter. Our hosts must have wondered: Who in his right mind would turn down a turkey from the Doukkala? Our demurrals were taken as good manners.

Khadija created a fait accompli by opening my door and jamming the disoriented fowl into the space where I'd hope to rest my feet, which I repositioned above the dash. Gallant Jamal offered to switch places with me. He didn't have to ask twice.

"God almighty!" sputtered Owen. "I don't want the damn bird!"

"It's too late now," I said. "Let's go."

"*Il'alleka* [Until we meet again]." We waved goodbye to Hamid and family.

"Wasn't that an elegant kaftan Atika lent me?"

"Well, *of course* it was," replied Jamal.

"What do you mean?" I asked.

"One would expect a wedding gown to be elegant, wouldn't one?"

Atika's generosity was hard to fathom. By lending me a kaftan from her trousseau, she'd been faithful to tribal tradition, which dictated that a guest be treated with the utmost respect. Jamal quoted a Moroccan proverb: "You will open the door to any stranger, and you will bestow upon him your hospitality for three days before enquiring as to the object of his visit." I leaned my head against the window so he wouldn't notice that my eyes were swimming.

Khadija's Turkey Couscous

Serves 8

4 tablespoons olive oil
2 medium onions, quartered
1 (7 to 8 pound) turkey, cut up
1 (24-ounce) can plum tomatoes
12 baby carrots
2 small turnips, peeled and quartered
2 mild Anaheim chiles
15 sprigs cilantro, tied with cotton string
15 sprigs flat leaf parsley,
tied with cotton string
10 cups water or chicken broth
8 threads Spanish saffron, crushed
2 teaspoons ground turmeric
2 teaspoons ground ginger

3 pounds butternut or pumpkin squash,
peeled and sliced
3 zucchini, peeled and cut into sticks
4 small yellow or green pattypan squashes
(optional), cut in half
1 cup fresh garbanzo beans, shelled or 1
cup drained canned garbanzo beans
1 cup fresh fava beans, shelled (optional)
3 teaspoons salt
1 teaspoon freshly ground pepper
1¾ cups couscous
2 tablespoons *smen* (see page 268), or butter
Harissa, for serving (see page 20)

In a *couscoussier* or large soup pot over medium high heat, heat 2 tablespoons of olive oil. Cook onions until soft, 4 to 5 minutes. Brown turkey parts, 2 to 3 minutes on each side. Add tomatoes, carrots, turnips, chiles, cilantro, parsley, 8 cups broth, saffron, turmeric, and ginger. Bring to a rolling boil for 6 to 8 minutes and then reduce heat to medium. Cover and cook until carrots are tender, 30 to 35 minutes. Using a slotted spoon, transfer vegetables to an ovenproof dish and keep warm in the oven.

To the broth, add the butternut squash, zucchini, pattypans, garbanzos, and fava beans. Cover and cook until tender, 15 to 20 minutes. Add to vegetables already in the oven. Discard cilantro and parsley. Transfer turkey to oven if tender. If not, continue simmering until ready to serve. Season broth with 2 teaspoons of the salt and all of the pepper.

Meanwhile, prepare couscous. In medium saucepan, bring remaining 2 cups broth, remaining olive oil, and 1 teaspoon salt to a boil. Remove from heat. Add couscous in a stream. Stir once. Cover and set aside until couscous is tender, 12 to 15 minutes. Add *smen* (or butter) and fluff with a fork. Transfer to a serving platter and, using your hands, create a steep mound. Garnish the face with cooked vegetables and arrange pieces of turkey around the perimeter. Serve with remaining broth and *harissa* on the side.

23

Unexpected Guests

It must have been for the parking attendant's benefit that Jamal extracted the turkey with the theatrical panache of a magician pulling a rabbit from a hat. In one fluid motion, he drew the unsuspecting bird from the floor of the front seat to within inches of the *gardien*'s nose.

"*Bibi kbir* [Big turkey]," declared Messaoud stoically.

Big droppings too.

"*Makaeen mooshkeel* [No problem]," he assured me, pointing to the mess on the floor mat. He knew that a generous gratuity would come his way for expunging the funky excrement.

Jamal checked his watch. "Please forgive me, but I must attend to my dear sisters."

He delegated custody of his rudely roused prisoner to my husband, who surprised me by handling the bird like a consummate farmer. Zemmouris were accustomed to buying their poultry "on the hoof," and no one gave him a second look.

I expected a more flamboyant reaction from the turkey's executioner-elect. Bouchaïb's eyes did widen a bit when he opened the front door, but other than that, his demeanor seemed uncharacteristically sober. "Nigel's friends arrived this afternoon from London," he informed me in the hushed tone of a butler.

"What?"

"Yes. They're having drinks on the terrace," he continued. "They told me you were expecting them." I *did* remember promising to host an English couple, friends of Nigel's, but they'd never contacted me to confirm their date of arrival.

Bouchaïb decided to billet the turkey in the utility room on the ground floor, the one adjacent to the Turkish toilet. I proceeded upstairs to introduce myself to our guests, Ian and Penelope. I couldn't help feeling that a critical piece of background information eluded me. I no sooner thrust forward my hand for a "Hello, I'm Kitty" when the wayward data surfaced. My husband appeared on the terrace at that very moment. I felt my face flush.

"And this is Owen," I introduced him. Several feathers had ridden upstairs on his T-shirt. I casually brushed them away, but Ian and Penelope followed their descent to the tiled deck. Owen saw no harm in relating the exotic events of the day, assuming that our guests, like us, were aficionados of organic farming.

"A free-range turkey will be spending the night with us," he began.

"What do you plan to do with it?" asked a horror-stricken Penelope.

Owen seemed puzzled by the naïve question and looked to me for a lifeline. I had none to throw his way. And besides, he was already out of range.

"Well, ahhh, Bouchaïb thought we'd roast it in your honor," he ad libbed.

Penelope blanched. "Didn't Nigel tell you?" she gasped.

"Tell us what?" asked Owen.

"Ian and I are vegetarians." The repartee was starting to sound like a comedy routine.

Nothing like the prospect of butchering a turkey to make visiting vegetarians feel at home! All hope of establishing a rapport with Nigel's friends went up in smoke, not scuttled by Ian and Penelope's dietary preference, but by the manner of its revelation to my humiliated husband.

Of the painful conversation that followed I remember mercifully little, except Owen's insipid smile as he listened to Ian expound on the esthetics of our *riad*'s orientation based on the principles of *feng shui*.

It had been a long day, made longer by the awkward moments on the terrace. I tactfully pinned the blame for my weariness on travel fatigue and suggested that we all get to bed early.

I didn't inform Bouchaïb of the contretemps until the following morning. Vegetarianism wasn't easily explained to someone like him, who, more than once in his life, had wondered about the source of his next meal.

The meat embargo didn't last long. Our guests announced their intention of shoving off sooner than planned — immediately after breakfast. They strategically positioned their bags in the foyer for a quick getaway. They seemed tired. Living under the same roof as the condemned bird must have kept them tossing and turning all night. Bouchaïb, on the other hand, bounced into the kitchen looking well rested. The menu for our upcoming feast — *dinde farcie au couscous zamita* and *purée de courge et patates douces avec confetti de poivron rouge* — must have given him sweet dreams.

Over croissants and coffee, I gave Ian and Penelope a crash course in the dos and don'ts of Moroccan touring and highlighted must-see destinations on their Michelin map. Then, Owen and I escorted them to their car on the main square.

"Well, *bon voyage*," I chirped. Maybe I was a bit too lighthearted in my delivery, considering the debacle of our guests' abbreviated layover at Dar Zitoun. Penelope read me like a book. If she hadn't guessed it before, she did then — my cheeriness that morning had nothing to do with excitement over their itinerary.

"Thank you for your hospitality," she said tepidly, looking up at me through the open passenger side window. And off they went.

Bouchaïb wasted no time in slitting the turkey's throat. He hung the unplucked bird upside down in the cool of the utility room to begin its *faisandage*, aging process.

"Fowl has to rest for two days before roasting," he asserted. Khadija would have done the same had she not planned on stewing the bird she prepared for us at the farm.

Maybe the turkey and I had something in common. I too was on the wrong end of a *faisandage*, thanks to almost everyone within the legal community, including the *greffier* in Casablanca. The news blackout from Maître Chentouf's office mystified me, especially as he'd appeared so earnest in his desire to help. Were his minions indeed combing the archives for my father's lost testament? Had they struck gold? I decided to find out, so I called him.

"Madame, you've been on my mind. Members of my staff are still on the hunt seven days a week. I'm sure they will have something positive to report in the near future," he assured me, borrowing lines from Maître Drissi's playbook of dilatory tactics.

A couple of days later, inasmuch as I had reentered the fray, I decided to visit the local tax collector in Azemmour. My goal was to secure a complete record of property tax payments for Dar Zitoun in order to close the gaps in my father's erratic accounting.

Bouchaïb had already "fixed things" with a friend of his, a cashier in that office, who'd offered to help me circumvent the normal scrum of petitioners, including the pervasive line jumpers. Was I about to become one of them? I'd never personally greased the palm of a civil servant before. The mere thought of it made me uncomfortable, particularly in regard to the protocol of bribe transmittal.

"Just slip Hassan this little *fabor* [tip]," counseled Bouchaïb, handing me a sealed envelope. "It's done all the time."

The man behind the wrought iron grill spotted me the moment I entered the packed office. He waded through the knot of Zemmouris to escort me to the section of counter where he had neatly clipped together the documents I was after. Before he dealt with those, he presented me with a separate tax statement marked, "*Impôts Hôtel* Dar Zitoun" and addressed to, "Monsieur Chandler, maître d'hôtel." I folded it and put it in my purse. For over thirty years my father paid the commercial rate. True, the house *was* the size of a boutique hotel, and during Daddy's lifetime, it welcomed an almost continuous stream of overnight guests, but every one of them non-paying. However, I wasn't there to debate tax status.

"Please sir, if it wouldn't be too much trouble, may I have a copy of these records," I asked, laying the plain brown envelope on the counter. My bribe didn't absolve me from the customary etiquette of clerical transactions.

"I need them for the *conservation foncière*," I added by way of justification. I shouldn't have bothered. The clerk was prepared to give me as many copies as I wanted even if I'd planned to line the parakeets' cage with them. He left the building and strode across the courtyard to another structure. The gang of petitioners in the office doubled in his absence. There had been no sighing or carping up until that point. That was about to change.

"You've got to have eyes in the back of your head when you come here," groused a businessman in coat and tie. His comment touched a nerve in the fellow next to him.

"*Bureau de merde* [Shithole of an office]!" replied the colorful character on the verge of going postal. "You'd get screwed in this damned place, even if you had eyes on the soles of your feet!"

Finally, like a prisoner exchange, the cashier's still-warm copies and my brown envelope crossed paths under the iron grill. "Are you able to certify them for me as well, monsieur?" I asked expectantly.

"*Malheureusement, non madame. Je suis désolé* [Unfortunately, no madame. I'm sorry]. For that you must go to the urban administration building." The cashier offered to take me there himself, but I declined. I had neither the funds for a second honorarium nor the heart to hold up the crush of unsmiling supplicants behind me any longer.

My first order of business on arriving home was to open the oven door to liberate a crisp piece of skin from the turkey, by that time, basted to a luminous brown. I was about to peel off another when the chef walked in and caught me in the act. "Katy!" he scolded.

"*Tu m'excuses*, Bouchaïb; I couldn't help myself," I apologized. "Ian and Penelope will never know what they missed."

"*Des gens bizarres* [Strange people]," he remarked with a shrug. Vegetarianism and animal rights were as much a mystery to him as Moroccan bureaucracy was to me.

Dinde Farcie au Couscous Zamita

(Roast Turkey with Couscous & Almond Stuffing)

Serves 8 to 10

1 cup slivered almonds
1⅓ cups water
1 teaspoon salt
4 tablespoons butter
1 cup couscous
1 cup (about 2.5 ounces) golden raisins, plumped in warm water and drained
8 pitted dates, coarsely chopped
12 sprigs parsley, chopped
3 tablespoons orange blossom water (see Note)

2 tablespoons sugar
1½ teaspoons ground cinnamon
1 teaspoon ground ginger
1 (8 to 9 pound) turkey
Salt to taste
1 teaspoon freshly ground pepper
12 fresh figs, halved
½ cup honey
2 cups chopped celery

Preheat oven to 325 degrees F.

In a medium skillet, toast almonds, stirring occasionally, until they turn a light gold, 5 to 6 minutes. Set aside.

In a medium saucepan over medium heat, bring water, salt, and butter to a boil. Add couscous in a stream. Stir once. Remove from heat. Cover and let stand until couscous is tender, 12 to 15 minutes. Transfer couscous to a bowl. Allow it to cool slightly. Combine couscous with the almonds, raisins, dates, parsley, orange blossom water, sugar, cinnamon, and ginger. Set aside.

Remove giblets from turkey and save for future use. Rinse turkey under running water and pat dry. Season with salt and pepper. Stuff turkey with couscous mixture.

Meanwhile, slice figs in half and baste cut surfaces with honey. In a grill pan or under the broiler, grill figs until nicely browned. Set aside.

Spread celery in a shallow roasting pan and set turkey on top. Insert a meat thermometer in the thickest part of the thigh, taking care not to contact the bone. Roast 2½ to 3 hours, basting with pan juices from time to time until thermometer registers 180 degrees F and juices run clear. Remove from the oven. Let rest at least 15 minutes before carving. Serve turkey with pan juices and braised celery in separate bowls. Garnish *zamita* stuffing with grilled figs and serve.

Note: Orange blossom water is available in Middle Eastern markets and in some liquor stores. If fresh figs are out of season, combine couscous mixture with chopped dried figs.

Purée de Courge et Patates Douces avec Confetti de Poivron Rouge

(Squash and Sweet Potato Puree with Red Bell Pepper Confetti)

Serves 4

1½ pounds butternut, Mediterranean, or winter squash
2 medium sweet potatoes
½ cup milk or broth
1 teaspoon salt
1 teaspoon *ras el hanoot* spice blend (see page 156)
2 tablespoons olive oil
2 medium onions, finely diced
1 red bell pepper, seeded, deribbed, and finely diced
1 teaspoon sugar

Preheat oven to 375 degrees F.

Place squash and sweet potatoes on baking sheet. Bake until soft, about 1 hour. Cool, peel, and scoop seeds from squash. Peel sweet potatoes. Puree vegetables with ricer or potato masher. Transfer to a medium saucepan. Stir in milk (or broth), salt, and *ras el hanoot*. Keep warm until ready to serve.

Meanwhile, for the confetti, in a large skillet, heat olive oil over medium heat. Add onion, pepper, and sugar. Cook, stirring occasionally, until onions are lightly caramelized, 15 to 20 minutes. Stir half the confetti into the puree. Transfer to a serving dish. Garnish with remaining confetti.

24

An Eclectic Neighborhood

L'amoureuse est sortie du fond de la rue:
Collier de perles (au cou), tatouage bleu (au menton),
Henné aux paumes des mains, couleur de jujube;
Je plaçais ma main dans la sienne et me mis à contempler.
Elle me dit: "Que regardes-tu donc, ô mon pauvre garçon?"
Je lui répondis: "Rien d'autre que l'oeuvre de Dieu."

The lover came out from the end of the street:
Strand of pearls (around her neck), blue tattoo (on her chin),
Hennaed palms, the color of jujubes;
I put my hand in hers and began to contemplate.
She said to me: "What are you looking at, oh my poor boy?"
I answered her: "Nothing more than the work of God."

— from *Chansons de l'escarpolette à Fes et Rabat-Salé*
(*Songs of the Swing in Fez and Rabat-Salé*)
Translated from Arabic into French by Jeanne Jouin

Dissatisfaction with my lawyer's performance had become almost intolerable, yet I decided against an active search for someone to replace him. My approach would be discreet and passive in nature, relying upon *mektoob*, a fatalistic openness — to the next first-rate Moroccan counselor I chanced upon. Of course, I said nothing about my resolution to Maître Drissi.

My father was not one to worry. "Sufficient unto the day . . ." he used to quote the biblical admonition from the Book of Matthew — let the future take care of itself. So I turned over the legal headhunting to a higher power.

I didn't have to wait long. By a stroke of luck, a friend of a friend put me in touch with one Monsieur Labadi, a member of an anti-corruption society. His affiliation with that august body would be advantageous to our cause, I reasoned. Whether it turned out to be an asset or a liability in the country's opaque judicial system remained to be seen. In any case, it gave me peace of mind and something to brag about to friends. The fact that Maître Labadi had run for public office for the opposition elevated his status even more. In our first conversation over the phone, he spoke with a contagious optimism that left me feeling ten pounds lighter.

His office was located outside the zone most favored by the legal establishment and some distance from the *conservation foncière*. Affixed to the stone façade near the building's entrance was a tarnished bronze plaque engraved with Maître Labadi's name, degree, law school affiliation — Montpellier, France — and the imposing words: "*Agréé près la Cour Suprême* [Licensed to practice before the Supreme Court]." That lofty-sounding phrase would have carried more weight if it hadn't also embellished the plaque in front of the office of our not-yet-released lawyer in Casablanca.

Owen and I were Maître Labadi's first clients of the day and had arrived early to boot. Since there was no directory in the foyer of the multistoried edifice and not a soul on the ground floor to offer assistance, we climbed to the second floor. Two doors accessed its landing, both locked. We assumed one of them led to his office, so we sat down on the stairs to wait for a secretary. A few minutes later, we heard a deadbolt slide.

An elderly woman in her bathrobe backed through the doorway of what was apparently a private residence. She had a fright upon finding us camped out behind her. We apologized profusely and explained our predicament. She smiled.

"*Pas de problème*," the woman assured us. "Many first-time clients have trouble finding Maître Labadi's office. It's on the ground floor, at the end of a dark, narrow corridor. *Voulez-vous prendre un petit café avec moi* [Care to join me in a cup of coffee]?"

Only in Morocco. Things may have turned out differently had we stumbled into an apartment building in Brooklyn. Reluctantly, we declined her kind offer. We didn't want to be late.

The introductory meeting with Maître Labadi went well. And, because the wiry law professor spoke as passionately about Moroccan cuisine as he did the law, we decided to seal our new alliance with a cook-off, pitting his wife's specialty, fish couscous, against a sub-Saharan recipe passed on to me by an acquaintance from the West African country of Togo. My choice was provisional; it hinged on my success in tracking down the recipe's essential flavoring agent — peanut butter. I suspected the sandwich spread was not a popular item in Azemmour. But one never knew.

While I began my hunt, Owen headed to the barbershop for a haircut and shave, with iPod and compact portable speakers squirreled away in the oversized pockets of his photographer's jacket. His music was a big hit on a previous appointment, so much so, that waiting clients, as well as the barber's assistant, began doing the twist to the riffs of Dire Straights' lead guitarist. Owen watched the hilarity unfold in the mirror.

My husband planned a more wide-ranging recital for his upcoming session at the coiffeur's, so I probably wouldn't see him again until lunch. That would give me plenty of time to corral the all-American product, if indeed it lay abandoned on some forgotten shelf of an *épicerie*. I'd also decided to pay a courtesy call on the *caïd*, the town's district commissioner. Maître Labadi thought it wise to notify this gentleman of my change in legal representation.

"Do you and the *caïd* know one another?" I'd asked our new lawyer.

"I'm sure he's heard of me," replied Maître Labadi.

He also wanted me to show the flag — to let the *caïd* know that Dar Zitoun was still under family control. A bug in that man's ear would be passed along to the *commissaire de police* and eventually trickle down to a patrolman working the graveyard shift on the kasbah beat, who could keep an eye on the *riad*. At least, that was the theory.

Vacant homes were magnets for squatters and thieves. Bouchaïb, though a respected figure in Azemmour, usually visited the house only once each day. True, he did maintain an apartment in the medina, but it lay some distance from Dar Zitoun, just across from the mosque, with his bedroom window directly below the minaret. I'd often wondered if the low rent made up for the *muezzin*'s jarring pre-dawn *adhan*.

My hunt for peanut butter proved unsuccessful, however, I did have luck at the *caïd*'s. He promised to add our home to the *chabakouni*'s watch list.

"Dar Zitoun is part of Azemmour's history," opined the commissioner emphatically. "We'll make sure nothing happens to it."

I was lucky to find him in the office. With restoration projects to oversee and festivals to plan for the coming year, he had much to keep him occupied. The town hummed with activity. How I wished my father could have lived to see it. His prediction about Azemmour was coming true. With mixed blessings.

Zemmouri *samsars*, the persistent Hadj Mustapha among them, lived in breathless anticipation of our medina following the Marrakech and Essaouira models of urban redevelopment. One negative aspect to such progress was the tendency of some new proprietors to disregard architectural norms. Gossip mills crackled with tales of cash payments to bureaucrats willing to bend the building code.

What would Dar Zitoun look like in a hundred years? Dramatic changes to its riverfront façade over the previous century had more to do with Mother Nature than with human intervention. In the early 1900s, landslides had undermined the cliff on which our *riad* stood, resulting in the disappearance of at least one-third of its massive structure.

* * *

Three months earlier, in California, news of a different sort of alteration reached me, as it usually did, in the middle of the night. "*Allô?*" I answered in French, as was my custom for all such calls.

"Katy!" exclaimed the familiar voice on the other end. I was too disoriented to chide Bouchaïb for having awakened me. He could never remember whether to add or subtract eight hours when calculating Pacific Time.

"The new embankment, it is level with our wall!"

"*Comment* [What]?"

"The new embankment, it is level with our wall!!!" he repeated.

It took me several seconds to assimilate the news, the likes of which I'd heard before. Again our garden wall was gone, not in body, but in spirit. Landfill for a riverfront promenade commissioned by local authorities had risen to the full height of the barrier we'd erected only two years earlier. A wall ceases to be a wall when it is no higher than the earth around it.

Bouchaïb was in a panic. "Now everyone has access to our garden and to the stairway leading to the back door," he went on. "This afternoon, I found two men smoking hashish under the olive tree."

I knew of the planned esplanade. Indeed, I applauded the municipal project that promised to benefit the entire community and add luster to the medina. But I hadn't foreseen the consequence it posed for our *riad*.

"What do we do?" I asked Bouchaïb.

My husband had been leaning close enough to the receiver to pick up Bouchaïb's breathless account. "Tell Bouchaïb, before he does anything else, he has to hire a night watchman to camp out in the *hammam*. Next, he must engage a mason to get started on a new wall as soon as possible," he advised. "Build it directly on top of the old one."

If the ancient inhabitants of Troy could rebuild the massive ramparts of their city nine times, surely we, the heirs to Dar Zitoun, could come up with a few hundred concrete blocks, some sand, and a little cement to restore a simple garden wall.

* * *

On our return the following summer, the great wall was there in all its glory, twenty meters long by two-and-a-half meters high. Its broad, whitewashed façade served as a canvas for graffiti vandals who, thanks to the adjacent promenade, had easy access. The public walkway gave Zemmouris a perspective on Dar Zitoun that was previously available only to the occupants of passing skiffs. I frequently saw strollers craning their necks to gawk at the *riad*'s soaring exterior.

The masons had embedded glass shards in their wall-capping layer of mortar. The sharp fragments didn't deter a cat from choosing the precarious spot to groom itself.

"For the job, we broke up empty wine bottles from the *marabout*," bragged Bouchaïb. That may have been of some consolation to our resident saint, Sidi Makhfi.

The workmen had done a first rate job, but obliterated the once-restored garden in the process. "Pink blooms will be cascading over the wall before you know it," Bouchaïb assured me, in reference to the wilted row of geranium cuttings he'd salvaged from the trampled flowerbed.

As I opened the hose bib at the top of the garden steps to water his not yet rooted plants, a trio of vivacious young women looked up at me from the promenade. I wasn't used to seeing these ladies out and about in broad daylight. They were in their early twenties, slender and pretty, and dressed in form-fitting clothes that would have been fashionable in California. In North Africa's religiously conservative culture, however, such dress was considered provocative.

Our *riad* stood halfway between a mosque and a house of ill repute. The solemn activities of one didn't interfere with the brisk business conducted in the other. I'd always wondered about the mysterious influx of gentlemen in sport coats, who walked purposefully down our alley as if on a mission. My lack of awareness spoke to the unobtrusive manner in which the town's ladies of the evening cast their nets. The business went on for years under my nose. I only learned of it after Owen's tutor Jamal enlightened me.

Zoubida and Fatiha were two of Azemmour's most renowned prostitutes, he confided. Everyone in the medina knew how the world's oldest profession lifted the former from poverty to a life of relative ease as owner of several *téléboutiques* popular with Zemmouris for placing international calls. Zoubida's legitimate businesses funded a pilgrimage to Mecca that earned her the title of Hajjah. Almost sixty years before, another prostitute's life story briefly intersected with my own. According to my friend Roselyne, The Villa Clara, a splendid house in Casablanca, once belonged to a certain Madame Clara who operated a brothel there during the French Protectorate. After World War II her exclusive *maison close* became the private maternity clinic where I was born.

Jamal introduced me to both Zoubida and Fatiha one day on a walk through the medina. "These narrow lanes have a way of swallowing poor women," he said with resignation.

Retirement hadn't broken Zoubida of the habit of wearing heavy make-up. Plump and outgoing, she was known for her philanthropy. Once a year, she distributed sacks of flour and sugar to local widows before the Feast of the Lamb.

Fatiha, on the other hand, still struggled to make ends meet. Jamal told me how her husband had repudiated her when she was in her late teens. Poor and illiterate, she turned to prostitution in order to support herself and her infant son. Her artfully hennaed ankles, come-hither eyes, gold-capped incisors, and brightly colored pantaloons made her instantly recognizable. Whenever our paths crossed, she would acknowledge me, even when she was engaged in whispered negotiations with a potential client.

On another occasion, I observed her from a distance as she splashed water over the pavers in front of her apartment, a one-woman campaign to prevent the dust in the lane from going airborne. She was unaware of my surveillance.

"Yussef!" she called for her son. "Yussef!" The harsh decibels launched a pair of pigeons that had been roosting on a parapet.

Fatiha cupped more water from her bucket. Suddenly, a little boy of seven or eight, all arms and legs, came running from the direction of the public square. Yussef may not have heard his mother's call, but someone had, and through the grapevine, word had reached him.

He did his best to conceal several *sfenj* strung on a leaflet of palm. Fatiha collared him. "Where did you get the money for those?" she demanded.

"I found a dirham in the street."

"Don't lie to me! You were begging, weren't you?" she scolded.

Not many tourists passed through Azemmour, but when they did, the insistent demands of *"un dirham, un dirham"* from children like Yussef were annoyingly commonplace. Visitors' complaints had no effect. Local officials pretended to disapprove, but they never did anything to stem the panhandling.

That didn't prevent Fatiha from dishing out punishment to enforce her own moral code. She slapped the back of her son's head, snatched the *sfenj* away, and set them on a ledge above the water meter. Yousef's wailing filled the air.

"*Amouee* [Mother]!" he pleaded, extending his arm for restitution. Fatiha yanked her son into their apartment and slammed the door. The doughnuts wouldn't remain on the ledge for long.

Just around the corner, unsynchronized recitations escaped from the Qur'anic preschool. Why not renew my acquaintance with its headmaster? Several years before, the wizened gentleman was most gracious when I brought a group of Americans by his schoolroom for an impromptu visit. I poked my head through the doorway. A score of boys with smudged faces sat on straw mats in the windowless space.

"*Salaam alaikum* [Peace be with you]," I greeted the headmaster. He raised his hand to cut off the chanting. Before the teacher could respond to my greeting, one daring little boy blurted out, "*Ash smeetek* [What's your name]?"

"Rachid!" The headmaster's rod quivered dangerously close to the knuckles of the boy who'd spoken out of turn. The *taleb*, the Qur'anic schoolteacher, ran a tight ship. No students dared cross him. Neither did their parents. "*Qtel-u-ana-hedfen* [Master, kill him and I will be there to bury him]," had once been a common expression with which a father relinquished control of his son on the first day of class. I hoped my visit hadn't put the boy in jeopardy.

Lawsuits against teachers for the mistreatment of students were unheard of, putting legal action against *conservateurs*, *greffiers*, et al., in the realm of the unthinkable.

The *taleb* himself didn't have an easy life. He relied upon the charity of parents, many of whom were poor themselves, for support. Living conditions for him would have been less difficult in the countryside, where farmers could pay him in kind — with a free-range chicken, a few eggs, some freshly churned butter, or a decaliter of wheat.

A woman squeezed past me to set a covered tagine in the corner for the *taleb's* lunch. I took advantage of the diversion to break away. The sound of the pupils' cacophonous recital and the tapping of the *taleb's* rod followed me down the lane.

"*Aiieee!*" Bouchaïb grimaced when I touched upon the visit to his alma mater. "I cried every morning when my father dragged me there," he continued. "I remember when Yunes wet his pants in class. The *taleb*, he got very mad."

"What did he do — the *taleb*?" I asked.

Bouchaïb recounted the meting out of corporal punishment as if it had taken place only the day before: "The *taleb* asked for help from the biggest boy in class. M'hamed was his name; I spit on his mother's grave. He pulled Yunes across his back, hooked him behind the neck and knees, and held him fast for the *taleb*'s rod. Yunes' derrière hurt for a week."

Bouchaïb winced in the telling. "*Le taleb n'était pas gentil* [The *taleb* was not a nice man]. I left his class after only two years."

Owen returned from the *coiffeur* with ears significantly more prominent. My husband couldn't remember whether, in his instructions to the barber, he'd linked the Moroccan verb for "take" or "leave" with the word "*shweeeya* [a little bit]." It must have been the latter. A closer cut would have exposed gray matter. On the positive side, Owen got the best shave of his life. His face was as smooth as a nectarine.

While my husband admiringly stroked his cheeks and neck, Bouchaïb and I put our heads together for the challenge of locating the elusive peanut butter. As so often was the case, the problem's resolution would ultimately involve Roselyne, who informed me of a just-opened *hypermarché* on the outskirts of Casablanca where homesick American expatriates could find a limited assortment of familiar groceries, from taco shells to Skippy peanut butter.

Couscous Togolais au Beurre de Cacahuète (Togolese Couscous with Peanut Butter)

Serves 4

3 garlic cloves, minced
1 chicken bouillon cube, crushed
½ teaspoon ginger powder
¼ teaspoon freshly ground pepper
8 chicken legs and thighs
2 large tomatoes, peeled, seeded, and coarsely diced
1 medium onion, coarsely cubed
2⅓ cups chicken broth

3 tablespoons peanut oil
1 tablespoon tomato paste
4 tablespoons smooth peanut butter
1 teaspoon salt
1 cup couscous
2 tablespoons butter
½ cup (about 4 ounces) dry roasted peanuts, coarsely chopped
4 scallions, thinly sliced, for garnish

In a large bowl, mix garlic, bouillon cube, ginger powder, and pepper. Coat chicken with the mixture. Set aside.

In a blender, pulse half the diced tomato, onion, and 1 cup broth until smooth. Set aside.

Heat 2 tablespoons of oil in medium casserole set over medium high heat. Cook chicken, turning with tongs, until browned on all sides. Add reserved tomato/onion mixture. Cover and cook until sauce bubbles, 10 to 15 minutes. Stir in tomato paste, peanut butter, and ½ teaspoon salt. Lower heat to medium. Continue cooking, covered, until chicken is tender, 30 to 35 minutes. If sauce becomes too thick, dilute with a few tablespoons water or broth.

In a medium saucepan, bring remaining 1⅓ cups chicken broth, ½ teaspoon salt, and remaining tablespoon of oil to a boil. Add couscous in a stream. Stir once. Cover tightly, remove from heat, and set aside until couscous is tender, 12 to 15 minutes. Add butter and fluff with a fork. Mound couscous in center of a shallow serving platter. Surround with chicken topped with peanut sauce. Garnish with peanuts, remaining diced tomato, and scallions.

25

Native Son

Jarndyce and Jarndyce [a fictitious eighteenth century probate case] drones on. The scarecrow of a suit has, in course of time, become so complicated, that no man alive knows what it means. The parties to it understand it least; but it has been observed that no two Chancery lawyers can talk about it for more than five minutes without coming to a total disagreement as to all the premises . . . The little plaintiff or defendant, who was promised a new rocking horse when Jarndyce and Jarndyce should be settled, has grown up, possessed himself of a real horse, and trotted away into the other world.

— from *Bleak House* by Charles Dickens

If I had been more obsequious at any time in my life, I couldn't remember when. But it took an exhibition of world-class groveling on my part to wheedle an audience with the president of the El Jadida tribunal through his puffed-up gatekeeper.

On the day of the appointment, Owen and I arrived twenty minutes early at the colonial-era building in hopes of learning why authorities had decided to refer our straightforward *acte de donation* to a higher court. Since there was no room left on the wooden benches in the lobby, we staked out positions against a wall outside the president's office.

The atmosphere was Dickensian. Hundreds of glum citizens bumped against one another in the current of dense foot traffic, like corpuscles moving through a capillary. Across the corridor, a sea of document-waving plaintiffs bellied up to a chest-high counter. Occasionally, a flock of supplicants, like blue jays harassing a crow, pursued a beleaguered official attempting to make good his escape. Every so often, in the blue haze of cigarette smoke, a shouting match would erupt between opposing litigants or between a client and his own counselor.

The scheduled time of our appointment came and went — fifteen minutes, one-half hour, and then forty-five minutes. My fidgeting bothered Owen.

"You've got to adopt a more Zen-like outlook," he advised. "Imagine you have all the time in the world. Keep calm, close your eyes, and breathe deeply."

The lady next to me, who had the demeanor and dress of a Moroccan living abroad, appeared to be more in need of relaxation exercises than I. She seemed on the verge of a nervous breakdown. "*Je suis Belge* [I'm Belgian]!" she proclaimed to no one in particular. "*En Belgique, ce n'est pas comme ça. Ils sont organisés. Ici, c'est un cirque* [In Belgium, it's not like this. They're organized. Here, it's a circus]!"

Owen and I simply listened, not wanting to associate ourselves with her rant, even though we agreed with everything she said. The bailiff ushered the woman into the president's office ten minutes later. She emerged in a daze soon thereafter.

"Madame," I said, touching her on the arm. She didn't respond. The defeated woman plodded past me like a zombie. I wondered how long she'd been engaged in her legal battle, and whether, eventually, I'd be reduced to the same mental state?

Owen and I would have to kill time in that hallway until who knew when, for, without resolution of the *acte de donation*, my brother's buyout could not be confirmed, and we were dead in the water.

Another fifteen minutes passed without my name being called. And I was one of the lucky ones. In all likelihood the majority of stoic souls around me, those without appointments, were destined to wander the halls for the entire day with nothing to show for it. My luck finally changed when an assistant to the president, who introduced himself as Chafiq, took me to see his boss.

"Yes, indeed, madame, your case must be reviewed by the *cour d'appel*," said the president. His reason: "Contradictory court records disagree on the size of your *riad's* footprint — by four square meters." For the life of me, I could not understand why the higher court needed to involve itself in such a trivial matter.

The chief executive did make one conciliatory gesture. He ordered his assistant to escort me to the *cour d'appel* to have our case placed on the docket.

"*A votre service* [At your service] *madame*," said debonair Chafiq. Had a gentleman finally come to my rescue? I became even more hopeful when I learned the meaning of his name — "the one filled with solicitude." He was unusually tall for a Moroccan and bore an uncanny resemblance to the subject of a portrait I'd discovered in Dar Zitoun's guest book just after Daddy's death.

* * *

The pen and ink drawing depicted an imposing black African with an eagle feather in his hair. The artist who drew it must have spent time at Dar Zitoun, although I'd never heard my father speak of him — John Houser, El Paso, Texas (I learned from the inscription on the portrait). The find so intrigued me that I wrote to Mr. Houser immediately upon my return to the United States.

A letter of condolence arrived from Texas the following week. In it, Mr. Houser told me of how my father had offered him (an acclaimed American sculptor I later found out) the use of Dar Zitoun as a studio. With a young man from southern Morocco as his model, Houser produced a series of working drawings for a clay bust of a sixteenth century Moroccan known as Estebánico. Mr. Houser also told me that his work in Azemmour had been commissioned by the city of El Paso as part of its XII Travellers Memorial to commemorate the most prominent explorers of the American Southwest.

I'd never read anything about this "Estebánico," neither at the lycée in Casablanca, nor during my college years in the United States. My curiosity prompted a call to Mr. Houser, who agreed to send what biographical information he'd collected on "the black Arab and native of Azamor [sic]" mentioned in the memoir of Captain Álvar Núñez Cabeza de Vaca, one of the "black Arab's" companions on an extraordinary trek across the North American continent.

In the early sixteenth century, invading Portuguese abducted the Moor from famine-stricken Azemmour and sold him as a fighting slave to a Spanish lieutenant by the name of Andrès Dorantes. Master and slave set sail on a disastrous journey to the New World. Of the two hundred souls who put ashore in La Florida, only Azemmour's illustrious native son and three Spanish officers survived. In a nine-year odyssey that took them from the Caribbean to the Sea of Cortez, the Moor was re-enslaved by local Indians, won fame as a healer, learned six Indian dialects, guided a Spanish expedition for the Viceroy, and met his death from a Zuni arrow at Hawiku Pueblo in 1539. Owen and I later visited the site in New Mexico on assignment for *Saudi Aramco World* magazine.

242

* * *

"Madame!" Chafiq roused me from my rêverie to begin what I hoped would be the final leg of my own twenty-first century odyssey, which was rapidly becoming as arduous and implausible as the Moor's.

Our chaperone stood apart from other bureaucrats, as a dynamic character in a sea of the uninspired. We had trouble keeping up with him as he navigated sinewy shortcuts into the bowels of the tribunal, en route to the archives. The cavernous repository was akin to an aging penitentiary in that it incarcerated four or five times more documents than planned for by its architect.

Chafiq and the archivist squeezed between teetering ramparts of overstuffed files. I wasn't optimistic. Surely, locating the pertinent papers regarding Philippe's *acte de donation* would take them the rest of the day. But I

underestimated the ability of the aged clerk in the tasseled fez. Within minutes, he returned with a folder titled "Chandler/Morse." Chafiq took charge of the dossier as soon as the archivist transcribed it in his log. As before, we were off to the races along a tight corridor and down the front stairs to the street. The "circus" the Belgian woman described had become a lot less intimidating with the lion tamer by our side.

The clerk of the *cour d'appel* was next on our list. Chafiq hailed a cab, whose driver turned out to be one of his cousins, who, for some reason, launched into a diatribe against members of the legal profession as soon as we pulled away from the curb. Our chaperone was quick to add that his cousin's generalizations did not apply to the esteemed Maître Labadi. "Indeed, many lawyers, they . . . " He finished his sentence by making a slithering motion with his hand. "But your esteemed counselor . . . my cousin and I are in agreement . . . he is a reputable man." Auspicious news.

"I hope we can get this done before the midday break," said Chafiq. "That way you won't have to spend the afternoon in town." I nudged Owen to see if he'd picked up on the solicitude for which our escort had been so aptly named.

Our taxi unexpectedly pulled over. Chafiq sprang from the front seat and dashed into the finest pâtisserie in El Jadida. I knew it well. Only the week before, I'd purchased a birthday cake there for Alia. I shouldn't have bothered. She seemed bewildered by all the fuss, the celebration of birthdays being outside the Moroccan tradition.

The aroma of fresh bakery drifted through the cab's window before Chafiq had a chance to climb back in. He passed a warm paper bag our way. "*Tenez* [Have some]," he offered.

"The baker too is a cousin of mine. He and I trained together in Marseilles," said Chafiq. "I helped out in his shop for a year or so. But the bakery business wasn't for me. I needed my sleep. I went to work at the tribunal as soon as the job opened up in the president's office." Imagine that: being taken around by a French-trained *boulanger/pâtissier*! No wonder I liked him. "*Ça alors* [Well, I'll be]!" I said with my mouth full of pâte feuilletée. I gave Owen another poke in the ribs.

While our *petit taxi* steered clear of pedestrians and mopeds, I picked Chafiq's brain on the finer points of *cornes de gazelles* and éclairs until our arrival at the *cour d'appel*. The cab driver refused payment. "Next time, *Insh'Allah*," he said, by way of goodbye.

As before, we had trouble keeping up with our indefatigable chaperone. He did give us a few minutes at the entrance to a working courtroom, which appeared for all the world a model of decorum. We continued along a colonnade and then up a curved staircase.

We hadn't appreciated the scope of Chafiq's connections until, unannounced, we walked into a magistrate's antechamber. "Bouchta here is one of my best friends," he told us. "You must record the nature of your visit in his official ledger." Chafiq pointed to the book on the front edge of the wide metal desk. "It's only a formality," he assured me. "Just write [I still recall his stilted salutation]: *Veuillez agréer, cher monsieur le juge, l'assurance de mes sentiments les plus respectueux* . . . [Please accept, dear judge, the assurance of my respectful sentiments . . . "

"You'll hear from our office within the week," promised the clerk after I'd completed my entry.

A surge of optimism swept over me. What progress we'd made that day! I could have hugged Chafiq, but that would only have caused him embarrassment. Instead, we repaired to his favorite oceanfront café for some warm *baghrir* pancakes with honey butter.

"Marseilles was too hectic for me," he confided. "I'm a product of the Doukkala. I grew up in El Jadida and spent my summers working on my uncle's farm, upriver from Azemmour, near Mehioula. Surely you've visited Mehioula?"

"I've never heard of it," I told him.

"It's just above the Oum er-Rbia on the dreamiest hillside in all of Morocco. When I was a boy . . ." Owen and I could have listened to him all afternoon.

Before long Chafiq glanced at his watch, took one last sip of coffee, and to my protestations, scooped up the bill. "One day, *Insh'Allah*, I'll come to see you at Dar Zitoun," he promised, and was gone. In the few short hours we'd known him, Estebánico's look-alike helped us make more headway in our quest than any of our paid professionals.

And so, on the following weekend, rather impulsively, we headed off to Mehioula, a village so insignificant that cartographers hadn't bothered to include it on their maps. Apparently, being located on a "dreamy hillside" was insufficient criterion to make it worthy of consideration. But that didn't matter to us. Owen and I both understood what motivating force lay behind our Sunday afternoon spin.

Baghrir (Semolina Flour Pancakes)

Makes 1 dozen

1¼ cups warm water (100-110 degrees F)
1 teaspoon active dry yeast
1 teaspoon sugar
½ cup flour
1 cup superfine semolina flour (see note)
½ teaspoon salt
1 egg, lightly beaten
¼ cup vegetable oil, for frying
Honey, butter, and apricot jam, for serving

In a bowl, combine water, yeast, and sugar. Stir. Set aside until mixture starts to bubble, 10 to 12 minutes.

In a shallow bowl, combine flour, semolina, and salt. Make a well in center. Whisk in egg and yeast mixture (in ¼ cup increments) to obtain a smooth, lump-free batter. Cover and set aside in a warm place for 2 to 3 hours. Gently remix.

To cook, heat a skillet over medium low heat. Grease with a piece of paper towel dipped in oil. Pour ¼ cup of batter into center of pan. Cook until moisture disappears from the surface, 1½ to 2 minutes. Cook on one side only. Do *not* flip. Transfer *baghrir* to a plate and cover with foil to keep warm. Proceed in this fashion with remaining batter. Serve warm with honey-butter sauce (1 part honey to 4 parts butter) and apricot jam on the side.

Note: You can purchase superfine semolina flour at health food stores and Italian specialty markets.

26

Mehioula

I'd already fallen in love with the hamlet's name, the elision of its melodious syllables, with the first forming on my lips, the second and third gathering steam between throat and palate, and the fourth propelling itself gently from the tip of my tongue. Me-hi-ou-la. That none within my social circle could enlighten me as to its etymology was but a minor disappointment.

My father had never taken me to explore upriver, nor had he spoken of the now defunct *auberge*, the inn that once thrived above a stand of bulrushes in an idyllic valley located less than fifteen kilometers from the Azemmour ramparts. Such an excursion would have required too many precious hours away from Dar Zitoun.

Chafiq told of how he played soccer with his friends on a sliver of sand the locals referred to as *"La Plage de Mehioula* [Mehioula Beach]."

"After a game, we'd go for a swim to cool off and then eat a couple of the oranges that rolled down the bank from the grove. The patrons of the *auberge* didn't seem to mind."

Auberges, like the one at Mehioula, appealed to urban *pieds-noirs*, Europeans born and raised in North Africa, who followed French tradition by spending Sunday in the country. The establishments, with their red tiled roofs, expansive orchards, and lovingly tended vineyards, oozed Provençal charm. As the years passed, I remembered French Moroccan inns less for their food than for their names: L'Auberge de la Forêt (Inn of the Forest), the more whimsical L'Auberge du Lièvre Volage (Inn of the Fickle Hare), and Le Sanglier Qui Fume (The Smoking Boar). The latter, in the High Atlas Mountains above Marrakech, was still the subject of international acclaim. Most, however, were but ephemeral features of the colonial era, and after Moroccan independence, were abandoned by their French proprietors. Chafiq hadn't been sure the *auberge* of Mehioula was still in operation.

Giving us directions was a challenge for Bouchaïb due to the dearth of road signs in the area, forcing him to dredge his memory for landmarks. "You'll know you're getting close when you reach the corn silo," he said, referring to one of the beehive-shaped granaries unique to the region.

Our trip took an hour. The tertiary roads we followed were barely wide enough to accommodate our rented Renault subcompact. The rare bicyclist or horse-drawn wagon we encountered on the irregular tarmac had to give way as we approached, as we did when confronted with an oncoming *grand taxi* or truck; might made right, or rather, might made for right-of-way.

We were forced to stop on several occasions to get independent confirmation of Bouchaïb's directions, once from a group of old men who were passing the time in front of a quiet, country *épicerie*. A disabled gentleman on crutches was eager to communicate with me in French. The well-spoken veteran of the Foreign Legion, who'd lost a leg in World War II, couldn't help getting sidetracked onto the defining event of his life and the far-flung battlefields to which fate had taken him. Owen and I were not unwilling listeners. To be honest, the tales of his heroic deeds quite fascinated us. Finally, he did get around to

Mehioula. "*Tout droit* [Straight ahead]," he pointed with his crutch. "In about two kilometers, when you reach a white farmhouse, veer left and then follow the road half-way around the hill."

Better yet, he informed us, one of his cronies happened to be going that way and would gladly ride along as our guide. We quickly agreed — before learning that the man in question was delivering a sheep to the organizer of an upcoming tribal festival. But we were already committed. The shepherd, whose face was as weathered and brown as the earth he'd been sitting on, slid his hog-tied ewe across the seat before he himself climbed in. The undemonstrative fellow had the air of someone for whom being chauffeured by a couple of Californians was a common occurrence. We often picked up hitchhikers in rural Morocco, especially in remote regions, though our passengers had always been of the two-legged variety. Transporting livestock was a first for us — or a second, if one took into account the turkey.

In time, we could have adjusted to the smell of unwashed wool tinged with manure, but not on so short a run. What I wouldn't have given for a Chevy convertible! The bleating cargo seemed as eager to reach its destination as we were to deliver it. Its owner smiled and uttered a few words of Berber whenever I turned around, but I found it impossible to breach the linguistic divide. The last time he spoke up, it was in a tone so assertive that the meaning was clear. We pulled over. The shepherd adjusted the hood of his burnoose, hauled the sheep from the car, and hoisted the animal onto his back.

"Mehioula," he said gruffly, motioning with his chin as he stumbled past my window. He headed in the direction of a dozen women and children bent over at the waist cultivating corn. On a hillside above them was the silo Bouchaïb had described. I caught sight of a barely legible sign where the paving ended — "Mehioula." I let the name melt in my mouth like a puff of cotton candy. Since no one was about, we parked in front of a dilapidated structure with a roof of fractured terra cotta tiles. Several goats grazed in the shade of an adjacent palm.

The slamming of our car doors spooked a host of sparrows from an overgrown hedge of bougainvillea that paralleled the road. I detected movement behind it a second or two before a rusty iron gate creaked open.

"*Français?*" asked a voice from the shadows.

"*Non. Américains.*"

A man in his early twenties stepped forward. "*Je m'appelle Hassan. Je suis le gardien.*"

"*C'est l'auberge?*" I asked.

"*Non, l'auberge est abandonnée* [No, the auberge is abandoned]," he told us. "Would you like to have a look around?"

"It's allowed?"

I wasn't accustomed to such liberal policy regarding private property. Bouchaïb and I had an ironclad rule with respect to visitors to Dar Zitoun: No one entered without first getting permission from either Nigel or me. The guideline occasionally got me in hot water with Azemmour's *caïd*, who showed up unannounced from time to time with foreign dignitaries in tow. Bouchaïb stood his ground and denied entry despite threats from the town's leading politician to return with a couple of gendarmes to break down the door. Had I been there in person, or had the *caïd* phoned or faxed, I would have acceded to his request. I wanted to believe that our *gardien* was always so scrupulous in hewing to the convention.

With Dar Zitoun vacant for months on end, however, the temptation for him to do otherwise was considerable: *Chez Bouchaïb: Menu prix fixe, 100 dirhams. Spécialités de la maison*: *bestila, tagine, couscous*. I dreaded the prospect.

"I'll show you around," declared Hassan. If the owners of the *auberge* were more permissive than I, why not accept their *gardien*'s offer.

The young man led us down a long series of stone landings to an abandoned villa — a replica of a Provençal farmhouse. The two-story structure stood lifeless behind closed shutters. Hassan unlocked its heavy wooden door, whose squeal of neglect echoed through a large, empty salon. The draft created by our entry caused spider webs to tremble in the room's enormous fireplace. I wondered when its bricks had last felt the lick of a flame?

On the second floor, our guide fought with the temperamental French doors that opened onto a terrace, where twin, stone pillars and a balustrade of theatrical proportions framed a spectacular panorama over an isolated stretch of the Oum er-Rbia. The Elysian ambiance was like few others I'd experienced. If eternity was to be spent on that balcony, so be it. I could tell Owen felt the same way. We soaked up the view in silence for several minutes.

We descended into the grove, where flowers piqued our olfactory senses and bees in profusion hummed around us, creating an auditory mantra that put me in a relaxing, meditative state. At that moment, California seemed as remote as another planet.

Hassan stood by with indifference. Like a U. S. Park Ranger assigned to the Grand Canyon, he spent every day along the same stretch of river. Why expect him to wax poetic over his surroundings in the same way that the odd tourist, like Owen or I, would have. However, the abundance of fallen fruit on the ground was something that *did* elicit a comment: "When the owners lived here, they employed my father to truck crates of citrus to Casablanca. Now, there is no one to oversee the farm's operation. *Dommage* [Too bad]."

Owen took the liberty of stashing a few specimens of the windfall into his photographer's jacket. By evening, the lemons would find themselves preserved in salt and the oranges swimming in sugar syrup.

I brought up another subject I thought likely to loosen the lips of our reticent guide. "Farmers were working in the neighboring cornfield when we arrived," I commented. "*Ana n'hibb kesksoo baddaz* [I love cornmeal couscous]."

Doukkala maize wasn't the variety we dipped in melted butter at Fourth of July cookouts in the United States, but one employed primarily as animal feed, although many local cooks also processed it into coarsely ground meal for making couscous.

Hassan's face lit up for only a second. "*Baddaz, numéro wahed* [number one]!" he said without elaborating.

We reentered the villa. Hassan showed us into the master bathroom with its oversized enameled fixtures, including a tub large enough to accommodate a Sumo wrestler.

"You don't find such quality anymore," he touted, sounding more like a real estate agent than a young man from the countryside.

We moved to the spacious *salle à manger*, where visiting *colons*, colonists, eager to recharge their batteries after a strenuous hunt in the surrounding hills, converged for elaborate repasts. In my imagination, I could hear the din of conversation and laughter beneath the room's twelve-foot ceiling, as wine flowed from bottles of robust Vieux Papes and chilled Gris de Boulaouane into cut-crystal glasses. By mid-afternoon, boisterous and somewhat tipsy bon vivants would spill down the veranda's steps onto the back lawn for interminable rounds of boules.

* * *

I'd been a spectator at many a game at the home of a childhood friend. For all I knew, Maria's father, an avid outdoorsman, may have been a Mehioula regular. A stonemason by trade who'd immigrated to North Africa from his native Portugal, he regularly augmented the family diet with squab, quail, pheasant, and wild boar. Mehioula would have offered the perfect base for men like him, devotees of *la chasse*, the hunt.

On Mondays, for him and other *pieds-noirs* sportsmen, it was back to Casablanca's *ville nouvelle*, the European domain of tree-lined boulevards and boutiques that also served as stomping grounds for my classmates and me. Well, not quite all of us. A loosely enforced convention confined what few Moroccan students were enrolled to *la ville indigène*, the indigenous town, whenever class was not in session. At the time, I never considered the morality of this ethnic segregation. It wasn't until I grew older that the unpleasant realization of French Morocco's mid-century apartheid began to weigh more heavily on my mind. How I wanted to believe that Mehioula reflected a less oppressive side of the French Protectorate, inasmuch as *pieds-noirs* farmers had nurtured the semi-arid land into a breadbasket of citrus and olive groves, wheat fields, and vineyards — an agricultural legacy that carried over well past independence in 1956 into the twenty-first century. But there was no getting around the fact that, even in a bucolic setting like Mehioula, everything in the former French Protectorate had revolved around the colonialist model, whereby France exploited a land that was not hers.

The nationalists' simmering resentment over foreign rule boiled over in the early 1950s. Every household in our peaceful Val Fleuri followed the disturbing accounts of assassinations, gun battles, and train derailments as the rebellion spread. I remember my mother giving me news of a bomb attack that killed eighteen people at the Marché Central on Christmas Eve, 1953. As a result, our shopping trips to the vibrant market became a lot less frequent. *Les évènements*, the events, as the French called them, were made real to me the following year on Bastille Day, when a bomb exploded in the Mers-Sultan district, less than a mile from our home. My parents, Philippe, and I huddled in terror, wondering if the wail of sirens would ever end.

All of the bad news inspired many *colons* to relocate to less volatile shores. In spite of the violence, my father chose to keep his family in Morocco. The new independent government must have felt less threatening to Daddy than to his peers. He was, after all, a British citizen, not a Frenchman. This distinction set him apart and kept him, and us, from the full ire of the nationalists. In any case, only a paltry clutch of girls awaited me at Madame Grandjean's classroom when I returned to the lycée. Luckily, my two closest friends were among them.

* * *

Mehioula's *gardien* brought us back to where our tour had begun. "You must come again," he said. His invitation may have had more to do with the twenty-dirham note that Owen discreetly slid into his palm than personal chemistry. Nevertheless, we didn't hesitate to take him up on his offer and returned whenever we had the chance.

When I reached the uppermost garden landing, a sudden gust of wind sweeping down the narrow gorge prompted me to wheel around for one last look at the derelict *auberge*. How remarkable that the lonely structure had aroused so many memories of my youth. On my return to Dar Zitoun that evening, I illuminated every lamp in the salon and prevailed upon Owen to insert a French cassette into my father's tape player. Edith Piaf and Charles Aznavour never sounded so good.

Preserved Lemons

12 small, unblemished lemons (Meyer or Eureka)
Sea salt
1 quart glass canning jar with gasket and lid

Wash and dry the lemons. Cut a dime-size slice from both poles of one of them. Set on end and cut ¾ of the way through. Rotate the lemon 90 degrees, turn upside down, and make a second cut (at a right angle to the first), ¾ of the way through. Pack both slits with as much salt as they will hold. Transfer the lemon to the jar. Proceed in this manner with remaining lemons, filling the jar as much as possible. Seal and set aside on the kitchen counter overnight.

Over the next few days, as the rinds begin to soften, force additional salted lemons into the jar until it is tightly packed. The goal is to keep the lemons submerged in their own juice. Seal the jar. Set aside on a kitchen counter for 4 to 6 weeks, until rinds are tender and the brine attains a syrupy consistency. Refrigerate to slow discoloration of the preserved lemons.

Mémé's Oranges Confites
Candied Oranges

2 large thick-skinned oranges
2 cups granulated sugar
⅓ cup water
2 tablespoons lemon juice

Using a microplane or fine grater, remove all zest from the oranges. Cut each orange into eight sections and slice away most of the pulp. Soak wedges in cold water for two hours. Drain and rinse. In a non-reactive pan over low heat, simmer wedges for 10 minutes in enough fresh water to cover. Drain. Repeat this step with more fresh water. Drain and set aside.

To the same pan over low heat, add sugar, water, and lemon juice. Simmer until sugar dissolves. Add orange wedges. Continue simmering over low heat until most of the liquid evaporates (about 1 hour). Let cool. Transfer wedges and syrup to an airtight container. Serve candied oranges on their own, with crêpes and sundaes, or in recipes like *Pudding de Petits Pains au Chocolat à l'Orange Confite* (see page 57).

27

The Loyal Bird

Gabby was one of the girls at the lycée who'd left Morocco after independence, emigrating with her parents to Montréal. Recently, she came across my website and emailed news of her upcoming visit to Morocco, the first since her departure from the country over forty years earlier. I volunteered to meet her at the airport.

I suspected that the man emerging from customs with a pair of binoculars around his neck was Gabby's husband. She'd already filled me in on Jeannot's passion for birdwatching. His relatively short stature and balding pate were qualities that didn't square with the Romeo I envisioned for the Lycée de Jeunes Filles' girl-most-likely-to-win-a-beauty-contest, who was turning heads even at the tender age of fourteen. But there she was, rolling a suitcase behind him.

I would have recognized her anywhere with her still striking figure. Her kohl-rimmed eyes and hennaed bangs were telltale vestiges of a *pied-noir* upbringing. She and I hugged each other for the longest time before regressing into giggling teenagers. How easily we slipped into the adolescent banter we once used to exchange schoolyard gossip. Owen and Jeannot stood by patiently until the initial torrent of reminiscences ran its course.

We were soon in Azemmour. Gabby was clearly taken with the town. When we were girls, she and I often visited the Casablanca medina on shopping excursions, but we never would have considered spending the night there, or for that matter, in the native quarter of any Moroccan city. Times had changed.

While Bouchaïb prepared dinner, I gave Gabby and Jeannot a tour of Dar Zitoun. They oohed and aahed at its sheer scale, decorative ceilings, massive doors, and ubiquitous zillij mosaics. I wasn't trying to dazzle them. The fact that the *riad* so impressed all who entered reflected on my father's vision and perseverance, not mine. I was simply one of the lucky beneficiaries to whom the house had passed (or rather, was in the process of passing). Nevertheless, I couldn't deny that the place was working its magic, and with each year, was becoming more a part of me. I suspected my father anticipated as much when he penned the line in his testament: *It is my wish that Dar Zitoun remain in the family.*

I let the Canadians reconnoiter while I went downstairs to help Bouchaïb. Jeannot later confessed to heading straight for the bookcase in the library. He appeared at the dinner table with his nose in a thin paperback titled: *Doukkala, fief de la fauconnerie au Maroc* (*Doukkala, capital of Moroccan falconry*).

"Katy, do you realize you live just a few miles from the heart of Moroccan falconry?" he asked. I did not.

"It says in this book that members of the Kwacem tribe are the only commoners in the kingdom legally authorized to capture and train falcons."

I couldn't imagine that Jeannot, a retired academic and self-proclaimed "birder," would approve of a sport, regardless of its ancient provenance, that condoned the entrapment and confinement of wild birds. For the Kwacem, whose forebears had hunted with falcons for over five hundred years, he was willing to make an exception. He peppered the dinner conversation with "raptors this" and "raptors that." The term wasn't new to me, although I associated it with the carnivorous velociraptors in the movie *Jurassic Park*. Jeannot straightened me out. True, the designation *did* apply informally to the terrifying prehistoric creatures, but also, in avian nomenclature, to the diurnal birds of prey that included the family *Falconidae*.

Jeannot cut short the lesson to seek more practical information from Bouchaïb, namely, on how to arrange an introduction to the Kwacem. Bouchaïb suggested we seek the services of his friend Miloud, a local *grand taxi* driver who was as familiar with the Doukkala's back roads as he was with the medina's alleyways. Bouchaïb soon had him on the phone, and in the space of thirty seconds, driver and professor had agreed to a time and place to rendezvous.

Miloud arrived early the next morning behind the wheel of a vintage Mercedes with a black velvet hangtag imprinted with a Qur'anic verse swinging from the rear-view mirror. Gabby, Jeannot, Owen, and I rode in relative comfort for most of the way, until we hit a stretch of *piste* outside the village of Had Oulad Frej. Without warning, Miloud swerved off the dirt road and skidded to a stop. "*Vite, vite* [Quick, quick]!" he ordered.

We scrambled from the vehicle. Fifty meters off, two figures with their backs to us stood knee-deep in a field of sugar beets. We followed our driver's lead, bounded over rows of vegetation, and then stole along a furrow of bare earth to close on a man sporting a falconer's gauntlet on his left hand. He was looking skyward crying, "*Woooyie! Woooyie!*"

By following his line of sight, we spied a solitary bird of prey. The peregrine soared on a thermal high above us. Its behavior soon changed, however, when a teenage girl, the old man's assistant, released a pigeon from a basket at her feet. The apparent surge in the falcon's adrenalin paralleled my own. It abandoned its wind-driven meanderings, folded its wings, and stooped toward its quarry. One heart-pounding near miss followed by another only heightened the suspense. A successful intercept on the third attempt culminated in a breathtaking burst of blue-grey feathers.

Normally, witnessing a kill would have been outside my comfort zone. As a girl, I had no interest in attending the popular bullfights that took place regularly in Casablanca's Les Arènes, not even when renowned Spanish matadors, like Dominguín and El Cordobés, were in town. I could never have developed an appreciation for the brave toreros' "artistry, grace, and elegance," as aficionados so poetically described the bullfighters' professional skills. That first exposure to falconry was somewhat different, however, because we'd come upon the training session by chance, and because everything had happened so quickly. Perhaps my fascination with the noble falcon trumped remorse for the demise of the lowly squab, the oft-featured ingredient in *bestila*, the crowning dish of Moroccan cuisine. What a revelation that falcons, too, were pigeon connoisseurs.

As to Jeannot's reaction, he was over the moon. "*Tu as vu ça* [Did you see that]?" he exclaimed. "*Incroyable, tout à fait in-croy-able* [Incredible, simply incredible]!"

He virtually flew over the crowns of foliage to get to the grisly scene: with the raptor furiously tearing feathers from around the wound in its lifeless prey. I expected the falcon to eat its fill. But the old man wouldn't allow his hunter to dine *sur place*. Squab, it turned out, was a take-away order. The falconer would later strip every ounce of flesh from its scrawny carcass, chop it up, and serve it à la tartare in measured amounts to his peregrines over the course of the day.

With a muted cluck of his tongue, the old man sweet-talked the raptor onto his leather gauntlet for hooding and tethering. With that accomplished, Miloud got around to formal introductions. "*Marhaba* [Welcome]," greeted the falconer, Abdallah, who, according to background provided by Miloud, was a descendant of Sidi Ali Bel Kassem, a tenth century saint from Marrakech.

"*Yallah fee dar* [Let's go home]," he said by way of invitation. We fell in behind him and his majestic bird, falconer and falcon cutting quite the exotic silhouette against the horizon.

Abdallah took us through a breach in the hedge of prickly pear cactus that encircled his modest homestead. Leaven-scented smoke from a domed, mud oven swirled around the front door. The high-ceilinged living room we stepped into was sparsely appointed. Aside from the perfunctory divans, the only other piece of furniture was a rustic cupboard holding a teapot, a platoon of decorative glasses, and several souvenirs of world travel, including a tin box embossed with the Eiffel Tower and a miniature of the Grand Mosque of Mecca, the latter, good evidence of our host holding the honorific title of Hadj. A stack of folded blankets in the corner of the room betrayed its secondary purpose — as sleeping quarters.

Abdallah coaxed his hooded falcon onto a perch and requested that we take our seats on the divans. Jeannot positioned himself immediately to the right of the stoic bird to better examine its talons, splayed out on the surface of a wooden block. Good thing the peregrine was hooded — unable to be tantalized by the brood of chicks that scuttled underfoot.

"Rabia!" called our host.

The girl who had assisted him in the field, his granddaughter, appeared at our table with a tea service that included a generous bouquet of fresh mint, a symbol of hospitality in North Africa. Abdallah handed a sprig to me.

"No other is as fragrant as the one we grow here in the Doukkala," he bragged.

He stuffed the pot with the entire bunch, which he chased with chunks of sugar loaf. While it steeped, a handsome, middle-aged woman with blue-black tattoos running vertically down the middle of her forehead and chin arrived with several warm anise-scented loaves of *hobz* and a small covered crock. There was no need for Abdallah's wife Meryem to disclose its contents.

"*Smen!*" I exclaimed, clapping my hands, even before she had a chance to lift the lid. The unique aroma identified the substance within.

Odiferous aged butter, more pungent than Gorgonzola, should be illegal — it is that good. Berber lore tells of a new father who buries an amphora of *smen* on the day of his daughter's birth and unearths the sublimely ripened substance for her wedding feast. I often use the condiment in my own cooking to enhance the flavor of couscous or *harira*. But the idea of serving it simply with warm bread had never crossed my mind. Not one milligram of Meryem's homemade delicacy went to waste.

"I hope I'll be able to find some of this in Montréal," said Gabby. Of that I had no doubt. Moroccan expatriates numbered in the tens of thousands in her adopted land.

"It's easy to make at home," I assured her. "I'll show you how. All you need is freshly churned butter, a little salt, and an infusion of oregano." I acquired my recipe from Mina, the caterer whose mother went through culinary training at Dar Zitoun.

While we sipped tea and gorged ourselves on bread and *smen*, Abdallah held forth on the historic highlights of Moroccan falconry: "The Romans hunted here with falcons. We know this because of the coins discovered at the ruins of Volubilis [an ancient Roman outpost between Meknès and Fez]. They're stamped with images of the birds . . . Sultan Moulay Ismael, a contemporary of Louis XIV, appointed an official falconer to his team of court advisors . . ."

To which Miloud added: "For Moulay Ismael, the falcon symbolized nobility, strength, and loyalty."

His strategically interjected comments made me suspect we weren't the first outsiders the cabbie-turned-falconry-expert had conveyed to the farm. He digressed with other details from Abdallah's curriculum vitae — how the Hadj and his falcons had headlined royal hunts organized by King Hassan II, and how, most recently, he'd been featured on Spanish and Japanese television. We were in the company of celebrity.

Our education entered a loftier realm when the Kwacem elder favored us with a recitation from Sura V, Aya 4 of the Qur'an, which Miloud translated for our benefit: " . . . good things are allowed to you, what you have taught the beasts and birds of prey, training them to hunt — you teach them of what Allah has taught you — so eat of that which they catch for you and mention the name of Allah over it . . . " In other words, our host was doubly blessed — in being able to supplement his modest farm income through an avocation that was sanctioned by God.

Jeannot next took the floor. I should have expected the retired educator to become more proactive in the falconry seminar. To that end he produced the book from my father's library and opened it to a tabbed page.

"I know you'll find this as enlightening as I did: 'The Alouite dynasty took great interest in it [falconry] . . . Sidi Mohamed Ben Abdellah built a hospital for wounded falcons . . . Once again we find this great interest in the Sultans Moulay El Hassan, Moulay Abdellaziz, Moulay Abdelhafid . . . through letters addressed to Sidi Boubker Ben Mustapha El Kasmi . . . ' "

The swarm of royal names had the predictably soporific effect on the rest of us.

* * *

My eyes glazed over and my mind began to wander — to my first, and long past, encounter with peregrines. It took place far from the Doukkala. Many years before, Owen and I honeymooned at the Grand Hotel du Sud in the Saharan oasis of Zagora. On the outskirts of town, a sign done in naïve style depicted a Tuareg (one of the legendary Blue Men of Morocco) and a camel. *Tombouctou, 52 jours* [Timbuctoo, 52 days], read its caption. An arrow pointed eastward.

The hotel's desk clerk appeared nervous on our arrival. On the far side of the lobby, an aristocratic Middle Easterner in white *gallabiya* and red-and-white *kaffieh*, dress typical of the Arabian Peninsula, was issuing orders to members of the hotel's staff as well as his own retinue of gauntleted attendants, each one in charge of a hooded peregrine. A hotel maid stood by with mop and pail in case a raptor answered the call of nature on the polished marble floor. No one dared suggest the hunting party wait outside. With a nod from the Arabian "prince," the entourage quit the opulent hall in a flurry of flapping wings.

* * *

Abdallah's booming voice cut short my daydream. "My father was a falconer, as was his father, and his father's father. It is in our blood. I think it is because these birds possess traits that are almost human — they mate for life, protect their young, and watch over aging parents. That is why we call the falcon *tahar el hor* [the loyal bird]," he explained. "And, most important of all, they respond only to men who are pure of heart." At that very moment, the falcon spread its wings, as if to emphasize the point.

"My father taught me how to communicate with these birds, and I am passing that knowledge on to my granddaughter," he told us. "This girl, she has a gift. She's more skilled than her brothers." Rabia lowered her gaze.

Except for Abdallah's praise, her prowess in the male-dominated sport would go unrecognized. Because of gender, the possibility of demonstrating her skill at the annual tribal festival was unlikely. Her grandfather put his hand on Rabia's shoulder. "Maybe next year they will accept her, *Insh'Allah*."

He gained stature in my eyes by weighing in on the side of his granddaughter, and by extension, on the side of feminism in a region so steeped in tradition. Women were making progress in Morocco, though the gains were more clear-cut in urban areas. Royal decree recently mandated ten percent of the seats in parliament be apportioned to women, and only the week before, local papers carried a story of nineteen women who matriculated into a government school dedicated to the training of *caïds*. These breakthroughs augured well for equal opportunity. Had Rabia lived in a less progressive Muslim country, her dream of becoming a falconer would have remained just that.

"Let's show them what you can do," encouraged Abdallah, pitching a gauntlet his granddaughter's way.

Rabia left us to retrieve a young peregrine from the outdoor aviary. We joined her and her trainee a safe distance from the farmhouse, where the raptor was less likely to be distracted. The girl loosed the short leather straps attached to the falcon's legs and released it into the wind. The furious action of its stiff-feathered wings cracked the air as it erupted from her wrist to climb aggressively into the sky. "*Woooyie! Hech! Ha! Hech!*" she cried, swinging an inanimate lure. For a second time that day, the speed and precipitousness of the raptor's descent almost stopped my heart. Surely, breaking a fall so abruptly violated a principle of physics.

"*T'barka'llalek* [Well done]!" congratulated Rabia's grandfather. He then turned to me.

"Sometimes I feel as close to these birds as I do to my own children," he admitted. "I never know if a falcon will return. It can fly away if it chooses, but it always comes home."

I wouldn't soon forget my day with the Kwacem. Nor would Jeannot. For my newfound Canadian friend, I imagined there'd be no scarcity of material to serve up at the next meeting of Montréal bird watchers.

Smen (Aged Butter)

Makes 1 pound

1 pound unsalted butter, at room temperature
½ cup water
1 tablespoon coarse salt
¼ cup dried oregano leaves

Place butter in a medium bowl. Set aside.

In a small saucepan, boil water, salt, and oregano until water reduces by half, 20 to 25 minutes. Strain this "oregano tea" through a fine-mesh sieve directly over the butter. Discard leaves. Blend tea thoroughly into the butter with a wooden spoon. Let cool. Transfer to another strainer. The next day, pat mixture with paper towels to absorb moisture.

Set aside at room temperature in a covered bowl for 2 days.

Spread mixture on a clean cutting board. Using paper towels, mop up any pockets of moisture. Spoon the mixture into a wide-mouth jar or clay pot. Seal. Store at room temperature until mixture acquires a pungent, Gorgonzola-like aroma, at least 2 to 3 weeks, and then refrigerate.

28

Of Dentists and Dromedaries

Our exhilarated foursome tripped back to Miloud's taxi and braced itself for the jarring run to the village. Once we rejoined the highway and could concentrate on something other than the road, I regaled Gabby and Jeannot with our soap opera of a probate.

"But how can it take this long?" asked my friend. "*Ce n'est pas possible. Quelqu'un veut vous créer des problèmes* [It's not possible. Someone is trying to create problems]."

Miloud was eavesdropping on our tête-à-tête. And, not being shy about offering a suggestion, he put in his oar. "Hasn't an *adoul* [a notary versed in Islamic law] explained to you the convention of *douze témoins* [twelve witnesses]?" he asked. For me, the intriguing term took the air out of the passenger compartment. I thrust my head between the seats to speak directly into our driver's ear.

"*Douze témoins?*" I repeated.

Miloud explained that the expression referred to an age-old method of establishing property rights in the absence of documents.

"Go on, Miloud," I pressed him.

"My father's father had no papers to prove ownership of the land his family had farmed for generations. Upon his death, a wealthy neighbor tried to wrest from the estate a field that had lain fallow for several years. Since my father was poor and couldn't afford the services of a lawyer to fend off the challenge, he hired an *adoul*. The public officer instructed him to assemble twelve witnesses — peers within the community who knew my grandfather and possessed enough knowledge of his affairs to give testimony on the matter of the disputed land." If the only document acceptable to the *conservateur* in El Jadida was my father's original testament, and if said testament had been carried away by the "great flood of Casablanca," then the *douze témoins* offered a commonsensical solution to our dilemma, a solution worthy of King Solomon, prophet Sulayman of the Qur'an.

"Must all the witnesses be men?" asked Gabby.

"Women can testify too, but you would need more of them because the Holy Qur'an states that one male witness is equal to two female witnesses," explained Miloud. He must have noticed Gabby's puzzled expression in his rear-view mirror and was quick to proffer what, to his mind, was a rational justification:

"Don't you see? Two women *are* needed. If one of them forgets what she is supposed to say, the other will be there to jog her memory."

Gabby bit her lip. Perhaps she was waiting for me to stand up for our sex. I had no intention of doing battle with Miloud over women's rights after his potentially game-changing counsel. The prospect of his *douze témoins* lifting me from my legal morass was too delicious to contemplate.

Miloud's bombshell raised an important question: Would I be able to muster twelve, cognizant Zemmouris who understood the connection between Monsieur Chandler, Dar Zitoun, and me? While I was making a mental list of candidates, I completely lost track of my geographic bearings. Being unfamiliar with the area didn't help. I assumed we would be going home via the same route we'd come earlier that morning — until our taxi became ensnarled in a traffic jam of horse and donkey carts — an unlikely event, if we were, as we should have been by that time, in the vicinity of El Jadida. Something was amiss.

"We're not in Kansas anymore, are we, Miloud?" I asked rhetorically.

"Kansas, madame?"

"Where are you taking us?" I reframed the question.

"*Settat,* madame. *C'est le* souk *aujourd'hui,*" he replied.

"Ah!"

Miloud had taken it upon himself to push on to the provincial capital. I couldn't argue with his reasoning: "Oulad Frej is so close to Settat," he explained, "I felt certain you wouldn't want your guests to miss its souk and camel auction." Technically speaking, he was referring to the auctioning of dromedaries, the one-humped members of the Camelid family that are native to North Africa and the Arabian Peninsula. If I'd realized the weekly souk in Settat coincided with our day-trip to Abdallah's farm, I would have suggested combining the attractions myself.

I was glad Bouchaïb hadn't got wind of our amended itinerary, or he would have badgered me for a kilo of camel meat. At the age of seven, I'd fallen in love with a snow-white bull calf in the oasis of Goulimine. No amount of pleading could convince my parents that the endearing creature would make an ideal pet. My infatuation grew even stronger after listening to my mother's story about a mounted battalion of indigo-robed Tuareg who swayed down Casablanca's Avenue d'Amade in a stirring parade to celebrate the end of World War II. Bouchaïb knew of my soft spot for the animals, the Settat butchers' stock-in-trade.

The auction ground lay on the far side of the souk. We had to circumvent a group of men in djellabah haggling over a hundred or so disheveled chickens, jammed ten-to-a-crate on a waiting *charette.* The hens' predicament rivaled that of an uncomfortable sextet of sheep whose insensitive owner forced them into a nose-to-nose "wheel" by interlocking their horns. Fowl and ruminants awaited transport to even less promising appointments. Amidst this uninviting atmosphere our driver chose to nosh.

"You go ahead; I'll catch up with you later," he reassured us before ducking under the awning of a tent café.

I marveled at his ability to keep appetite whetted despite the sensory stimuli arrayed in opposition, most notably the swirling bouquet of guano, made even less bearable by the incessant bleating and cackling of farm animals and the overall noise of electrically amplified barkers. To Cuban-French author, Anaïs Nin: "A souk is . . . a strange mix of din and odiferousness." And so it was that day.

Being at a country souk was a new experience for Gabby. When she was growing up, her mother had deliberately avoided the indigenous rural markets in favor of what she considered the more hygienic *marchés* of the big cities.

With Miloud savoring a smorgasbord of local fare, Owen took command of our leaderless squad. This made me apprehensive. And for good reason. Like a homing pigeon, he headed straight for the plein-air dental surgery. He was in luck. The rest of us were not. A white-knuckled *tbib asnan,* tooth doctor, had engaged a resentful crown with the beaks of his forceps. Neither the practitioner nor the tooth's exquisitely uncomfortable owner seemed to mind an audience. In a show of strength and callousness, the dentist half lifted his arched-back patient from the chair as Gabby, Jeannot, and I looked on in horror.

Snaggled, bloodstained trophies from patients past lay heaped on an iron stand behind the *tbib asnan*'s chair. They advertised his prowess to one and all. Owen zeroed in for a closer look at the macabre assemblage of ivory. Many teeth were incomplete, suggesting that root tips abandoned in unsuspecting mandibles and maxillas were likely to require the exodontist's ministrations on another occasion. Nevertheless, my husband was impressed by the bold confidence of the exodontist, a man who'd learned his trade through apprenticeship — at the side of a master extractor.

Owen had plenty of experience in the business himself from volunteer work he'd done at a free clinic. The fact that he still remembered most of his dental Arabic, even after all the intervening years, proved the adage coined by linguists: "Use a foreign phrase one hundred times; and it's yours."

"*Hul bezef* [Open wide]!" directed Owen, who couldn't resist getting involved.

The *tbib asnan* slid his grip to the end of the forcep's handle in order to gain greater mechanical advantage. Owen's body English paralleled the direction in which his Settat counterpart leaned into the task at hand. Mercifully for us, and for the patient, the battle was soon over. "*T'fil* [Spit]!"

The patient hocked up a repulsive red glob into a piece of cloth, laid a ten-dirham coin in the dentist's palm, and lumbered off, Quasimodo style, cradling the side of his face with his hand. I gave thanks for American dentistry, lidocaine, and nitrous oxide.

We moved on to the sector of the *souk* set aside for dromedaries. Turbaned, sober-faced attendees wandered haphazardly among the arrogant looking beasts destined for the auction block. A calf on wobbly legs suckled from its mother, whose nostrils twitched in response to tormenting flies. The animal the nomads called *Ata Allah* (Gift from God) regarded me with indifference through a tussock of thick lashes.

A camel behind Gabby startled her with a sudden loud bawl. I should have warned her that the animals make the frightening sound whenever they get to their feet, giving them the unwarranted reputation of being cantankerous.

A "ship of the desert's" ability to go for several days without food or water makes it ideally suited to the arid regions of North Africa, where it serves not only as the principal beast of burden, but also as a source of milk, leather, fur, and meat. For that reason, both breeders and prospective buyers have a number of qualities to consider before deciding to purchase an animal that is up for auction.

"What's that?" asked Gabby, crinkling her nose and pointing at a froth-covered, pink sack that protruded from the mouth of a couched dromedary, one set apart from its brethren. "That's the bull's soft palate," I said with authority. Some years before, in researching a human-interest story for a magazine, I accompanied a Moroccan veterinarian, a graduate of the University of Minnesota's College of Veterinary Medicine. The specialist in camel fertility was the first scientist in the world to successfully isolate luteinizing hormone, the substance that triggers ovulation.

"The male camel's soft palate inflates during the rutting season," he'd told us. To which Owen quipped, "I'm glad we humans don't share that adaptation. If we did, I never would have gotten my prom date off the front porch of her father's house."

I thought the perplexed scientist would have been accustomed to American humor after his years of study in St. Paul. But then, he probably hadn't come across anyone quite like my husband, who, armed with the arcane information on dromedary husbandry, would pose a menace to respectable dinner parties for a decade to come.

The severed head of a dromedary was on display outside a butcher's tent. The unfairness of it all! The proud animal had suffered too many cruel indignities during the course of its hard life to wind up en brochette, or minced, doomed to peer out at the world from the inside of a sausage casing. I suppose I would have felt differently had I been born a Tuareg.

Miloud reappeared with a weighty purchase wrapped in butcher's paper.

"Bouchaïb's order," he announced. "Two kilos of camel loin and a kilo of *chama dial j'mal* [fat from the hump]."

If ever I needed proof that Bouchaïb was cleverer by half than I, there it was. Maybe a little *chama dial j'mal* would be just the ticket to woo an irresolute witness to a meeting with our yet-to-be-hired *adoul*.

29

Twelve Witnesses

A travel piece on adventure tourism had seduced Gabby into contracting with a Moroccan outfitter to provide the appropriate four-wheel drive vehicle, equipment, and supplies for her and Jeannot to traverse the High Atlas Mountains. Watching our friends depart from the car rental agency in El Jadida, I pictured the more perilous leg of their journey — on a one hundred kilometer *piste* that Owen and I had bounced along on many years before between El Ksiba and Imilchil, a mile-high Berber town renowned for its annual marriage festival. Our journey had claimed a muffler and spare tire, the latter ruined by an upthrusting boulder in the roadbed that perforated the underside of our relatively low-riding coupe. Neither mishap was likely to befall Gabby and Jeannot in their all-terrain Land Rover.

From Imilchil, they would follow another unpaved road that dogged the Todra River, until it spent itself in the Saharan oasis of Tineghir.

A week later, we met up with Jeannot and Gabby, bronzed and mellow, at Mohammed V airport. "I shouldn't have waited so long for this reunion," admitted my misty-eyed friend, as she let go of my arm to slip behind the barrier at passport control.

I wanted to believe that Dar Zitoun and Azemmour had helped her unwind from the demands of her hectic urban lifestyle. The *muezzin*'s evocative call to prayer, the sound of children at play, and the soothing white noise from our fountain all had played their part. If her job hadn't compelled her to return to Canada, I was sure she would have stayed another month.

As for me, I felt happier in our *riad* than I did anywhere else, even when faced with imbroglios at the *cour d'appel, tribunal,* and *conservation foncière.* That wasn't to say that the unresolved status of my father's estate hadn't worn me down. But when I closed the massive doors to the atrium, the *riad* became my cocoon, a quiet place in which to restore my mental equilibrium. A friend, a physicist by profession, framed "The Dar Zitoun Effect" in more scientific terms in our guest book: "It impedes the build-up of nervous system entropy." Whatever it was that happened to me within the confines of those stone walls would give me strength for the coming challenge — identifying twelve upstanding Zemmouris who would be willing to testify on my behalf.

My first order of business was to run Miloud's ingenious idea about the *douze témoins* past Bouchaïb. I did so after lunch the following day. After all these years, I looked upon him as a member of the family. Long gone was the humiliating separation of servant from master so typical of the colonial era. Yet at mealtimes, Bouchaïb still donned a butler's bearing to play his part in a make-believe *Upstairs, Downstairs* scenario. He bowed slightly with left hand tucked behind his back whenever he set a plate before me. Could it be that he imagined himself a maître d'hôtel and our scarred and wobbly dining surface the chef's table at the Ritz? "Bon appétit, madame." He couldn't bring himself to forego tableside formality even though he knew full well that twenty minutes later the two of us would be working side-by-side in the scullery.

"You didn't know about the *douze temoins*?" he asked. Being fond of Bouchaïb the way I was didn't blind me to his shortcomings. At times, he could be maddeningly uninsightful.

"How would *I* know about the *douze temoins*?"

"Well, you should have asked me about it," came his predictable reply.

"How could I ask about something I never knew existed?" I argued. I was getting nowhere, so I saved my breath. Bouchaïb seemed unfazed by our little tiff, if indeed he realized one had taken place. He was used to tuning me out as soon as I raised my voice.

"Let me see," he said. He slid a chair over to the kitchen table. With a paring knife, he whittled away at a blunt-nosed pencil before beginning the list of Zemmouris who could vouch for my father's ownership of Dar Zitoun. If the forthright citizens were also ones with whom I was acquainted, we had a match, and Bouchaïb could put a checkmark after their names. The first six came easily:

— Hadj Khalid, the owner of the granary
— Ahmed, the electrician
— Ouadoudi, the plumber
— Hisham, the barber
— Messaoud, the custodian at the Peugeot's parking lot
— Redouane, the shoeshine man on the square, the only Zemmouri other than the *samsar* to address me as Mademoiselle Chandler

More names would come to Bouchaïb in due course. I knew from previous campaigns that once he understood the mission, my battles became his.

On *that* day in the kitchen, he lacked his usual energy. Something about him had changed. He seemed wan. When had this developed? Had I been too absorbed in my own problems to notice his declining health? I swallowed hard as my next thought crystallized: He looked like a man living on borrowed time. I pulled a chair close to his to peruse the names he'd written down. His labored breathing made me feel ashamed for having been short with him. I hoped my impatience wasn't the cause of his suffering. Was diminished vigor behind his surrender of second-floor duties in favor of Leila, and his recent decision to fast during Ramadan, an attempt to get right with his god before it was too late? He carried on with the conversation as if nothing was amiss.

"You must give each witness a *fabor* for their time," he reminded me, unaware that my mind had left the station on an unrelated train of thought.

"Of course. Just tell me what is required," I quickly agreed.

"And, when we're finished, we must celebrate with my *bestila aux pigeons* and your *bestila à la glace*."

"Whatever you say, Bouchaïb."

If I hadn't been so concerned about his health, some harmless teasing would have been in order. I could have suggested we include a tagine of the specially delivered camel meat, about which Bouchaïb said nothing, thinking, no doubt, that Milloud had kept me in the dark about the transaction.

Bestila au Poulet (Sweet & Savory Chicken Pie)

Serves 8

This traditional and symbolic dish is served to newlyweds in the hope that their life together will be as sweet as a *bestila*. In this recipe, I substitute Greek phyllo dough for the *warka* I use when in Morocco.

2 tablespoons vegetable oil
1 onion, finely chopped
8 skinless, boneless chicken thighs
25 sprigs fresh parsley, minced
20 sprigs cilantro, minced
¼ teaspoon ground turmeric
8 threads Spanish saffron, crushed
½ cup water
1 teaspoon ground ginger
2¼ teaspoons ground cinnamon

3 eggs, lightly beaten
1 teaspoon salt
½ teaspoon freshly ground pepper
1¼ cups powdered sugar
½ cup (about 3 ounces) whole blanched almonds
2 sticks (8 ounces) butter, melted
12 sheets Greek phyllo dough
Cinnamon, for garnish
Powdered sugar, for garnish

In a large, enameled saucepan or a Dutch oven, heat oil over medium heat. Cook onion, stirring occasionally until golden, 6 to 8 minutes. Add chicken thighs, parsley, cilantro, turmeric, saffron, water, ginger, and 1¼ teaspoons of the cinnamon. Cover and cook until chicken is tender, 20 to 25 minutes. Using a slotted spoon, transfer chicken to a bowl and set aside to cool. Shred meat. Set aside. Leave sauce in pan and reduce by two-thirds. Add beaten eggs, salt, pepper, and ¾ cup of the powdered sugar. Stir continuously until eggs are set. Set aside.

Coarsely grind almonds in a blender or food processor. Transfer to a bowl and add remaining powdered sugar and remaining cinnamon. Set aside.

Unwrap phyllo on a damp cloth. Separate 12 sheets. Rewrap and refrigerate remaining phyllo for later use.

Stack sheets on a flat work surface. Using a sharp knife and a 12-inch-diameter pizza pan as a template, cut through stack to create rounds. Discard scraps.

Paint pizza pan with melted butter.

Layer 3 rounds of phyllo on pan, lightly brushing each with melted butter. Sprinkle the third round evenly with ½ of the ground almond mixture. Layer and butter 3 more rounds. Spread evenly with chicken/egg mixture, leaving 1½ inches of the perimeter uncovered. Layer and butter 3 more rounds. Sprinkle with remaining ground almond mixture. Layer and butter the last 3 leaves. Make sure the top round is generously buttered. Tuck phyllo perimeter under the *bestila* as you would a bed sheet. At this point, *bestila* can be baked or frozen.

Preheat oven to 400 degrees F. Bake *bestila* until golden brown, 20 to 25 minutes. Place a cake decorating template or a paper doily on the surface of the *bestila* and, using a fine-mesh sieve, sprinkle evenly with powdered sugar. Alternatively, dust the surface with powdered sugar and crosshatched lines of ground cinnamon to create diamond-shaped patterns over the crust. Serve hot.

Bestila à la Glace (Ice Cream Pastry)

Serves 6

In Azemmour, every tiny *bureau de tabac* sells ice cream bars. In this recipe I substitute lumpia wrappers for the *warka* I use when in Morocco.

Vegetable oil for frying
5 (7 or 8-inch) Filipino lumpia wrappers (see Note)
1 cup almonds
¼ cup powdered sugar
1 tablespoon ground cinnamon
3 chocolate-coated ice cream bars
1 pint fresh raspberries
1 pint fresh strawberries, cut in half
1 tablespoon granulated sugar
2 tablespoons Chambord raspberry liqueur

In a heavy frying pan, pour vegetable oil to a depth of ½ inch. Heat over medium heat until a piece of lumpia wrapper sizzles instantly. Carefully lay a wrapper into the hot oil. Cook until golden. Transfer to a baking sheet lined with a paper towel. Proceed in this manner for remaining wrappers, interspersing with paper towels. Set aside.

Coarsely chop almonds. Combine with powdered sugar and cinnamon. Set aside.

Cut ice-cream bars into bite-sized pieces and return to freezer.

In a bowl, sprinkle berries with sugar and liqueur. Mix gently and set aside.

Set a fried lumpia wrapper in the center of a serving platter and sprinkle with a portion of chopped almond mixture. Repeat process with a second and a third wrapper. Arrange ice cream pieces over third layer. Add last wrapper and top with macerated berries. Garnish with chopped almond mixture. Serve immediately.

Note: Lumpia wrappers are available in Asian and most Middle Eastern markets.

30

Palpitations

Seven years after my father's death, our third lawyer, Maître Labadi, finally received formal confirmation from the Casablanca tribunal regarding the lost testament. The terse communiqué, however, shed no light on the circumstances surrounding the disappearance — whether it was due to flooding (as the archivist claimed), negligence on the part of his staff, or willful suppression. The news on the El Jadida front wasn't much rosier. Though we'd won a judgment at the *cour d'appel*, the new *conservateur*, the fourth with whom we'd dealt, requested an attestation of the court's verdict, on which the ink was not yet dry — "in case the justices were having second thoughts about their decision."

In case the justices were having second thoughts? I'd never heard of anything so absurd! The appeals court had ruled. Its decision should have been final, unless overturned by a higher authority, like the *cour suprême*. What right had the registrar to second-guess the judiciary? Since challenging him on the matter was out of the question, there was nothing to do but allow the wheels of *in*justice to turn at their usual glacial pace while we proceeded with plan B, the *douze témoins*. For this we'd need the services of a local *adoul*.

"Bouchaïb, shall I touch base with the witnesses?" I asked.

"No, no," he insisted. "I'll take care of that later, after I go home for a short nap. For some reason, I'm feeling a little tired this afternoon. If you'd like something to do, you can have the miller grind some wheat. Remember prices are inflated with Ramadan now upon us."

"If you're feeling unwell, Bouchaïb, shouldn't we call the doctor?" I asked.

"I'll be fine after a cup of oregano tea and a little lie-down."

"Please, Bouchaïb; let me ring the *gendarmerie*," I suggested. "They'll send *le médecin de garde* [the doctor on duty] to your apartment."

"*Mais non, Katy!*" He had enough of my fussing. "*Laisse-moi me reposer* [Let me rest]!" He folded the list of names, stuffed it into the pocket of his *gandoora*, and set off in search of forty winks and a quorum — the remaining six witnesses.

The alley was almost dead. It would remain so during the daylight hours of Ramadan, the twenty-eight days of fasting that commemorated the first Qur'anic revelation to the Prophet Mohamed. The medina's diminished energy seemed in consonance with that of its fasting inhabitants, who were required to abstain from food and drink between sunrise and sunset in order to reaffirm their submission to Allah and to demonstrate the power of shared sacrifice.

The urban pulse quickened noticeably around twilight, before the point in time when one could "no longer differentiate a white thread from a black one." I found this a more poetic method of confirming the end of the daily fast than the blast of a Ramadan horn, the wail of a siren, or even the *muezzin*'s call to prayer.

Self-purification through fasting is one of the five pillars of Islam, the acts of faith considered mandatory by Sunni Muslims. However, compliance is less than universal, even with the media promoting the practice as a national obligation. Those who observe state edict and their religious duty stay up half the night in order to partake of specially prepared dishes, as food becomes an obsession. Indeed, the editor of a popular women's magazine once told me that Ramadan was the best time of the year to sell cookbooks.

If Bouchaïb's prediction about the cost of wheat held true, then I'd have to dig deeper into my pocket, just like all of the other shoppers stocking up for the holidays. But, why had I become so caught up in the urgency of it all? I wasn't famished. A hearty breakfast and a three-course lunch kept a steady level of glucose coursing through my arteries. Nevertheless, off I hurried to the local grain merchant's before the afternoon shadows grew longer. Chin on chest, the dealer was having a catnap on the stoop in front of his store. I tapped him on the shoulder. "A sidi [Sir]," I said.

"How much is the wheat?" The man pointed to a piece of slate with the number "1400" scrawled on it in chalk. I assumed that was in *rials* — making the staple seventy dirhams per decaliter. The price had doubled since the month before. I ordered two decaliters.

The merchant filled the cloth bags I'd brought along for the purpose, and after taking my payment, resumed his attitude of repose. Our transaction hadn't awakened the granary's off-duty director of vermin control. The cat, surprisingly sleek by Zemmouri standards, was curled up contentedly on a sack of grain.

Down the street at the miller's, housewives were less talkative than usual. Tending to domestic chores on an empty stomach was difficult enough, especially for women who ran errands on foot and lacked most of the modern conveniences that we in the West take for granted.

"You get used to it," Mrisha, an observant Muslim mother of six once explained. The puffiness under her eyes told a different story. Pre-pubescent children were exempt from the fast, as were pregnant women, the infirm, and anyone in transit. Of course, nothing prevented people from doing what they wished in private, but in public at least, fasting was the rule.

I surrendered my two decaliters of grain to the miller's flour-dusted assistant and issued instructions for processing: one to be coarsely ground into semolina for couscous and the other finely ground into flour. I was fortunate to have caught him while the milling machine was idle. With a flick of the switch, the air vibrated with such an intense, unmuffled rattle that it made communication possible only for lip-readers. I covered my ears and stepped outside as a torrent of semolina spewed from the grinder into a large metal basin.

If Leila's country cousin Najwa had been in town, I would have employed her to mill the durum wheat in the artisanal manner using her hand-powered *raha*, as she'd done for me the year before. I had neither the coordination nor the arm strength to match her operation of the heavy stone quern, but I did show middling aptitude when it came to preparing our own Dar Zitoun "house blend" of raw couscous granules, by "rolling" Najwa's semolina with tiny amounts of flour, salt, and water.

Predictably, the bakery next door to the miller's was doing box-office business selling Ramadan pastries — deep-fried coils of honey-drenched *shabakiyah*, sweet couscous with dried fruit, and a blend of toasted flour, sugar, and ground sesame seeds called *selloh*. With these confections stashed away in their *couffins*, last-minute shoppers rushed home for the *ftoor*, the first meal after sundown, begun, according to custom, with *harira* (a hearty fava bean and lentil soup), dates, hard-boiled eggs, and mint tea.

I was in less of a hurry than they, until a breathless boy appeared at my side. "Madame Katy! *Bouchaïb m'rid* [Bouchaïb is sick]!" he sputtered. To reinforce the message he mimicked someone who was short of breath. I left my semolina and flour in the miller's

286

safekeeping and ordered the fleet-footed messenger to alert the *gendarmerie*, in case no one in Bouchaïb's household had thought to call.

Bouchaïb, *attends-moi* [wait for me], I pleaded silently as I hurried down the nearly empty street. We had competent physicians in Azemmour, but the town wasn't equipped to handle serious cases, if indeed that was the nature of Bouchaïb's problem. Medical evacuation to the *polyclinique* in El Jadida could take as much as an hour. Adrenalin got me to the Melhaj apartment in minutes.

"*Entre*, Katy," said a tremulous Leila.

I didn't bother to remove my shoes as I usually did whenever I entered her immaculate living quarters. Bouchaïb lay on a divan with his head propped up awkwardly, a heavy woolen blanket pulled up to his chin. Smoldering crystals of musk magnified the ominous atmosphere in the salon. I knelt by his side.

"Bouchaïb, *qu'est-ce qui se passe?*" I asked tenderly. I could have used Owen's help, but he was off somewhere in search of an igniter switch for the stove. I hadn't seen him since lunch.

Errand boy and physician soon joined us, the latter toting the signature black leather bag that was still associated with the healing profession in a country where house calls were not yet relics of a bygone era.

"Katy, I'm sorry," apologized Bouchaïb. "Usually the oregano tea helps me, but not today."

"Bouchaïb, don't talk anymore," I urged him. "Save your strength."

After a quick examination, the doctor took a vial of tiny white tablets from his bag. He showed me the label before addressing his patient. "*Nitroglycérine*," he announced. "It'll make you feel better." For good measure, he administered a *piqûre de calmant*, an injection of anti-anxiety medication. Almost every doctor's visit involved a shot of something. Indeed, patients expected it. I wished he could have given a second ampoule to Leila.

"Our new neighbor is a cardiologist. He's director of a private hospital in Casablanca," I informed *le médecin de garde*. "Should I apply for a consultation?"

"By all means," replied the Azemmour GP.

There was an opening at 7:00 am on Monday, two days hence. "We'll be there," I told the scheduler. I thought it best to keep Bouchaïb in the dark about the appointment until the last minute, as many in his generation grew up hearing horror stories about hospitals and avoided them like the plague. So I waited until Sunday evening to broach the subject with the man of the hour. Owen thought we ought to leave for the city immediately, just in case we encountered problems with the morning traffic.

"Bouchaïb, a cardiologist in Casablanca would like to take a look at you," I mentioned casually. "Your friend Miloud is standing by on the square to take us there."

"*Tout de suite* [Now]?" he asked, eyes widening.

"Come as you are, Bouchaïb. You won't need a thing. You'll be home by tomorrow evening."

Miloud delivered us to the Hôtel de la Corniche at the south end of Casablanca's beachfront boulevard. We asked for a room with two double beds — one for Owen and me and one for Bouchaïb. I should have requested a bed for myself, and another for Bouchaïb and Owen, since my husband was the one with apprehensions about our patient making a break for it in the middle of the night.

A married *nesrani* couple and a *gandoora*-clad Moroccan seeking joint berthing? I suspected the clerk on duty would find our request odd. He did indeed, and duly summoned the hotel manager, who made us settle for communicating rooms. I vetoed Owen's cockamamie scheme of tethering his ankle to that of our flight risk using twenty feet of plastic twine.

My husband's fretting was for naught. Bouchaïb, erstwhile stranger to the mosque and connoisseur of fine wine, awakened in time for pre-dawn prayers. His mood was sober.

"*Je te pardonne* [I forgive you]," he said to me (though I knew he meant to say "*pardonne-moi* [forgive me])" in a melodramatic confession for unspecified sins, followed by a request to use my cell phone. I assumed it would be to impart a "last word" to Leila.

"Sami? *Labass . . .*" I didn't catch much of the exchange, except that his devoted wife was not on the other end.

"My brother will pick us up in front of the hotel." Bouchaïb had a brother?

A prosperous-looking man behind the wheel of a Mercedes Benz arrived within the hour. He embraced his ailing sibling. I made a mental note to investigate the Melhaj family genealogy once our patient was back in the pink.

A burst of air, lightly perfumed with disinfectant, preceded the nurse steering an empty wheelchair our way. She collected her incoming patient and delivered him to the reception area.

"*Le docteur arrive,*" she assured us.

Dr. Hamdi descended a long flight of stairs taking two or three at a time. He was dressed head-to-toe in surgical greens. My first impression of him: an overachiever, a man of limitless energy, just the sort of physician I had hoped for. I thanked him for seeing us on short notice.

"Let's get him to his room," Dr. Hamdi ordered the nurse.

Owen and I followed them down the hall. Bouchaïb didn't utter a word. He appeared to be cowed by the elegance of the facility (a far cry from the government-run health center in Azemmour) and frightened by whatever lay ahead. I was unaware that the cardiologist had already scheduled two invasive diagnostic tests to immediately follow a physical exam.

Bouchaïb looked like a deer in headlights when his gurney emerged from the private room. Luckily, the Moroccan medical establishment didn't yet subscribe to the American convention of informed consent that required disclosure of all serious risks associated with a procedure before it was administered.

Owen asked to be Dr. Hamdi's shadow for the morning — inasmuch as he'd worked in operating rooms himself and understood the protocol. He never would have sought such a courtesy in the United States, but in Morocco, hospital rules were more relaxed and generally left to the physician's discretion.

"*Allons-y* [Let's go]!" replied Dr. Hamdi without hesitation.

My husband donned surgical scrubs and a protective lead apron before entering the catherization lab where Dr. Hamdi was preparing for Bouchaïb's angiogram and transesophageal echocardiogram. The doctor provided a simultaneous report of his findings for Owen's benefit. Bouchaïb's coronary arteries appeared normal, but two of his valves showed signs of significant malfunction. The cardiologist recommended medical treatment rather than surgery; the long-term prognosis, he said, was not encouraging.

I was so relieved that Bouchaïb survived the ordeal that I chose to focus on the relative health of his coronary arteries rather than dwell on the dire condition of his valves.

Because post-operative bleeding kept us at the clinic longer than expected, we thought it prudent to stay the night in Casablanca. Bouchaïb's brother offered to put us up at the apartment of his first of two concurrent wives.

As for sleeping arrangements, we had our choice from among eight divans that lined the salon of the palatial residence. Owen dutifully arose every two hours to conduct flashlight examinations of the dressing on Bouchaïb's groin. Shakespeare's "misery acquaints a man with strange bedfellows" was never so apt. Sami chauffeured us back to Azemmour in the morning.

Over the course of Bouchaïb's recovery, half of the medina's inhabitants must have drifted by the Melhaj apartment to hear his "war stories." The convalescent-turned-raconteur embroidered what Owen had related to him concerning their brief tenure in the operating room, about which the patient himself had little recollection. This didn't hamper his delivery of an animated first-hand account, complete with mimed gesticulations that kept well-wishers marveling at medical techniques few of them thought possible.

We asked Bouchaïb to have his son make a copy of the CD included in the discharge dossier from the clinic. We wanted to have it on hand in the United Sates should a second opinion (from an American cardiologist) become necessary. The disc contained only X-ray images from the angiogram and ultrasound. When the copy of the CD failed to materialize, Owen pressed Bouchaïb again. At first he was noncommittal. Then, in a vignette of low medical comprehension colliding with high technology, he took my husband aside to plead his case for withholding the disc in question, one Bouchaïb imagined to be more X-rated than X-ray: "Please, Monsieur Owen, don't make me do it. My son has never seen me naked."

31

The Headwaters

Thirteen centuries earlier, in the year 681 of the Christian era, one luminous morning in spring . . . standing on the promontory that overlooks the town of Azemmour at the mouth of the river Oum-er-Bia and the ocean, Hineb looks at the shimmering waters . . . A pathway bordered with aspens, birches and sycamores descends steeply from the heather-covered promontory. At eye level, it widens and breaks into two directions. One goes towards the village and the port then continues, paved, to the Jewish neighborhood. The other one goes almost immediately to the fields of barley and spelt. The earth has awakened, Oum-er-Bia has nourished it during its slumber, and the verdure has returned . . . To the east, where the view ends in the tender green of fields on the side of the slope, is the forest. If there is only the sea to stop it, who has ever known where it begins?
— from *La Mère du Printemps* (*Mother Spring*) by Driss Chraïbi

During his recovery, Bouchaïb had time to come up with names for the list of prospective witnesses. He often did so in the predawn hours, even before the *muezzin* had arisen to warm up his amplifier. Our convalescent got a kick out of unveiling a new *témoin* whenever I dropped by for a progress report on his health. Son Omar he dispatched like a personal marshal to summon provisional draftees to the side of his divan. All of them signed on.

Bouchaïb had already engaged an *adoul* from the medina to spearhead our legal stratagem. The septuagenarian gentleman he chose began taking testimony from our witnesses, one at a time. I understood the rationale for handling depositions in that manner, as well as the *adoul*'s practical reason for doing so. Three people couldn't possibly fit into the confines of his four-square-meter office, already over-furnished with a desk and two chairs.

In the space of a week, we were ready to do battle at the *conservation foncière*. Or so I thought. It took but a single sentence from the *conservateur* to defeat us:

"The invocation of *douze témoins* may not be employed by foreigners," he sneered at the *adoul*. "You should have known this." How dashing the hopes of a *nesrani* petitioner must have made the day for that awful man!

My suddenly hangdog paralegal became more milquetoast than macho when face-to-face with the arrogant bureaucrat, who, for good measure, leveled a verbal broadside at him in Arabic. After all, the *conservateur* was secure in his position of authority. No one of the *adoul*'s lowly rank dared cross him, and he knew it.

This wasn't the scenario I'd expected. I set sail that morning full of hope. But my ship foundered on the shoals of the *conservation foncière*. The *adoul* and I slinked from the wreckage, with nary a word passing between us on the drive back to Azemmour. All of our preparations for naught! For me the effect of the *conservateur*'s pronouncement was like getting word of a death in the family.

That evening on the terrace, an unknown force drew me up a ladder that led to the roof. There, under the Milky Way's canopy, with the dark presence of the river far below, I experienced an epiphany. In the grand scheme of things, was my taking formal possession of Dar Zitoun the be-all and end-all of my Zemmouri experience? My life would forever be linked to the Oum er-Rbia. Why make myself ill over the transfer of title? A change in modus operandi was in order. I'd had my fill of bureaucrats.

I adopted the guiding principle of a recovering addict, abandoned my pursuit of the *duplicata de titre foncier*, and let fate take over. I'd used that approach before. It worked well for a time, but then, little by little, I was pulled back into the morass. For the sake of my mental health, I had to insulate myself from lawyers, judges, *adouls*, and *conservateurs* — in short, from anyone involved in the toxic legal system that so dominated my thoughts. And so I granted power of attorney to Professor Mesoori, a retired Moroccan academic and old friend. He would deal with the issues related to probate while I tried to implement the hackneyed advice that well-meaning friends so freely offered — relish what was left of the Moroccan fall "one day at a time."

Achieving that nebulous goal would be my challenge. To that end, I began each day in front of my bedroom window with fifteen minutes of sun-drenched reflection, which invariably yielded to thoughts of Dar Zitoun's visionaries — Mohammed Ben Driss, for his inspiration in building the "house of the pasha," and the "superbly eccentric" Englishman (my father) who'd saved the *riad* from demolition two centuries later.

By the time the sun had warmed the medina sufficiently to coax the breeze ashore, I could hear water gently lapping at the promenade's embankment. The waves were unrelated to the power of the river, whose upstream dams robbed the waterway of its dynamism, save for the ebb and flow of the tides. Four times each day, during the periods oceanographers refer to as "slack water," the Oum er-Rbia achieved its most languorous state, becoming as still as a lake, more picturesque than functional.

In all the hours I'd spent daydreaming on the terrace, I'd never given much thought to the river's headwaters, until I came across El Jadida-born Driss Chraïbi's novel, *La Mère du Printemps* (Mother Spring). The prolific author posed a compelling question about the "green blood from the mountain": "If there is only the sea to stop it, who has ever known where it begins?" Tracing my finger along a wispy blue line on a map to find the answer wouldn't suffice.

With Bouchaïb much improved, thanks to the drug regimen prescribed by his cardiologist, I resolved to make a journey of discovery — to learn first-hand the source of the natural watercourse.

"*Un voyage d'exploration? Pour quoi faire* [What for]?" asked Bouchaïb dubiously. I didn't have an answer.

Our *gardien* had lived in Azemmour virtually his entire life. He swam in the Oum er-Rbia as a boy, spent thousands of hours angling for *ashabel*, and may have courted a nubile Leila along its banks. But he was never tempted to visit its source. The water flowed; that was enough for him. In fairness, he never had the luxury of getting involved in something that didn't affect him financially. His skeptical demeanor changed suddenly to one much sunnier. Something was afoot.

"Since you'll be passing through Khenifra, we could use a few liters of olive oil," he suggested. "The best olive oil comes from that region, you know. Now that I think of it, I could use a bottle or two myself." His ability to gain the advantage put a smile on my face. I'd opposed the purchase of camel meat out of principle. Olive oil was a different matter.

At the town of Boujad, in keeping with our number-one rule of Moroccan travel, Owen and I turned onto a partially paved road that promised a more exciting, though less comfortable, approach to Khenifra, a city bisected by the Oum er-Rbia. In the nineteenth century, it served as a haven for bandits who preyed on passing caravans. Later, it became known as the "city of beautiful women." The nickname intrigued me. Was it part of a marketing ploy cooked up by an enterprising staff member in the national tourist office?

I got my answer about ten kilometers outside of Khenifra when we came across farm workers engaged in the wind winnowing of wheat. Since we'd just traversed a particularly rough stretch of road, we welcomed an excuse to pull over. The stop also gave Owen the opportunity to photograph the age-old process for separating grain from chaff.

Encounters with foreigners in that remote place must have been a rare occurrence for what appeared to be an extended Berber family, whose members suspended their chores to gather round our car. Our arrival also attracted the attention of a young mother, who emerged from a stone farmhouse cradling an infant. Owen caught sight of her before I did. *"Ay Chihuahua!"* he gasped. My reaction was equally strong, though unexpressed.

"Was this the face that launch'd a thousand ships . . .?" Owen quoted Christopher Marlowe. In this case, a thousand sheaves, in the form of a bride's price, was more like it.

"She's Julia Roberts' doppelgänger!" my husband went on, "without make-up or haute couture." She was what a couple of virile Moroccan men would have characterized as a *meshoui*, a double entendre primarily used in reference to succulent whole roasted lamb. Emissaries from sultans past must have had standing orders to steer young women like her directly to the gates of the royal harem.

The chance meeting with the farmer's wife left Owen weak at the knees. He was still muttering to himself when we reached Khenifra, the capital of the Zayane Berbers, of which "Julia" and her family were members.

* * *

The Zayane constituted a pocket of resistance against French colonizers in the early twentieth century. In 1914, its tribesmen famously defeated over a thousand French cavalry in the battle of Elhri, popularly dubbed the "Moroccan Dien Bien Phu." Many rural Zayane were disciples of transhumance, migrating seasonally with their cattle between highlands and lowlands. Their motto reflects a spiritual attachment to ancestral lands: "The mountain is my being, the Oum er-Rbia is my belt, and the plain is my pasture."

Most of this background information I acquired as a girl of eight or nine, when my brother and I accompanied Daddy on a whirlwind tour to drum up support among Berber chieftains for the *Grand Gala de Marrakech* (later renamed *Festival National de Folklore*), a celebration of tribal music and dance that he co-founded in 1958 with French author Jean Mazel. My father also had a secondary objective for our expedition: to scout the Berber homelands for talented musicians, singers, and dancers — rising stars who'd be willing to enlist in his upcoming production. By the time school reopened in the fall, I had learned to identify many of the indigenous communities by their dress. I can still pick out the Riffians of the north (with more than thirty tribes), the Berrabers of the Middle Atlas (the Zayane among them), the Shleuh of the south, and the Harratin, Zenega, and Saharaoui of the Sahara. There are well over one hundred tribes in all.

* * *

Our first order of business in Khenifra was to fill Bouchaïb's request for olive oil — to guarantee a steady supply of his garlic vinaigrette. We happened upon an archaic granite *maâsra*, mill, turned by a blindfolded dromedary and a mule half its size. The odd couple plodded in circles, even without the motivating influence of a stick-wielding youth.

No other advertisement was needed for the cottage industry housed in a whitewashed processing plant. Inside, pungent oil oozed from the hemp filters of a press. The assertive aroma reflected the region's striking, red-ochre terroir.

I feared for the safety of the bottles of the lustrous, green-gold commodity arrayed on an uneven sill across from the processing equipment. Not so the miller. He was more concerned with making a sale. To increase the odds of that happening, he produced a loaf of warm *khobz* for dipping into a saucer of the robust and earthy oil. We wrapped a half-dozen bottles of it in towels and stashed them in our cooler. I wasn't about to let high temperatures in the trunk turn Bouchaïb's get-well elixir rancid.

Our errand completed, we checked into the hilltop Moha Zayani Hotel near the center of town. Around sunset, the maître d' showed us, his only customers that evening, to a table on the terrace. We were perusing the menu when a long-winged stork glided just meters over our heads. He was in the vanguard of a squadron that stretched off in a seemingly endless line toward distant hills, like airliners on final approach. A lifeless rodent, reptile, or amphibian, victuals for ravenous chicks back at the nest, dangled from each stout bill.

These storks migrated from the Alsace region of eastern France to winter in Morocco, where their ubiquitous roof and chimney-top nests were hard to miss. Khenifrans' tolerance of the messy aeries bespoke the widespread belief that the birds assured *baraka*, God's blessing. I wondered if our waiter subscribed to the traditional notion too, considering the extra effort it would take him to give the restaurant's deck a good swabbing at the end of his shift. The wildlife display, worthy of *National Geographic*, conspired with light, setting, and ringside seats, to create an ethereal mood that left me feeling temporarily disconnected from reality. We stayed well past dinner, until darkness rang down the curtain on the air show.

Morning clouds resembled tumbling curds of cauliflower. I crossed my fingers, hoping against rain, knowing that my selfish desire didn't have a chance against the invocations of a few million farmers praying for a downpour.

We opted to head directly into more mountainous territory on a road that skirted an isolated body of water called Aguelmane Azizga, Blue Lake. Not a soul was around to offer directions.

"How far have we gone?" asked Owen, after we'd been climbing steadily for half an hour. "Didn't the concierge at the Moha Zayani tell us we'd see a sign to Les Sources at twenty kilometers?"

Fat raindrops began to wallop the car as a forest of cedars closed in around us. Fortunately, before humidity fogged up our windshield, the elusive road sign we'd been searching for came into view, and one hundred meters further on, a troupe of Barbary apes. I'd seen macaque monkeys on a visit to the Rock of Gibraltar, but never encountered them in their native habitat. A female, with baby clinging to her side, approached our car for a handout. Like tourists the world over, we were only too eager to reinforce the bad habits of resident fauna. The segments of tangerine Owen tossed their way were of no interest to the stray dog that had joined in our reception. The scruffy and scarred mongrel appeared indifferent to the primates or, perhaps, had learned from experience to give them wide berth.

A "Les Sources" sign led us onto a logging trail layered with stones so sharp they would have shredded our tires had we driven over them much longer. After backtracking to the main road, we realized that a prankster had deliberately repositioned the sign to throw sightseers like us off-course. The discovery prompted Owen to recite Yogi Berra's famous admonition: "When you get to a fork in the road, take it," to which my husband added, "And look where that's gotten us."

The minor setback didn't diminish our spirits. After all, without the wrong turn we would have missed the simians. Within a kilometer, a second road sign validated our decision to follow the "other fork." Simply knowing we were on the right trail allowed me to lean back and enjoy the landscape, which at that point, was beginning to look familiar. I'd probably traveled the same road with my father all those years before.

An hour of hairpin turns from Aguelmane Azigza brought us to a tiny hydroelectric station. Judging from the speed with which the exuberant headwaters surged toward it, the power plant's turbine would have been put to the test that day. The facility was the first of a series of dams that would tame the careening water as it flowed downstream.

Below the station, on the edge of a rapids created by the outflow, a Zayane laundress was doing her washing. Her colorful unmentionables were draped over nearby bushes to dry. If there'd been an inner tube lying around, I'd have been tempted to flop into the stream for a whitewater ride that would have made headlines: *A Nesraniya Possessed*. "See you in Azemmour in three or four days," I'd have informed Owen. In fact, the realities of cold water, downstream pollution, and concrete *barrages* conspired against so fanciful an adventure.

Above the plant, the then vacant cabañas that lined both sides of the race saw occupancy rates soar when lowlanders sought respite at Les Sources during late-summer scorchers. The fact that the springs had also become a popular destination on the "Hippie Trail" of backpackers from the Continent forced Moroccan day-trippers to make for the mountains earlier than planned in order to stake out a good spot next to the turbulent channel.

"Many European students come here to relax and smoke hashish," declared our *guide officiel*.

The young man with a brass badge had attached himself to us as soon as we'd parked our car. We could have managed to find our way to the springs without his assistance; the trail was well marked. But guides like him were a means of improving the country's dismal unemployment statistics, and for officials higher in the food chain, to supplement their incomes through licensing such positions. Our guide claimed to be a part-time "student." I had to give him an "A" in English, which he spoke almost without accent. The faint odor of hashish emanating from his djellabah, however, made me suspect that second-hand smoke from visiting hippies had found its way into his lungs the night before.

"Thirty-five sweet water and five salt water springs join forces here," he began his monologue. I dipped my finger into one of them for a taste. It was indeed brackish.

Above the cabañas, a natural catchment basin collected water from a score of springs. I climbed to within meters of the most conspicuous contributor — a segmented waterfall some thirty feet high. With fine mist from its plunge pool settling on my face, it suddenly dawned on me that without the cascade and the springs, there would be no Oum er-Rbia, no Mehioula, no Azemmour, no Lalla Bahria, and no . . . I quickly suspended that line of thinking and picked my way down the slippery trail before emotions got the better of me.

Leeks with Bouchaib's Garlic Vinaigrette

Serves 4

12 baby leeks
2 teaspoons Dijon mustard
1½ teaspoons salt
½ teaspoon pepper
3 teaspoons granulated sugar
2 garlic cloves, finely minced
¾ cup extra virgin olive oil
2 tablespoons red wine vinegar
2 tablespoons water
⅓ cup minced parsley

Trim and discard green tops and roots from leeks. Rinse under running water, taking care to remove soil from between leaves. Place in a pan of boiling water and cook until tender. Drain. Transfer to a serving dish. Set aside.

In a bowl, whisk mustard, salt, pepper, and sugar. Add garlic, olive oil, vinegar and water, and continue whisking until mixture emulsifies. Stir in parsley. Spoon dressing over leeks and serve.

32

A Banquet for the Vanquished

"We must set a date for the *diffa* [banquet]," suggested Bouchaïb out of the blue.

"What *diffa?*" I asked.

"*Pour les douze témoins,*" he stated testily, at what he thought was my forgetfulness.

I assumed that news of the debacle at the *conservation foncière* had filtered down to the Zemmouri witnesses, who surely understood that celebratory dinners, by definition, were held when one had something to celebrate.

Bouchaïb made me see the error in my reasoning: The promised celebration was part of a verbal compact I'd made with the *douze temoins*. Disappointing my steadfast defenders in Azemmour simply wouldn't do. They'd done their part. It was time for me to do mine. A *diffa* for the vanquished. What a novel idea!

"I'll let Mina know about the *bestila* menu you've planned," I told Bouchaïb. "She can take charge in the kitchen." Our *cuisinier's* face sank.

"*Pas question, Katy, laisse-moi faire le nécessaire.*" I'd stepped on Bouchaïb's toes without meaning to. In his prime, he'd catered New Year's Eve celebrations for two hundred of my father's friends, as well as countless other dinner parties, to say nothing of the farewell galas for the members of my culinary tours. But that was before the advent of dodgy heart valves.

"Under two conditions," I bargained.

"*Oui, madame,*" he answered formally, with tongue in cheek.

"That you hire Mina as your *sous chef,* and that you take on a couple of local fellows to wait on tables."

"*D'accord,*" he agreed.

"And don't forget about Leila, Alia, Owen, and me. We'll do whatever we can to help," I added.

"But there are only the *douze invités.* That's nothing for me," he argued.

"Bouchaïb, you've always cautioned me to plan for uninvited guests," I parried.

"*Bon, d'accord* [Oh, all right]," he capitulated.

The phone rang just as we completed our negotiations. Professor Mesoori was on the line. We'd not spoken since I turned over the handling of my legal affairs to him through power of attorney. He was getting the runaround from Maître Labadi. The El Jadida lawyer had been quick off the mark when I first took him on two years before. Within a week of plunking down a hefty cash retainer, he steered the *acte de donation* through the court of appeals. However, the professor informed me that Maître Labadi had accomplished precious little since. Once again, our probate dossier had lapsed into gridlock. At least, when it came to sandbagging, the highly touted member of Transparency International didn't discriminate.

My mild-mannered friend hadn't called to complain, but simply to touch base. "I'm an old hand at playing the waiting game. Everything will work out. Don't worry," he reassured me. Delegating oversight of the title transfer to someone I trusted, someone who understood the system, allowed me to focus on the more pleasurable aspects of life at Dar

Zitoun, the gala for the witnesses being foremost among them. Bouchaïb and I fixed a date for the following weekend.

At dusk that Saturday, as Owen and I took our evening constitutional around the perimeter of the town square, a car that had just passed us screeched to a halt. The young man who leapt from the vehicle and ran in our direction was grinning from ear to ear.

"Katy! Owen! *Je tombe des nues* [I fall from the sky]!"

Luckily, I recognized Professor Mesoori's nephew Smaïl before we had an awkward moment. He'd spent a month with us in California to improve his English when he was in his teens. According to his uncle, he'd gone on to become a horticultural specialist who, unbeknownst to us, had recently taken over the position of managing director at a wholesale flower-exporting concern just north of Azemmour.

I would have spirited him away to Dar Zitoun to get caught up, but he and his impatient companions were bound for a party at the Royal Golf Resort. He did, however, accept a rain check — to the celebratory dinner for the *douze témoins*.

The next day, while Bouchaïb and I were sequestered in the kitchen, a courier from Smaïl's company surprised us with no fewer than ten dozen pink and white carnations, which I immediately set about arranging in and around the fountain. The apple hadn't fallen far from the tree. Daddy, impresario extraordinaire, used to buy up the local flower vendor's entire stock to prepare for such occasions at Dar Zitoun.

While I was tending to the flowers, Leila and Alia were eradicating cobwebs from every corner and fenestration, mopping zillij floors, and polishing brass trays to a blinding sheen. Owen's mission for the day was to replace the candles in the atrium's sixteen hanging lanterns. From time to time, both he and I popped into the kitchen to offer assistance.

I was happy to have so many things to keep my mind occupied. They helped mitigate the feeling of homesickness that always came over me a few days before my departure. We were, after all, only part-time residents of Dar Zitoun. Our return to California was fast approaching. I accompanied Bouchaïb for a quick trip to the épicerie and then turned my attention to boxing up books in the library, sprinkling mothballs between the woolen blankets in the *coffre*, and locking away any unopened bottles of wine in the bar.

The scent of the cinnamon and saffron in Bouchaïb's *bestila au poulet* stole into the atrium each time he opened the kitchen door to issue an order.

"Alia! Run to the *ferran* for *khobz*!"

"Leila! You need to wash the dessert plates!"

Bouchaïb still relished the opportunity to showcase his culinary virtuosity, but he had lost a step or two since his encounter with the cardiologist. His once balletic moves between sink, stove, and cutting board were more constrained. Part of me was relieved to see that he'd adjusted to his new condition, though I couldn't help being dismayed by the slowdown. Temporal and relatively trivial issues surrounding our upcoming departure and the *diffa* took a back seat to concerns over his health.

"*Bouchaïb, ça va* [are you okay?]"

"*Ça va shweeya* [A bit okay]," he answered in a mélange of French and darija.

The word "shweeya" bothered me.

"You want me to take over?" I asked.

"*Katy, ne te casse pas la tête* [quit worrying about me]," he said brusquely to get me off his case.

I wagged my finger in his face: "Bouchaïb, you must take care of yourself. You can never leave us, that's an order!"

"Me? Leave this place? Never!" he vowed. "Your father, when he was alive, he made me promise that I would always look after you and Dar Zitoun. *Mektoob*."

I retreated upstairs for a few quiet moments on the Glaoui's bed before our guests arrived. The breeze wafting through the shutters that afternoon carried with it the scent of autumn. Undulating reflections from the river played in hypnotic sequence on the room's white ceiling, while forty feet below, the tide pulled the Oum er-Rbia out to sea. I imagined myself stepping into a skiff and drifting with the river. Like a particle of Daddy's remains, I knew that I too would always return to the *riad*'s shore.

"*Clang, clang, clang!*" went the knocker on the front door. Instinctively I made a dash for the back stairway, forgetting that Bouchaïb and I had designated his daughter to serve as co-hostess for the evening. Alia had grown into a lithe young woman almost a head taller than her father, yet due to her sheltered upbringing, always at her mother's side, she was still as bashful as a little girl and unmindful of her striking good looks. The hem of her kaftan swept against the tiles of the foyer as she approached the door. The heavy boards and battens of the time-worn portal all but prevented her demure query from reaching the ears of the *témoins* waiting outside.

"*Shkoon* [Who is it]?"

Epilogue

Bouchaïb Melhaj, loyal employee and friend of forty years, passed away in the fourteenth year of probate. He is buried in the cemetery below the shrine to Moulay Bouchaïb, patron saint of Azemmour.

In the sixteenth year of probate, the *conservateur* in El Jadida transferred (into my brother's name and mine) the title to Daddy's *riad*.

Dar Zitoun currently awaits the *samsar*'s clients and the next generation of *cuisinières*.

Glossary

A:

Adoul: A notary versed in Islamic law

Aïd el Kebir: "Great Feast" to commemorate the sacrifice of Ibrahim (Abraham)

Al hamdullilah: Allah be praised

Al Jum'ah: Friday, the day of communal prayer

Allah eeshoof: God watches

Allah-u'Akbar: God is great

Ana: Pronoun, "I"

Argan oil: Highly prized oil extracted from the drupes of the *Argania spinosa*, a thorny bush endemic to southern Morocco

Arrondissement: Urban subdivision

Ashabel: Species of shad

Ah williwilli: Expression of helplessness

B:

Barabool: Satellite dish

Baraka: God's blessing, good fortune

Baboosh: Backless leather or velvet slippers; also, small snails

Baghrir: Semolina pancakes commonly served for breakfast

Beidaouia (Casablancaise): Woman from Dar Beida (Casablanca)

Beldi: From the *bled*, the countryside

Besh hal: How much?

Bestila: Flaky Moroccan pastry filled with a sweetened mixture of shredded chicken and flavored with saffron and fresh herbs

Bibi beldi: Free-range turkey

Bismillah: In God's name

B'lati: Wait (verb)

Blesh: It's not necessary

Brochette: Kabob

Boulangerie: Bakery

C:

Canoon: Small charcoal brazier

Caïd: Mayor

Calèche: Horse drawn cart

Carossa: Handcart

Chabakouni: From the French "*ça va cogner* [It is going to hit]" — a term for the paramilitary police

Charette: Donkey (or horse) cart

Collaborateur: A Moroccan who collaborated with the French authorities during the *Protectorat*

Commissaire de Police: Police superintendent

Conservateur: Registrar of Deeds

Conservation Foncière: Office of the Registrar of Deeds

Couffin: Straw basket

Couscous: Durum wheat staple of the Moroccan diet, also the dish in which it is the principal ingredient

Couscous *baddaz*: Cornmeal couscous, a specialty of the Doukkala

Cornes de Gazelle: A crescent shaped pastry filled with almond paste

Cuisinier: Cook (m)

:

Dada: A freelance woman cook, often descended from sub-Saharan slaves

Darija: Dialectical Moroccan Arabic

Dar Zitoun: House of the Olive [Tree]

Derbouka: Clay goblet drum

Diffa: Feast, banquet

Dirham: Unit of Moroccan currency

Djej: Chicken

Djellabah: Long, hooded robe worn by men and women

Doukkala: Fertile plain south of Casablanca

ع:

Eau de Javel: Bleach

Eeyeh: Yes

Epicerie: grocery store

Epicière: Grocer (f)

F:

Fabor: Free, a gift

Ferran: Public oven

Fkih: Herbalist, practitioner of native medicine

Fonctionnaire: Government functionary

Fundook: Hotel

G:

Gandoora: Sleeveless, ankle length garment

Gardien: Watchman

Goûter: Afternoon snack

Greffier: Clerk of the court

Grand taxi: "Big taxi" used to ferry passengers from town to town

G'saa: Large, round, shallow earthenware platter

H:

Hammam: Communal bath

Harira: Lamb and bean soup traditionally eaten to break the fast during the month of Ramadan

Harissa: North African hot sauce

Hayiti: Wainscoting used to decorate the sides of a tent

Henna: Powdered leaves from the *Lawsonia inermis*, made into a paste to tint hair and create temporary tattoos

H'shooma: Shameful

I:

Il'alleka: See you soon

Insh'Allah: If God wills

J:

Jinn (*jnoon*, plural): Mischievous spirit(s) created by Allah from fire

K:

Kasbah (medina): The older, native quarter of a North African city

Kefta: Ground meat

Keskes: Couscous pot or *couscoussier*

Khobz: Round loaf of bread

Khamsa (*Khmissa*, plural): Five fingered symbol representing the hand of Fatima, a talisman meant to ward away the evil eye

Kool: Eat

Koolshee: Everything

Kreeb: Someone close to you

Kwacem: Tribe of falconers

L:

Lah: No

Lalla: Arabic equivalent of "Madame"

Luisa: Lemon verbena (*Aloysia citrodora*), commonly used to make an infusion

M:

Mabool: Crazy

Makaeen mooshkeel: No problem

Marabout: A religious teacher or holy man. Also the tomb of a venerated saint

Marhaba: Welcome

Mashrabiya: Turned-wood partition

Medina (kasbah): The older, native quarter of a North African city

Mehraz: Mortar and pestle

Mektoob: "It is written", fate

Mellah: Jewish quarter

Meskeen (*meskeena*): Poor thing

Mezzian: Good

Minaret: A slender tower from which the *muezzin* calls the faithful to prayer

Mrouziya: Tagine of lamb in honey sauce

Muezzin: Man who calls the faithful to prayer

Municipalité: Town hall

N:

Nesrani (*nesraniya*): Foreigner

Neqqasha: Henna artist

O:

Oum er-Rbia: "Mother of Spring", one of Morocco's principal rivers

P:

Petit taxi: A "small taxi" that ferries passengers within city limits

Pied noir: "Black foot", anyone of European descent who was born in North Africa

Piste: Unpaved road

Plombier: Plumber

Procédure: Procedure, legal process

Procuration: Power of attorney

Protectorat: The historical period, from 1912-1956, when the French ruled Morocco

Q:

Q'dra: Aluminum soup pot

Qaddid: Salted, sun dried lamb preserved in lamb fat

Qur'an: Islam's holy book, revealed by Allah, through Gabriel, to the Prophet

R:

Ras el hanoot: "Top-of-the-shop," an herbalist's finest spice blend

Riad: Traditional Moorish house with an interior courtyard with central fountain

Rial: The currency of Morocco between 1882 and 1921

S:

Safee: Enough

Saïd (*Saïda*): Mr. (Mrs.)

Salah: Prayer

Salaam alaikum: "Peace be with you," a classical Arabic greeting

Samsar: Real estate agent

Sarwal: Pantaloons, especially those worn by women under their djellabah

Sfenj: Doughnuts

Smen: Preserved butter, a condiment

Shkoon: Who is it?

Shokran: Thank you

Shoof: Look (imperative)

Shweeya: Slowly, a little bit

Sidi: Sir

Souk: Open air market

T:

Tagine: Glazed, earthenware, cooking implement topped with conical lid. Also refers to the stews cooked in such vessels.

Tangia: A Marrakech specialty also called "bachelor's stew"

T'faya: Sweet mixture of caramelized onions, cinnamon, and sugar

Téléboutique: A boutique where one can make long distance calls

Témoin: Witness

V:

Ville nouvelle: "New town" (as opposed to the medina or kasbah)

W:

Wakha: OK

Walakeen: But

Warka: Rounds of paper-thin pastry dough similar to Greek phyllo

Y:

Yallah: Let's go!

Z:

Zabibah: A callus that results from a Muslim repeatedly touching his forehead to the ground during prayer

Zeitoun: Olive

Zemmouri, (Zemmouria): A man (woman) from Azemmour

Zillij: Zellige, terra cotta (natural clay) tilework

Also by Kitty Morse

A Biblical Feast: Ancient Mediterranean Flavors for Today's Table (2nd edition)

Cooking at the Kasbah: Recipes from My Moroccan Kitchen

The Scent of Orange Blossoms: Sephardic Cuisine from Morocco

Couscous: Fresh and Flavorful Contemporary Recipes

The Vegetarian Table: North Africa

Edible Flowers: A Kitchen Companion

Edible Flowers Poster

365 Ways to Cook Vegetarian

The California Farm Cookbook

Come with Me to the Kasbah: A Cook's Tour of Morocco

Acknowledgments

For their invaluable feedback I owe a debt of gratitude to cousins Stephanie Louise Meyer and Abderrahim Youssi; friends Whitney Robinson, Tershia d'Elgin, Edith Fine, Ann Carli, Julie Pendray, Martha Stoddard Holmes, Laura Baldus, Sarah Ben Daou Fishburn, Andrea Peterson, Patricia McArdle, Robert Doddridge, Enid Norman, Lenore Hughes, Michael Wolf and his pack of Wolfwriters, Abderrahmane and Roselyne Rahoule, Yves and Marie-Paule Ménahèze, Amy Fishburn, Peggy Fishburn, Jim and Froukje Frost, Mohamed Ben Daou, Lamia Lahlou, Ida Rigby, Deborah Richkin and Julie Castiglia. *Merci mille fois* to my mother Nicole Darmon Chandler and my aunt Martine Darmon Meyer.

Most of all, I want to thank my husband Owen, in-house editor, photographer, and taste-tester extraordinaire. Without his help and doggedness, *Mint Tea and Minarets* would never have seen the light of day.